UNI┌─────────────┐NGHAM
W│ D0301377   │WN
FRO└─────────────┘HE LIBRARY

.OAN

OWL

Post-Franco, Postmodern

Plate 1. Pedro Almodóvar directs Victoria Abril in *High Heels*. (Courtesy of Miramax Films Release and Pedro Almodóvar)

Post-Franco, Postmodern

The Films of Pedro Almodóvar

Edited by
Kathleen M. Vernon and Barbara Morris

Contributions to the Study of Popular Culture, Number 43

GREENWOOD PRESS
Westport, Connecticut • London

Library of Congress Cataloging-in-Publication Data

Post-Franco, postmodern : the films of Pedro Almodóvar / edited by
Kathleen M. Vernon and Barbara Morris.
    p.   cm.—(Contributions to the study of popular culture,
ISSN 0198-9871 ; no. 43)
    Includes bibliographical references and index.
    ISBN 0-313-29245-0
    1. Almodóvar, Pedro—Criticism and interpretation. I. Vernon,
Kathleen M. II. Morris, Barbara B. (Barbara Bryce).
III. Series.
PN1998.3.A46P67   1995   1003209948
791.43'0233'092—dc20   94-32047

British Library Cataloguing in Publication Data is available.

Copyright © 1995 by Kathleen M. Vernon and Barbara Morris

All rights reserved. No portion of this book may be
reproduced, by any process or technique, without the
express written consent of the publisher.

Library of Congress Catalog Card Number: 94-32047
ISBN: 0-313-29245-0
ISSN: 0-198-9871

First published in 1995

Greenwood Press, 88 Post Road West, Westport, CT 06881
An imprint of Greenwood Publishing Group, Inc.

Printed in the United States of America

The paper used in this book complies with the
Permanent Paper Standard issued by the National
Information Standards Organization (Z39.48-1984).

10 9 8 7 6 5 4 3

In order to keep this title in print and available to the academic community, this edition
was produced using digital reprint technology in a relatively short print run. This would
not have been attainable using traditional methods. Although the cover has been changed
from its original appearance, the text remains the same and all materials and methods
used still conform to the highest book-making standards.

Copyright Acknowledgments

The editors and publisher gratefully acknowledge permission to reprint the following copyrighted material:

"*Pepi, Luci, Bom* and *Dark Habits*: Lesbian Comedy, Lesbian Tragedy." © Paul Julian Smith 1992. Reprinted from *Laws of Desire: Questions of Homosexuality in Spanish Writing and Film 1960–1990* by Paul Julian Smith (1992) by permission of Oxford University Press.

"Melodrama Against Itself: *What Have I Done to Deserve This?*" by Kathleen M. Vernon. © 1993 by the Regents of the University of California. Reprinted from *Film Quarterly* Vol. 46, No. 3 (Spring 1993), pp. 28–40, by permission.

"Almodóvar's Laws of Subjectivity and Desire" by Barbara Morris, an earlier version of which appeared in *España Contemporánea* Vol. 6, No. 1 (Spring 1993), pp. 61–75. Used by permission.

"Almodóvar's City of Desire" by Marvin D'Lugo. Reproduced from *Quarterly Review of Film and Video*, Vol. 13 (4), 1991, pp. 47–65 with permission from Harwood Publishers.

"From Matricide to Motherlove: *High Heels*" by Marsha Kinder, an earlier version of which appeared as "Review of *High Heels*." © 1992 by the Regents of the University of California. Reprinted from *Film Quarterly* Vol. 45, No. 3 (Spring 1992), pp. 39–44, by permission.

Contents

A photographic essay follows p. 97

Acknowledgments

We wish to thank a number of individuals and institutions for their help in the preparation of this book. The early stages of research for our work on Almodóvar were funded by Fordham University, the U.S.–Spanish Joint Committee for Educational and Cultural Exchange, and the Program for Cultural Cooperation Between Spain's Ministry of Culture and North American Universities. The staff at the Filmoteca Española and the library of the Filmoteca, especially Dolores Devesa, were extremely helpful in facilitating our access to both films and written sources. Paco Pozo of Alphaville Cinema's Bookstore provided us with all manner of Almodo-variana. John Tilly of Cinevista was wonderfully generous in sharing with us its extensive collection of publicity photos. At Photofest, Harold Mandelbaum helped us find exactly the stills we needed. Michel Rubin of El Deseo was the model of kindness and efficiency in helping us secure permissions. The enthusiasm and professional know-how of our editors at Greenwood Press, Peter Coveney and Elisabetta Linton, eased our passage through every stage of the publication process. Our thanks to Lisa Abrams for typing a portion of the manuscript, to Lou Charnon Deutsch for her advice on the arts of photo reproduction, and to Marvin D'Lugo for bibliographical assistance and general counsel. Special thanks to Cliff Eisen for his technical and moral support.

Introduction: Pedro Almodóvar, Postmodern *Auteur*

Kathleen M. Vernon and Barbara Morris

As in many discussions of the postmodern, much of what has passed for critical commentary on Pedro Almodóvar's films has tended toward the form of a catalogue, a tautological list of distinctive features (characters or plot elements) that permit the phenomenon to be identified with itself. What has often been lost in the ensuing debate between enthusiastic proponents and impassioned detractors is a clear sense of the stakes of the argument within the larger context—social, historical, technological, national, and international—in which these cultural manifestations have arisen.

Our purpose in this introduction is to provide such a contextualization. In particular, we are concerned to offer the American audience for Almodóvar's films some understanding of the complex cultural realities from which they spring. It is not a question of "interpreting" the director's films for a public less versed in some subtle Spanish subtext; their broad-based international success has clearly shown that these movies need no translation. Rather, we are interested in analyzing the conditions and consequences of this success as understood within the framework of relevant cultural and social institutions.

To that end, we begin with a brief prehistory of the Spanish film industry during the period following the Spanish Civil War. The next section examines Almodóvar's artistic origins within the youth culture movement, the so called *Movida*, which emerged in Madrid after the death of dictator Francisco Franco. In identifying a number of the sociohistorical and political catalysts that gave rise to the *Movida*, we seek to evaluate its putative role as the most visible projection of some Spanish version of postmodernism. The introduction concludes with a study of the impact of the Almo-

dóvar phenomenon, both textual and extratextual, on that critical and
commercial institution known as the cinematic *auteur*.

POST-FRANCO PREHISTORY: SPANISH CINEMA
BEFORE ALMODÓVAR

Despite the director's celebrated disavowals of the past, his claim to
"start after Franco," to tell stories "as if he [the dictator] had never existed,"[1] Almodóvar's films, just as the Spanish audience and film industry
for whom and within which they were created, at least initially are a
product of that history. Beginning well before the end of the Civil War,
the Franco regime sought to establish its control over the national film
industry. In November 1937, the Nationalists created the Supreme Board
of Film Censorship based in Salamanca, Franco's headquarters, and by
1943 a full range of measures to regulate film production were in place.
Though originally designed to safeguard Spanish audiences against ideas
and even actors deemed inimical to the values of the new government,
these regulations almost delivered the final blow to a domestic film industry ravaged by the war and the ensuing exile of Republican talent.
After attempts to limit the Spanish public's access to American films during the period of greatest rapprochement to the Hitler and Mussolini
governments, the Ministerial Order of April 1941, imposing obligatory
dubbing of all foreign films, effectively opened the floodgates to an irresistible onslaught of technologically and artistically superior Hollywood
products that could now compete on linguistically equal footing with
Spanish cinema. Even the policy of awarding subsidies to films considered in the national interest was linked to the financial reward of import
licenses for foreign films. Thus a film ranked in the highest category by
the National Entertainment Union could earn fifteen import licenses; one
with a lower ranking, ten; and so on.

Although this system was modified over the years, a pattern had been
set. The regime might determine the kinds of pictures made in Spain, as
testified to by the scores of tendentious historical epics, folkloric musical
comedies, and religious dramas that dominated Spanish production in
the forties and fifties, but its policies unwittingly encouraged a kind of
escape hatch for the Spanish moviegoing public in imported, foreign
films. While these films were subject to (often notorious) censorship and
many were banned outright, in general, American films, with their emphasis on entertainment over controversy or critique, were treated with
a lighter hand than the more socially conscious cinemas of Italy, France,
or later, Britain.

That an artistically and sometimes even commercially respectable Spanish cinema began to develop and then blossom in the fifties and sixties
can be attributed to a convergence of diverse and sometimes contradic-

tory forces. As hard-line ideological pressures began to ease as the regime consolidated its hold on power and sought reintegration into the international community, after years of ostracism as a result of the nation's wartime Axis alliances, certain sectors in the government saw the value in using Spain's film industry to develop a product that would rehabilitate Spain's image abroad as a modern (in both industrial and cultural terms) nation.

For those working on the creative side of the industry, this relative liberalization came just in time. The year 1947 had witnessed the founding of the first Spanish film school, the I.I.E.C. (Institute of Cinematographic Research and Experimentation, its name changed in 1962 to the E.O.C., Official Film School). Luis García Berlanga and Juan Antonio Bardem, who would collaborate on two of the most significant films of the fifties (*Esa pareja feliz* [*That Happy Couple*] and *Bienvenido Mr. Marshall* [*Welcome, Mr. Marshall*]) before going their separate but equally influential ways, met in the classrooms of the Institute. The school had other important functions, as noted by Vicente Molina Foix: "It offered students the almost miraculous opportunity of seeing otherwise inaccessible foreign films."[2] Another significant influence was the Spanish film club movement. In 1955 the Salamanca club, founded by university student Basilo Martín Patino, organized the "Salamanca Conversations," which brought together directors, would-be directors, critics, and theoreticians of widely differing political stripes, from liberal Falangists and social activist Catholics to Marxists. The participants issued a much-cited manifesto criticizing the Spanish film industry for its many aesthetic, material, and political deficiencies.

While the real impact of the Salamanca meeting was and is open to debate, the late fifties and early sixties saw a change in governmental film policy that led to the birth of the "New Spanish Cinema." As Peter Besas describes it, under the guidance of Director General of Cinematography José María García Escudero, the government allowed for the creation of a two-tier film industry. By retooling the subsidy system and finally establishing written norms for censorship (prior to 1963, censors judged films on a case-by-case basis, with the outcome always in doubt), the government continued to promote regime-approved entertainment for the Spanish mass audience while approving the production of a small number of "serious" films—often critical of the regime—made largely with the foreign film festival market in mind.[3] Directors like Carlos Saura, Mario Camus, Basilo Martin Patino, and José Luis Borau, who debuted under such a system, or Víctor Erice and Manuel Gutiérrez Aragón, who made their first films somewhat later, learned to work with the art of the possible, eluding the censors' sanctions by elaborating a highly metaphorical, elliptical style in order to communicate their critical vision to an artistically and politically informed elite both inside and outside of Spain.

By the early seventies, even before the death of Franco, further changes had begun to transform the context for making, distributing, and viewing cinema in Spain. With the closing in 1971 of the Official Film School, would-be *cinéastes* found the access to professional training in directing, scriptwriting, and technical subjects increasingly difficult. While private film schools as well the newly created Facultad de Ciencias de la Información e Imagen at the Madrid Complutense University helped to fill the gap, what resulted was a greater fragmentation and dispersal among cinema professionals, no longer united by their common experience in the E.O.C.[4] Despite the release of important films such as Saura's *La prima Angélica* and *Cría cuervos* or José Luis Borau's *Furtivos*, metaphorical cinema began to lose its hold as the (artistically at least) dominant cinematic discourse. While censorship continued in one form or another until the end of 1977, opposition to the Franco regime no longer provided the discursive and/or thematic center it once had. Recognizing how the cultural policies of the sixties had already fragmented the public for Spanish films between the minority-oriented New Spanish Cinema and a series of low-budget subgenre pictures destined for the mass market, producer José Luis Dibildos launched the *tercera vía* (third way) comedy, seeking to attract a broader and increasingly sophisticated urban audience who longed (it was supposed) to see their own lives reflected more directly on the film screen.[5] While the *tercera vía* and its more cosmopolitan successor, the "New Spanish Comedy" of Fernando Colomo and Fernando Trueba in the late seventies and early eighties, sought to reconstitute the audience for Spanish cinema from among the emerging generation of young, relatively affluent urban dwellers throughout Spain, the regional cinemas of newly automous Catalonia and the Basque country offered a further challenge to that centralizing impulse.

An air of crisis has pervaded the Spanish film industry of the eighties and nineties, with the notable and unexpected exception of the films of Pedro Almodóvar. Despite a temporary increase in government subsidies in the mid-eighties under the Socialist Ministry of Culture and Directors General of Cinematography Pilar Miró and Fernando Méndez-Leite, the total box office gross of Spanish films continues to decline.[6] The fact is that Almodóvar's success has come at a time when, as Wendy Rolph reports in her "From Rough Trade to Free Trade: Toward a Contextual Analysis of Audience Response to the Films of Pedro Almodóvar," a diverse but shrinking group of Spanish films competes for the attention of a dwindling filmgoing audience (thanks to competition from television and video) with the ever more popular products of the American cinema industry. This conundrum highlights a central issue in analyzing Almodóvar's creative trajectory, one that will occupy the contributors to this volume in varying degrees. Despite the director's outsider status vis-à-vis the Spanish cinema establishment, Almodóvar and his films are heir to an ambivalent legacy generated by over half a century of tensions between government-sponsored attempts to define and perpetuate a national cultural tradition and the sundry enticements of an apparently liberating but no less restrictive transnational culture industry. His skill in negotiating such creative and commercial faultlines no doubt represents an important factor in his global appeal.

MADRID AND THE *MOVIDA*

With Franco's death in 1975, Spain embarked headlong on a belated journey into the late twentieth century. Although the sixties had heralded a relative political and cultural *abertura* (opening), the chief aftershock of 1975 was the final dissolution of the political and psychological frontiers that had ensured the tacit acceptance by Spaniards of Franco's sinister slogan: "Spain is different." In the rush to full membership in the global market economy, deals were struck and trade agreements negotiated; the abolition of censorship brought a tidal wave of films, books, television programs, and music from abroad that had been prohibited outright or severely limited in distribution.

Eager to demonstrate their distance from the past, young Spaniards identified with and imitated various tendencies in pop culture and politics that held sway in Europe and the United States at the time: punk rock, glam rock, the last gasps of the hippie movement (known as *el rollo* in Spain), the drug culture, women's and gay liberation. The loosening of immigration policies encouraged a large influx of Latin Americans with their respective cultural traditions. In the stew of these diverse influences, the younger generation—for whom anti-Francoism had never provided a sense of purpose or self—gave themselves over to a sometimes frenzied search for appropriate modes of expression.

The image of the new Spain that was being fashioned at the hands of technocrats and media experts had little in common with Franco's seamless iconography of a unified, Castilian nation that celebrated a monolithic history of reconquest and empire. The rise of regionalism, validated politically by the autonomy granted to Catalonia and the Basque provinces and reinforced by the resurgence of languages suppressed by Franco (Catalán, Basque, Galician), signaled not only a challenge to Madrid's political dominance but also the flowering of diverse regional cultures.

This impulse toward political and cultural decentralization also benefited Madrid, where the *Movida* that was incubating among the capital's marginalia began to coalesce in the late seventies. In its vanguard was a small coterie of friends, including Almodóvar, painter Guillermo Pérez

Villalta, painter and graphic artist Ceesepe, fashion designer Sybilla, photographer Alberto García Alix, drag artist and actor Fabio de Miguel, musicians Alaska and Ouka Lele, and television personality and producer Paloma Chamorro. The range of ages among the participants spanned almost a generation, embracing all those who had been unable to live the international youth culture explosion of the sixties but were determined to do so with a vengeance in the eighties. Nurtured in the underground, the *Movida* was characterized by intense activity in the plastic arts and design—from painting and graphics to comic books—as well as music and fashion. Unlike the avant-garde in Barcelona, which was fostered and promoted by existing cultural institutions and organizations, the *Movida* was in no way a collective cultural movement with a focused agenda. On the contrary, pop culture artists in Madrid expressed an intense disdain—at least initially—for the institutionalization of culture that had been perpetrated in Spain during the Franco years and later, as part of the political program of the former anti-Francoist opposition that came to power.

Almodóvar's beginnings as a filmmaker are a reflection of these circumstances and attitudes. With no access to professional training after the closing of the Official Film School, he rounded up friends, often during parties, and filmed them in Super-8mm shorts with provocative titles. First shown at friends' homes and later in Alphaville Cinema's Sala 5, his films featured live soundtracks with Almodóvar speaking all the dialogue, singing songs, and playing musical accompaniments on a cassette deck. Although light-years from mainstream cinema, his work also differed radically from that of his underground colleagues, such as Iván Zulueta, whose feature-length *Arrebato* (*Rapture*, 1979), a lyrical parable of cinema's vampiric voyeurism, was a cult hit.[7] In fact, Almodóvar found himself rejected by other underground filmmakers, who considered his work overly narrative and insufficiently experimental. As he notes: "In my films there was always a story to tell, and that was not accepted, it was too Hollywood, and not conceptual enough for the independent and underground guys who improvised with a camera."[8] Almodóvar's response to his critics in the Catalonian conceptual movement was a short with the pointed title *Film político* (*Political Film*, 1974), which the director describes as follows: "[It] was only one scene where I defecated in a very explicit way and then wiped my ass with a photo of Nixon. It's very profound and very hermetic."[9]

Despite its claims to apoliticism, however, the *Movida* thrived in part thanks to the populist policies of the Socialist mayor of Madrid, Enrique Tierno Galván, "the old professor" and a hero of the anti-Francoist opposition, who led the capital through the years of the transition to democracy. His support of free expression and insistence on returning the streets to the people liberated *madrileños* from what had been the constant scrutiny of the police and paramilitary Civil Guard. The *Movida*'s new night life transformed the cityscape into a warren of all-night bars and clubs, and Madrid's enormous flea market, the Rastro (later immortalized in the opening scenes of *Labyrinth of Passions*), became a favorite meeting place for the hip and would-be famous. Indeed, much of the "fauna almodovariana" of the director's early films was inspired by the milieu of Madrid street life. At age fifteen, Alaska, a punk rock musician, became one of the protagonists of *Pepi, Luci, Bom y otras chicas del montón (Pepi, Luci, Bom and Other Ordinary Girls)*. Fellow denizen of the *Movida* Ceesepe designed posters and titles for several of Almodóvar's films (Plate 2), and Pérez Villalta did one of the sets for *Labyrinth*.

With the loosening of the Franco regime's cultural straitjacket, young *madrileños* turned away from the musical Marxism of the *cantautores* (singer–songwriters of protest songs) from Catalonia, Portugal, and the southern cone of South America, who had been so popular with their older siblings in the sixties and seventies, preferring instead Anglo-American rock. Punk and heavy metal music exerted a tremendous influence on rock musicians in Madrid, who felt closer in spirit to the alienated youth of urban culture in London and New York than to the French and Italian neighbors with whom Barcelonans had enjoyed long-term cultural relations. Although few bands enjoyed much longevity (relative exceptions were Radio Futura, Gabinete Caligari, and the permutations of Alaska's bands: Caca de Luxe, Alaska and the Pegamoides, and Alaska and Dinarama), an extraordinary proliferation of punk rock groups provided the *Movida*'s nightly sound track.

Paloma Chamorro, the host and producer of the Buñuelesque-titled television program "La edad de oro" (The Golden Age) that did much to promote Spanish punk rock and the *Movida*, contends: "In Spain we were playing at 'no future,' putting on the punk aesthetic, its radicalness. . . . In Spain we like labels, even when misused. . . . Things were actually just the opposite. . . . We went from having Franco to not having Franco."[10] In their search for appropriate forms of expression, the young iconoclasts of the *Movida*'s first wave were spurred to try on and cast off identities with dizzying aplomb. Such celebratory displays of cultural transvestism, which the Spanish and international media would later conflate with postmodernism, were directly related to the euphoric sense of unlimited possibilities that came with "not having Franco."

Almodóvar's early films represent a willed break with previous Spanish cultural modalities. His first film, *Pepi, Luci, Bom*, is not only about the *Movida*, it is of the *Movida*. Its poor sound quality and inconsistent matching, no doubt products of its micro budget and sporadic production, mark it as an underground film, as do the imprecise narrative and the connections, however naturalistic, to pornography. Both *Pepi, Luci, Bom* and *Labyrinth* constitute a chronicle of the *Movida* as well as an almost utopian rendering of Madrid as *locus amoenus*, a space of infinite possibilities. Marvin D'Lugo contextualizes the protagonizing role attributed to the Spanish capital in Almodóvar's first seven films in his essay "Almodóvar's City of Desire." As explored by D'Lugo, as well as by Paul Julian Smith and James Mandrell, the city of Madrid provides the setting in which individual desires freely circulate, setting the stage for a potentially radical reformulation of cultural—and sexual—identities and values. For Smith, in his *"Pepi, Luci, Bom* and *Dark Habits*: Lesbian Comedy, Lesbian Tragedy," the director's first and third films foreground the spectacle of lesbian desire in a self-conscious celebration of the breaking of sexual taboos, both societal and cinematic. James Mandrell's "Sense and Sensibility, or Latent Heterosexuality and *Labyrinth of Passions,"* on the other hand, questions the real story behind that "crazy comedy" of identities borrowed and cast off, reading the film as an allegory of Almodóvar's career and his progressive integration into mainstream, commercial cinema and its compulsory heterosexuality.

As reflections and expressions of the Spanish youth culture explosion of the late seventies, these films served to propagate a kind of mythology of the *Movida*'s headiest movements, attitudes quickly internalized in the *Movida*'s increasing tendency toward self-portraiture. In the jumble of characters populating Almodóvar's film universe—the unlikely alliances and love affairs across barriers of age, class, religion, and sexual orientation, for example—certain proponents saw proof of the *Movida*'s fundamentally all-inclusive nature. This aspect is stressed by Borja Casani, founder and editor of Madrid's premier postmodern magazine, *La luna de Madrid*,[11] in his utopian assessment of life in the Spanish capital during the period: "[T]he *Movida* was interclassist. Madrid differs from all other cities in the world because its populace is interclassist by nature, everyone mixes with everyone. . . . There is a tribal mentality. The people, instead of recognizing each other by class, do so by tribes. . . . The *Movida* was everyone who was connected by the bar culture."[12] As represented in Almodóvar's early films, this image of the *Movida*'s post-Franco identity cruising in a classless city of unending possibilities came to provide the central emblem of what the second wave would label as a prototypical Spanish brand of postmodernism.

FROM MARGINS TO MARKETS

By the early eighties, following the apparent consolidation of Spanish democracy that was confirmed by the election of a Socialist government in October 1982, the *Movida* entered a new phase, a more self-conscious second wave that had a pronounced and problematic relation to the media.[13] Borja Casani, both participant and observer, noted that "[W]hen the interest in politics waned, the communications media began to look at the cultural movements, the festivities, the fads, the ceremonies that were being produced. . . . [E]veryone attempted to publish in their newspapers what they called signs of the postmodern."[14]

The media's subsequent fetishization of the *Movida* reinvented the underground as a cultural commodity available for export to other regions of Spain while it also offered proof to the world of Spain's ultra(post)modernity. Spain's incorporation into the European Economic Community in 1986 thus coincided with its emergence from near isolationism to a new protagonizing role in the European cultural consciousness. Javier Mariscal, the Valencian artist best known for his creation of the mascot Cobi for the 1992 Olympic Games in Barcelona, defended the image of the new Spain forged in the media frenzy of the eighties, saying: "I think we are the first generation that has crossed international borders without a beret and without an inferiority complex; the first that has known how to sell, in a dignified and correct manner, a totally modern image of Spain, a Spain at the same time attached to very strong roots."[15]

In many ways emblematic of the second wave's seemingly incompatible concern with marketability on the one hand and the politics of identity on the other, Almodóvar's films of the period embody the working out of this paradox. The director's first international success, ¿Qué he hecho yo para merecer esto? (What Have I Done to Deserve This?), without totally abandoning the outrageous plot twists and cartoonish characters of the first films, turns to the story of a struggling working-class family in Madrid's high-rise Barrio de la Concepción. Indeed, films like *What Have I Done* and Almodóvar's next picture, *Matador*, reveal a much more complex relation to Spain's historical and cultural past than the director's much-cited disavowals of historical memory would suggest. As Kathleen Vernon argues in her "Melodrama Against Itself: *What Have I Done to Deserve This?*," the filmmaker's purposeful juxtapositions of neorealism and Hollywood melodrama foreground the impact of the material and moral poverty of working-class immigrants lost to Francoism's "progress" in alienating urban developments, even while its conclusion plots the utopian future of the post-Franco, postpatriarchal family. In a related vein, Leora Lev's essay, "Tauromachy as a Spectacle of Gender Revision in *Matador*," analyzes the ways the director's fifth film brilliantly rewrites the social, sexual, and aesthetic iconography of the bullfight, Spain's *fiesta nacional*, rescuing the *corrida* from its role as folkloric fetish in a Franco-sponsored tourist industry. *Matador*'s gender-bending masquerade on Andalusian themes echoes a broader recontextualization of traditional Spanish cultures, also evidenced in the *Movida*-inspired boom in flamenco music and *sevillana* dance clubs.[16] The commercial viability of such explorations of Spanish "authenticity" both at home and abroad was not lost on decision makers at the Ministry of Culture, who awarded *Matador*, the first Almodóvar film to qualify for government financial support, the maximum subvention of 50 percent of production costs. By the director's own analysis, it was the international endorsement received by *What Have I Done?* that made his cinema suddenly palatable to the cultural establishment: "Although they didn't like my films at all, when they discovered that my cinema was appreciated abroad, . . . that *What Have I Done?* got excellent reviews upon its premier in the U.S. and various European countries, . . . I was categorized as exportable."[17]

THE POSTMODERNISM DEBATE

The first issue of *La luna de Madrid* featured an article by Borja Casani and José Tono Martínez, "Madrid 1984 ¿La posmodernidad?," that theorized a connection between the *Movida* and postmodernism.[18] An intense debate quickly arose on the (im)possibility of applying the European theoretical frame of postmodernism to Spain, with the participants citing recent translations of Jean-François Lyotard, Jean Baudrillard, Jürgen Habermas, and Hal Foster. To some, post-Franco Spain seemed the epitome of the postmodern, the incarnation in practice of European theory—from its multilingual, multicultural mix to its alleged toleration of drugs, pornography, and homosexuality. They argued for the postmodern as a quintessentially Latin, Mediterranean phenomenon in view of the region's distinctive modernity, "less rigid, mechanical, and at bottom, less repressive." This view was crystallized in Italian philosopher Gianni Vattimo's paraphrase of Walter Benjamin, acclaiming "Madrid, capital of the Twentieth Century."[19]

A more cautionary view of postmodernism emerged from other quarters, however. Casani, for one, observed that the gay and punk movements imported from Britain and the United States marked not the beginning but the end of the influence of liberatory discourses and that the eighties inaugurated, rather, the postmodern simulacrum of culture.[20] Spanish philosopher Eduardo Subirats, among others, pointed out the pitfalls of postmodern thought that many in the *Movida*—including its eventual institutional and governmental supporters—heedlessly embraced. For Subirats, the dangers were clear: the surrender of historical memory, viewed as the great liberation of mankind, to the simulacrum of technological perfection could only lead to an ecstatic fascination with the dissolution of the subject and the spectacle of the end of the world.[21] In the context of posttotalitarian Spain, of course, any unproblematized celebration of postmodernism's end of history raised an alarming echo of Franco's own attempts to impose an end to politics and ideology—as theorized by the technocrat-led governments of the late fifties and sixties—through the creation of a prosperous consumer society.[22]

During those years, in the absence of any legal means of political expression, the anti-Francoist opposition had turned to Marxism and Marxist rhetoric as the only viable option for voicing their dissent. When members of this group of so-called *progres* (progressives), many of whom had come of age in the political ferment of the sixties, finally came to power in the seventies and eighties,[23] the younger generation rebelled. This intergenerational conflict often informed and occasionally displaced more dispassionate appraisals of Spanish postmodernism and its some-time standard-bearer, the *Movida*. For Spaniards in their teens and twen-ties, the latter was a conspicuous and dramatic reaction against what they saw as an obsession with political concerns that had nothing to do with them. Speaking for many in the *progre* generation, Juan Luis Cebrián, editor of Spain's most influential newspaper, *El país*, countered by ac-cusing the *Movida* and, in turn postmodernism, of being "the prelude to a kind of cultural fascism that has repudiated the left's collective cul-tural mission."[24] In defense of the *Movida*, Almodóvar stated that frivolity became, for all practical purposes, a political posture in itself, and that the seeming apoliticism of the era was the only sane response to the left's "pointless political activity."[25]

AFTER THE FIESTA

Whether done in by the internal contradictions that once fanned its creative flames or by media and government bureaucrats who co-opted its energies in the interest of promoting and selling the image of a hip Spain abroad, by 1985, when foreign journalists were descending on Spain to document a decade of democracy, the *Movida*'s vitality as a public, street-level enterprise was on the wane. Reflecting the tenor of the times, Almodóvar continued to capitalize on the wave of international interest in Spain even as he went on to produce, write, and direct one of his most personal films, *La ley del deseo* (*Law of Desire*), which Bar-bara Morris analyzes as a masochistic camp of the family romance in "Almodóvar's Laws of Subjectivity and Desire." With its seriocomic treat-ment of incest, transsexuality, and homosexual romance, *Law of Desire* solidified the director's growing international reputation as a filmmaker of ambidextrous appeal, able to bridge the gap between art and/or cult film audiences and a mainstream, commercial public. The 1988 release of *Mujeres al borde de un ataque de nervios* (*Women on the Verge of a Nervous Breakdown*) delivered on that promise as the film garnered un-precedented critical and commercial success both at home and abroad, capped by a nomination for best foreign film Oscar.

As the last film in what might be termed Almodóvar's *Movida* cycle, *Women on the Verge* marks an ending to an interfilmic tale of upward social mobility: from Pepi's low-rent apartment block to Pepa's penthouse terrace, from the underground punk aesthetic (or lack thereof) to glossy, high-comedy production values. For some commentators, the film's widespread international appeal only confirmed their suspicions that the *Movida*'s postmodern stylizations masked the triumph of a yuppified consumer capitalism in Spain over more progressive political impulses. And yet, as Brad Epps shows in his study, "Figuring Hysteria: Disorder and Desire in Three Films by Almodóvar," there may be more to the film than meets the eye. Linking *Women on the Verge* to *Labyrinth* and *What Have I Done?*, he discovers traces of hysteria's "crisis of signification" traversing the film's deceptively conventional surface, highlighting tensions between body and image, class and gender, language and desire.

If Almodóvar's first seven films celebrate, in one form or another, the *Movida* generation's exploration of multiple life possibilities in a newly liberated Spain following the death of Franco, his three most recent films suggest a somewhat darker reappraisal of postmodern Spanish reality. Víctor Fuentes's reading of *Atame* (*Tie Me Up! Tie Me Down!*) in his retrospective look at "Almodóvar's Postmodern Cinema" finds in the Spaniard's edgy rewriting of the captivity narrative an ebbing of the earlier films' carnivalesque imperative. For if the film continues to affirm eros's transformative power over the pair of unlikely lovers, it nevertheless suggests that their love can develop only in isolation from a larger society no longer open to the collective ravages of desire. On the other hand, despite *Tacones lejanos*'s (*High Heels*) primary setting in the closeted public spaces of controlling patriarchal institutions—the television station, the court house, and the jail—as Marsha Kinder argues in her essay, "From Matricide to Mother Love: *High Heels*," the film marshals the negative oedipal narrative of a daughter's passionate love for her mother to explode the psychic and societal strictures of the patriarchal law from within. Clearly, then, this apparent retreat into the more private realm of individual desire does not necessarily signal a loss of subversive intent or effect.

While surely not the last word in the director's cinematic chronicle of urban life in *fin de siglo* Madrid, his latest film, *Kika*, recapitulates a number of themes and motifs from earlier pictures, but with an ominous twist. The director's coda to his own summary of *Kika* emphasizes this darker turn:

Kika is an attempt at comedy of a very hybrid sort, one that goes from light in the first part to dark and poisonous at the end. It has a number of parallels with *Women on the Verge* in its humor, its focus on female characters and on urban life. But if the "thesis" of *Women on the Verge* consisted in portraying an idyllic city that was eminently livable (pharmacists didn't ask for prescriptions, taxi drivers were real guardian angels, and friendship was a secure refuge) and where the only source of tension lay in the fact that men leave women, in *Kika*, the city is an aggressive inferno and men don't leave women but they lie to them, they refuse to talk to them, they spy on them, and if it comes to that, they kill them.[26]

Thus, Kika and the other characters in the film find themselves under siege, not only by uncommunicative boyfriends or the serial killer who lives upstairs, but also by a voyeuristic media apparatus that has replaced the state or the police as the principal threat to individual liberty and the authentic expression of desire.

PEDRO ALMODÓVAR, POSTMODERN *AUTEUR?*

Contemporary academic film theory and criticism have generally rejected the notion of the cinematic *auteur* as grounded in a romantic/ literary inheritance blind to the realities of the film work's formal, industrial, and ideological determinants. Nevertheless, as recent studies by Dudley Andrews, Timothy Corrigan, and James Naremore testify, the reports of the *auteur's* demise have been greatly exaggerated.[27] Still, the models of *auteur*ism at work today bear scant resemblance to the term's original meaning in the *Cahiers du Cinéma* writings of soon-to-be filmmakers François Truffaut, Jean-Luc Godard, and Claude Chabrol (among others), who sought through their against-the-grain readings of classic Hollywood cinema to distance themselves from the excessively literary *cinéma de qualité* of their immediate French forebears.[28] As imported and translated into American film critical discourse by Andrew Sarris in the sixties, the French strategy (*politique des auteurs*) became a "theory" that championed the personal vision expressed in the small, low-budget, art house picture as opposed to the mainstream entertainment cinema produced by Hollywood.[29]

While *auteur*ism certainly favored the distribution and reception of European and other foreign films in the United States, as the framework for a certain critical and spectatorial "horizon of expectations," it also produced some notorious distortions in evaluating their impact. As a marketing tool, a kind of star system evolved that effectively allowed the films of certain "name" directors to compete for audience dollars on the restricted art house circuit. But as Peter Lev points out, the limited release options that restricted spectators' access to European and other international cinemas tended to impose a monolithic reading of all such films—even those that had been broadly popular in their own countries—as art pictures intended for a minority audience.[30] The emphasis on the director as an artist whose works could best be appreciated by an international cultural elite likewise produced decontextualized readings that ignored the historical, national, and/or regional contexts that informed the films in question.[31] The star system also generated a form of tokenism whereby Third World and/or emerging cinemas were identified with a single director in the cinematic consciousness of American spectators, critics, and distributors. Thus, where France, Germany, or Italy might be represented by a number of figures, Mexican,

Spanish, Indian, or Senegalese cinema, for example, was perceived as wholly embodied in the persons of Luis Buñuel, Buñuel (later Saura, and still later Almodóvar), Satyajit Ray, or Ousmane Sembene, respectively. The persistence of these tendencies is noted by Georgia Brown in an article in the *Village Voice*, in which she laments the general provincialism/chauvinism of New York film reviewers (and consequently, spectators). Her prime example, appropriately enough, concerns Spanish directors Almodóvar and Bigas Luna:

Reviews of Bigas Luna's *Jamón Jamón* in both the [New York] *Times* and the *New Yorker* simply assumed the director must be a follower of Almodóvar since Almodóvar is the only contemporary Spanish director they know and his films arrived here *first*. In fact, the influence, if any, goes the other way 'round since Bigas Luna was making his singular, macabre, sex-obsessed melodramas before Almodóvar picked up a camera.[32]

This inattention to historical and cultural specificity as well as national context has characterized more theoretically inflected treatments of the cinematic author as well. As Dudley Andrew notes, both structuralist and poststructuralist readings "suppress the search for [a film's] human source," demoting the *auteur* to a "name for certain regularities [or irregularities] in textual organization."[33] While certainly valuable in their emphasis on the text as a structured play of forces, relations, and discourses rather than a site of unified, final meanings authorized by their source, in practice such approaches run the risk of being reappropriated by an ahistorical neoformalism.

Ideological critics, such as Roy Armes in his work on Third World cinema or Claire Johnston on women directors, in contrast, have sought to recuperate the *auteur*'s expressive stance as linked to a project of collective political opposition, whether against neocolonialist economic and cultural hegemony or bourgeois, capitalist patriarchy.[34] Under such a view, *auteur*ism is thus conceived as offering an alternative mode of cinematic production to the industrial/narrative model of "classic (Hollywood) cinema" as well as access to a form of cultural and political agency.[35]

More recently, however, Timothy Corrigan, in *A Cinema Without Walls*, has called into question the continuing relevance of the binary distinction between the model of *auteur*ist expression (whether personal and aesthetic or collective and political) and that of textual organization, in the face of recent technological, social, and economic developments that have radically destabilized traditional patterns of viewing, marketing, and distribution. If, as we noted above, the economics of marketing functioned as one determinant among many in the production and reception of the director's role within the context of the international art cinema of the fifties, sixties, and seventies, in Corrigan's view, "The international imperatives of postmodern culture have made it clear that commerce is now much more than just a contending discourse: . . . he or she [the *auteur*] has rematerialized in the eighties and nineties as a commercial performance of 'the business of being an *auteur*.' "[36]

In the case of Pedro Almodóvar, even the harshest critics of his films would recognize his mastery of this latter role. In fact, some of the more serious academic and media critics in Spain, perhaps nostalgic for the model of the traditional *auteur*, have repeatedly acknowledged Almodóvar's marketing savvy while denying him access to the status of artist, tellingly enough, most often on the grounds of his deficiency as a writer (not director) of films.[37] Underlying this essentially modernist model of the film author is the assumption that commercial control is incompatible with artistic accomplishment. For the postmodern *auteur*, however, the creation and mobilization of a celebrity persona has become at least as important as the making of films. As Corrigan notes, "More recent versions of the *auteur*ist position have swerved away from its textual center. . . . [T]he *auteur*–star is meaningful primarily as a promotion or recovery of a movie or group of movies, frequently regardless of the filmic text itself."[38]

Thus what begins as a marketing technique, the dramatization of self as a means of selling the creative product, soon exceeds that function: the star–director's offscreen, celebrity image displaces the film or films being promoted as the center of interest, as a text to be "read." Even a casual survey of the extrafilmic material generated by the Almodóvar publicity machine reveals the accuracy of this description.[39] In interview after article, feature after puff piece, feuilletonesque accounts of the director's upbringing compete for reader interest with discussions of the films, perhaps not surprisingly, since both his biographical and his fictional story lines share a capacious disregard for traditional notions of verisimilitude. Just as his films flaunt the tension between their loving cultivation of the hoariest narrative conventions and the characters' "modern" disdain for conventional morality, the narrative of his own unlikely origins takes the familiar nineteenth-century plot of the poor boy from the provinces who makes good in the cosmopolitan capital to its contemporary extremes.

Though details and emphasis vary from telling to telling, the outline of the story runs as follows.[40] Born in Calzada de Calatrava, a small rural town in La Mancha, where his father worked as a mule driver, Almodóvar spent his school-age years in Cáceres, the provincial capital of Estremadura, studying in a Salesian seminary where he excelled as a choir soloist. In the late sixties he left the provinces for Madrid and a job with the telephone company. Combining his day job with involvement in experimental theater, he also began to write and shoot films in Super-8 format. And the rest, as they say, is history. Despite a lack of formal film training, by the late eighties Almodóvar had become Spain's most successful director both at home and abroad.

Although the purpose of this book is clearly not to dwell on the extratextual manifestations of the *auteur*–star persona to the exclusion of his films—rather, the contrary is true—some attention to the broader performative context of what might be termed the Almodóvar phenomenon is essential in order to understand the way in which Almodóvar's cinema lays siege to the traditional notion of the *auteur*, reinscribing it as a postmodern phenomenon. While the history of world cinema might well be characterized as the story of the unexpected results of the always vexed contest and collaboration between art and commerce, even materialist historians have tended to cast the tale as a contest between the forces of light and darkness, the creative individual against the money-driven demands of the Hollywood studio or the multinational conglomerate. And yet, as Corrigan convincingly argues, such a story line hardly describes the art and/or business of filmmaking today, if it ever did. In his view, the directors he deems "*auteurs* of commerce" (a group that includes Francis Ford Coppola, Steven Spielberg, Brian De Palma, and R. W. Fassbinder, among others; Almodóvar is not mentioned) are not mere pawns in the publicity-making apparatus of some transnational culture industry. Instead, they "monitor or rework the institutional manipulations of the *auteur*ist position within the commerce of the movie industry . . . consciously employ[ing] the public image of the *auteur* in order to then confront and fragment its expressive coherence."[41]

Almodóvar's active interventions in the commerce of moviemaking have taken many forms. Like Coppola, although with greater success to date, he has mounted his own production company, El Deseo, S.A., which he directs with his brother Agustín. Made possible by the Spanish film industry's Miró Law financing scheme of the mid- and late eighties that made government subsidies available to filmmakers themselves, El Deseo has given the Almodóvars access to bigger budgets and greater international exposure thanks to recent cooperative arrangements with the French company Ciby 2000, the coproducer of *Tie Me Up! Tie Me Down!* and *Kika*. But it is through his continuing cultivation and manipulation of the spectacle of a protean public persona that Almodóvar most effectively confounds received ideas of artistic coherence and authority. Refusing to be typecast by his own repeated self-characterization as Almodóvar the autodidact filmmaker, the director has also generated a range of alternate identities, available to be assumed at will: from his early eighties role as Patty Diphusa, the ingenue-like porn star turned memoirist,[42] or as half of the punk rock duo Almodóvar and McNamara (Plate 6), to his more recent incarnation as arbiter of the international fashion scene thanks to his collaboration in *Kika* with *haut* European designers Gianni Versace and Jean-Paul Gaultier.[43]

While clearly of a piece with the *Movida*'s own brand of cultural trans-vestism, these practices of authorial masquerade have further implica-tions for the interpretation of Almodóvar's films as well.[44] In an essay collected in the critical anthology *The Construction of Authorship. Textual Appropriation in Law and Literature*, legal scholar Rosemary J. Coombe addresses the notion of the celebrity image from the other way round, as it were, defining it not as the product, and hence the property, of the media star but as the object of the creative reelaborations of the audience, for whom the star image becomes "a cultural lode of multiple meanings, mined for its symbolic resonances and, simultaneously, a float-ing signifier, invested with libidinal energies, social longings and political aspirations."[45] For Coombe, recent legal decisions that have extended the media figure's proprietary rights over any publicly recognizable manifes-tation of his or her image (from singing style to mannerisms and ges-tures) have placed a brake on popular cultural practices that appropriate and rewrite media imagery in subversive and politically expressive ways, such as in gay male appropriations of female stars, lesbian reworking of James Dean, or middle-class women's use of characters from *Star Trek* in the creation of fan magazines.[46]

Seen from this angle, the star functions in a continuum with his or her audience rather than across a great divide. As Coombe notes, the most successful of postmodern performers are themselves cultural *bricoleurs* who "mine media history for evocative signifiers from our past."[47] Thus Almodóvar's manipulations of his many-layered celebrity persona, like his flagrant borrowing and reworkings of familiar cinematic—especially Hol-lywood—styles and genres in his films, divert and disperse any claims to extracinematic authority not simultaneously authorized by his spectators' own active reelaborations of shared cultural codes and references.

In the face of such challenges to the notion of directorial authority, then, our goal in this volume is certainly not to restore the figure of the *auteur* to its former glory by offering a unitary or exhaustive interpreta-tion of the director's work. While the essays are guided by a shared im-pulse to redirect the focus away from the Almodóvar phenomenon as a publicity-generated event and toward the analysis of the director's indi-vidual films, the fact of the book's collective authorship necessarily works against the temptation of a totalizing reading. Furthermore, all of the readings are themselves vigorously intertextual, attentive to the play of sources and discourses that traverse the filmic texts under study.

If there is a point of convergence to be found in the diversity of critical and theoretical approaches to the films analyzed in the collection, and reflected in this introduction, it is in regard to our collective insistence on exploring the local, Spanish context of the director's work (although without neglecting its interface with varied international sources). Rather than an attempt to circumscribe future readings, this concern with the films' "Spanishness" stems from a recognition that we have perhaps not yet arrived at Corrigan's "cinema without walls," in a world where national and linguistic boundaries have ceased to shape the spectators' horizon of response. The world may indeed "dream itself to be American,"[48] but as Almodóvar's films have demonstrated, the cultural specificity of Spain's appropriations of its own American dream(s) has something important and perhaps unexpected to tell us about the present moment in both cultures. As John Beverly and José Oviedo have noted in regard to the similar but different context of contemporary Latin America, "Postmodernism itself . . . is bound up with the dynamic of the interaction between local cultures and an instantaneous and omnipresent global culture, in which the center–periphery model of the world system dominant since the sixteenth century has begun to break down."[49]

In Luis García Berlanga's brilliant 1952 film, *Bienvenido Mr. Marshall*, the filmmaker explored the paradoxical role of the fantastical products of the Hollywood dream machine in offering Spaniards a mirror in which to take the true measure of their own wishes and desires. Set in the forgotten Castilian *pueblo* of Villar del Río, the very embodiment of Spanish marginality vis-à-vis the geopolitical and economic realities of the Cold War West, the picture nevertheless promoted cinema itself as the primary vehicle for challenging the dual hegemonies of American cultural and political domination. In it, when the townspeople learn of the imminent arrival of an American delegation that is sure to shower their Spanish hosts with money and gifts (so they are promised by the band of government bureaucrats who announce the visit), they concoct a script to transform their village into a movie set version of Andalucía, the stereotypical tourist poster image of Spain (the natives suppose) near and dear to American hearts. But where *Mr. Marshall*'s Yankee visitors unwittingly passed up the chance to witness the spectacle prepared for them by the town's inhabitants, thus losing the opportunity to contemplate their own countenance in the inverted image of the margin's vision of the center, some forty years later, American audiences have finally taken up Almodóvar's playfully sly invitation to do the same.

NOTES

1. Quoted in Peter Besas, *Behind the Spanish Lens: Spanish Cinema Under Fascism and Democracy* (Denver: Arden Press, 1985), 216.

2. Vicente Molina Foix, *New Cinema in Spain* (London: British Film Institute, 1977), 9. In addition to Molina Foix, Peter Besas, and John Hopewell, *Out of the Past: Spanish Cinema After Franco* (London: British Film Institute, 1986), offer detailed overviews of the history of Spanish cinema.

3. Besas, 69–83.

4. As María Antonia García de León reports in her valuable sociological study

of Almodóvar, the loss of the film school tended to reinforce the determining role of socioeconomic class. She cites the case of Almodóvar's more or less contemporaries, directors Fernando Trueba, Oscar Ladoire, and Felip Vega, the "Yucatán School," so called for the name of the café where they used to hang out; their common origins include their attendance at a Catholic private school, the same private college preparatory school, and the Complutense Facultad. As she notes, such an education places them at the antipodes of Almodóvar's social milieu, a factor clearly reflected, despite generational affinities, in their very different film careers. María García de León and Teresa Maldonado, *Pedro Almodóvar, la otra España cañí* (Ciudad Real: Biblioteca de Autores y Temas Manchegos, 1989), 42.

5. See the discussion in José Enrique Monterde, *Veinte años de cine español* (Barcelona: Ediciones Paidós Ibérica, 1993), 54–65.

6. For relevant statistics and an attempt to explain the current situation of the Spanish film industry, see John Hopewell, " 'Art and a Lack of Money': The Crises of the Spanish Film Industry, 1977–90," *Quarterly Review of Film and Video* 13.4 (1991): 113–122.

7. Zulueta, a prolific director of shorts but little inclined to make more feature-length films, designed posters for *Dark Habits, Labyrinth of Passion,* and *What Have I Done to Deserve This?*.

8. Quoted in Miguel Albaladejo et al., *Los fantasmas del deseo: A propósito de Pedro Almodóvar* (Madrid: Aula 7, 1988), 30.

9. Albaladejo et al., 30.

10. Quoted in José Luis Gallero, ed., *Sólo se vive una vez: Esplendor y ruina de la movida madrileña* (Madrid: Ardora, 1991), 149. Gallero's book, which its author deems "a collection of vibrant and disordered fragments . . . [which] ought to be read like a novel" (11), constitutes an invaluable source for understanding the *Movida*'s multiple and often contradictory impulses. All translations from the book are ours.

11. On the role of *La luna*, see Malcolm Compitello, "Translating Postmodernism," paper presented at the November 1992 MMLA Convention. Almodóvar's connections with the paper go back to its inception. His fantasy-memoir "Patty Diphusa" was commissioned initially as a serial in *La luna*, for which he wrote a number of other pieces.

12. Cited in García de León and Maldonado, 132. As García de León notes, such comments evoke echoes of certain aspects of punk ideology. She cites Malcolm McLaren of the Sex Pistols regarding punk's dream of a classless society.

13. There is considerable dissension among both participants and observers concerning the *Movida*'s history and parameters. Nanyé Blásquez considers the beginning of the *Movida* to be the day F-23 (23 February 1981), when Civil Guard commander Antonio Tejero Molina attempted a military coup by taking the Spanish Parliament hostage. The failure of the coup resulted in a joyous celebration of the strength of the young democracy. Others, such as Casani, pinpoint three periods: the punk scene and underground before 1981; the consolidation of the *Movida* and the publication of *La luna de Madrid*, 1981–1986; and the commercialization of the *Movida* and its international acclaim after 1986. Juan Luis Cebrián, editor of *El país*, Spain's premier daily, founded shortly after Franco's death, places the *Movida* in the context of the *desencanto* (disenchantment following the initial euphoria after the dictator's death) as another element in the

political transition, but with cultural aspirations other than the traditional Left's Christian Marxism. In Gallero, i, 11–12, 313.

14. Gallero, 9.

15. Gallero, 371.

16. Carlos Saura's trilogy of flamenco dance films, made in collaboration with choreographer/dancer Antonio Gades—*Bodas de sangre* [*Blood Wedding*] (1980), based on the García Lorca play; *Carmen* (1983), inspired by Prosper Merimée and Georges Bizet; and *El amor brujo* [*Love, the Magician*] (1986), based on Manuel de Falla's ballet—offers a further problematization of the consequences of this artistic and commercial exploration of "Spanishness."

17. Nuria Vidal, *El cine de Pedro Almodóvar*, 2nd ed. (Barcelona: Destino, 1989), 188. Translation ours.

18. Borja Casani and José Tono Martínez, *La luna de Madrid* 1 (November 1983): 6–7.

19. Gianni Vattimo, preface to the Spanish edition of *La sociedad transparente*, trans. Teresa Oñate (Barcelona: Paidós, 1989), 67–68.

20. Gallero, 248.

21. Eduardo Subirats, *La cultura como espectáculo* (Mexico City: Fondo de Cultura Económica, 1988), 218–219.

22. The principal exponent of such views was Gonzalo Fernández de la Mora, in *El crepúsculo de las ideologías* (Madrid: Ediciones Rialp, 1965).

23. This group would include Socialist Prime Minister Felipe González and most of his cabinet as well as a number of well-known filmmakers, including Pilar Miró, who as head of the I.C.A.A. (Institute of Cinema and Audiovisual Arts) in the eighties was responsible for the Miró Law regulating government subsidies for filmmakers and producers.

24. Gallero, 314.

25. Gallero, 219.

26. Pedro Almodóvar, "Narra en su propia voz, el argumento de su última película, *Kika*," *Interfilms* 5.62 (November 1993): 39. Translation ours.

27. Dudley Andrew, "The Unauthorized Auteur Today," in *Film Theory Goes to the Movies*, ed. Jim Collins, Hilary Radner, and Ava Preacher Collins (New York: Routledge, 1993); Timothy Corrigan, *A Cinema Without Walls* (New Brunswick, N.J.: Rutgers University Press, 1991); and James Naremore, "Authorship and the Cultural Politics of Film Criticism," *Film Quarterly* 44.1 (Fall 1990): 14–22. For an invaluable account of the historical and theoretical stakes of the debate on the notion of authorship in film, literature, and critical theory, see John Caughie, ed., *Theories of Authorship* (London: British Film Institute, 1981).

28. The relevant essays have been collected and translated in Jim Hiller, ed., *Cahiers du Cinéma* (Cambridge, Mass.: Harvard University Press, 1985).

29. Andrew Sarris's influential writings for the journal *Film Culture* are collected in his *The American Cinema: Directors and Directing* (New York: E. P. Dutton, 1968).

30. Peter Lev, *The Euro-American Cinema* (Austin: University of Texas Press, 1993), 9.

31. A notable example is Sarris's "existentialist" reading of Tomás Gutiérrez Alea's *Memories of Underdevelopment*. See Andrew Sarris, "A Tale of Two Circles (Films in Focus)," *Village Voice*, 14 February 1974, cited in Tomás Gutiérrez Alea,

director, and Edmundo Desnoes, author, *Inconsolable Memories*, Rutgers Films in Print (New Brunswick, N.J.: Rutgers University Press, 1990), 201–202.

32. Georgia Brown, "Woman on the Verge," *Village Voice*, 2 November 1993, 3.

33. Andrew, 78.

34. Roy Armes, *Third World Film Making and the West* (Berkeley: University of California Press, 1987). Claire Johnston's principal publications include *Notes on Women's Cinema* (London: SEFT, 1973); *Dorothy Arzner: Towards a Feminist Cinema* (London: British Film Institute, 1975), as editor; "The Subject of Feminist Film Theory/Practice," *Screen* 21.2 (1980): 27–34.

35. Writing on the notion of cinematic authorship in the context of Spanish national cinema, Marvin D'Lugo has identified a similar function, arguing: "Though obviously not a Third World culture, historically Spanish cinema has occupied roughly the same position as culturally colonized national cinema in the Third World. That culture of dependency has contributed in no small way to the emphasis upon author cinema as perhaps the single dominant feature of film production in Spain for the last four decades." Thus, observes D'Lugo, for opposition filmmakers from Juan Antonio Bardem and Luis Berlanga in the fifties to Saura in the sixties and beyond, *auteur*ism offered a vehicle for social critique as well as for the development of an "anti-hegemonic style that was a rebuke to the Francoist ideology of representation." Marvin D'Lugo, "Authorship and the Concept of National Cinema in Spain," *Cardozo Arts and Entertainment Journal* 10.2 (1992): 599–600. The essay is reprinted in *The Construction of Authorship*, ed. Martha Woodmansee and Peter Jaszi (Durham, N.C.: Duke University Press, 1994).

36. Corrigan, 104.

37. See, for example, Vicente Sánchez Biosca, "El elixir aromático de la posmodernidad o la comedia según Pedro Almodóvar," in *Escritos sobre el cine español 1973–1987*, ed José A. Hurtado and Francisco M. Pico (Valencia: Filmoteca de la Generalitat Valenciana, 1989), 115, under the subheading "Almodóvar's Errors": "Almodóvar's cinema is criticized for its 'weakness in plotting' . . . its 'clumsy scripts' . . . for his films being merely 'a series of half-baked jokes badly strung together.' " And more recently, apropos of *Kika*: "[In the film] we discover nothing new: Almodóvar is a brilliant inventor of plot ideas, a savvy promoter, an imaginative director, and a bad writer of films [*un mal escritor de películas*]." Angel Fernández-Santos, "La ley del desastre," *El país*, 30 October 1994, 27. The Spanish press's treatment of acknowledged *auteurs* like Saura on the one hand and Victor Erice on the other has been varied. When Almodóvar replaced Saura as the best-known and most marketable Spanish director abroad, he also took over the latter's role as the director most Spanish critics seem to love to hate. For a survey of critical attitudes toward Saura, see Manuel Palacio, "La obra de Carlos Saura en la crítica especializada española," in *Le cinéma de Carlos Saura* (Bordeaux: Presses Universitaires de Bordeaux, 1984). In contrast, Víctor Erice, director of *El espíritu de la colmena (The Spirit of the Beehive*, 1973), *El sur (The South*, 1983), and *El sol del membrillo (The Quince Tree Sun*, 1992), has generally received enthusiastic reviews in both the general and the specialized press. Nevertheless, the anomalous nature of his directorial career—he has made only three feature films in twenty years, preferring to support himself by making television

advertising—perhaps no less than Almodóvar's, puts into question modernist notions of the *auteur*.

38. Corrigan, 105.

39. See the bibliography.

40. Consult the excerpts from representative Spanish publications reproduced in García de León and Maldonado, 26–28. Each of the press books for Almodóvar's films contains a similar biographical abstract. The press book for his most recent film, *Kika*, takes the reader over familiar ground, and adds some existential asides ("His education with the Salesian fathers only taught him to sing Gregorian Chant and to lose his faith in God."). Virtually all extended treatments of Almodóvar and his films in the U.S. press inevitably return to this same seemingly irresistible tale of upward social and artistic mobility. For example, see Ben Brantley, "Spain's Bad Boy Grows Up," *Vanity Fair* 53 (April 1990): "Pedro Almodóvar was born in the repressive age of Franco and spent the first eight years of his life in a bleak impoverished village called Calatrava de Calvera" (185).

41. Corrigan, 107.

42. The memoirs of Patty Diphusa, whom Almodóvar characterizes as "belonging to the species of those wayward girls of Warhol and Morrisey and the first Divine (*Pink Flamingos* and *Female Trouble*), Anita Loos's Lorelei, the Holly Golightly of *Breakfast at Tiffany's* . . . with the amoral and witty tone of Fran Lebowitz and even Dorothy Parker," were first published in serial form in *La luna de Madrid* and later collected with a number of Almodóvar's other occasional pieces. Pedro Almodóvar, *Patty Diphusa y otros textos* (Barcelona: Anagrama, 1991), 11, translation ours. There is also an English translation: *Patty Diphusa and Other Writings*, trans. Kirk Anderson (Boston: Faber and Faber, 1992).

43. See the pieces in *W* and the Style section of the Sunday *New York Times*: William Middleton, "Almodóvar's Reel Camp," *W*, April 1994, 76; and Amy M. Spindler, "Dressed to Thrill: In Pedro Almodóvar's Films, Fashion Sparks the Passion," *New York Times*, 13 March 1994, sec. 9, pp. 1, 4. Published some two months before *Kika*'s scheduled New York premiere, these articles provide proof of the auteur–star's extracinematic reach.

44. To the extent that this celebration of the protean possibilities of authorial masquerade has resulted in the apparent downplaying of Almodóvar's "personal" identity as a gay male/gay male director, the response among the Anglo-American gay male community has sometimes been uneasy and even distrustful. (On that issue, see the chapter by James Mandrell included in this volume.) In an interview with Brad Gooch—reported in Gooch's "The King of Kink," *Out* (May 1994): 57, 114—Almodóvar adds fuel to the fire, explaining his preference for what might be called a serial view of gender/sexual orientation/identities:

You know, I could be married in two years and I don't want anyone saying nothing against that. To be gay is not something that determines my life. It's a part, but not the most important part. Because sometimes you live your homosexuality throughout your life. But I remember that I lived my life many different ways. At one time, all heterosexual. Another time, bisexual. Another, closer to drag queen—not drag queen, but punk with makeup and so on. In the last years my masculinity has grown more and more. It's good to go through all the phases so as not to be left with the sensation of something you haven't done.

45. Rosemary J. Coombe, "Author/ing the Celebrity: Publicity Rights, Postmodern Politics and Unauthorized Genders," *Cardozo Arts and Entertainment Re-*

view 10.2 (1992): 365; reprinted in *The Construction of Authorship*, ed. Martha Woodmansee and Peter Jaszi (Durham, N.C.: Duke University Press, 1994).

46. Coombe, 366–67.

47. Coombe, 370–371. The paradigmatic example, explored at some length by Coombe, is, of course, Madonna.

48. Corrigan, citing a phrase of Stuart Hall's, 4.

49. John Beverly and José Oviedo, eds., *The Postmodernism Debate in Latin America*, special issue of *boundary 2* 20.3 (Fall 1993): 3. For a rethinking of the breakdown of the hierarchies of the center–margin model in the specific context of Spanish media, with a particular eye to the national/regional interface, see the discussion in Marsha Kinder, "Micro- and Macroregionalism in Catalan Cinema, European Coproduction and Global Television," in her *Blood Cinema* (Berkeley: University of California Press, 1993). She cites Almodóvar, along with Bigas Luna and Eloy de la Iglesia, as filmmakers who succeed in "breaking through to an international market by politicizing marginality."

Pepi, Luci, Bom and Dark Habits: Lesbian Comedy, Lesbian Tragedy

Paul Julian Smith

PEPI, LUCI, BOM: LESBIAN COMEDY

A medium shot of two women knitting indoors: Pepi (Carmen Maura) is thirtyish and wears a dress with black, white, and red stripes; Luci (Eva Siva) is "fortyish and submissive,"[1] with sculptured hair and a neat blue cardigan. They quarrel over the knitting, and Pepi, now in close-up, eyes her companion lasciviously and strikes her on the arm. In a series of reverse-angle shots, Luci modestly explains to the admiring Pepi how she likes to be dominated. Pepi pricks her arm with the knitting needle, with a smile of complicity; and, on hearing the doorbell, disappears out of frame.

Cut to medium long shot from Luci's point of view of Bom (Alaska), a teenage punkette in a black dress and a leopard-print coat. We see a close up of Luci's reaction, her mouth gaping in wonder at this vision. In medium long shot, with Luci still sitting in the center, Pepi moves into frame on the left, Bom on the right. The latter lifts her leg toward the wall. A match on action shows her completing the gesture from the side: now her leg arches over the top of the frame; Luci's hesitant face is below on the right; and the admiring Pepi is in the center. A stream of urine crosses the screen and bathes the now ecstatic Luci.[2]

Almodóvar has proudly called *Pepi, Luci, Bom, y otras chicas del montón* (*Pepi, Luci, Bom, and Other Ordinary Girls*) his "dirtiest" film, claiming that he wanted to show behavior typical of pornography within a naturalistic and everyday atmosphere, free from exhibitionism.[3] And it is clear that the humor of this scene lies in the contrast between banal, domestic reality (knitting classes) and perverse sexual practice: after urinating on her newfound partner, Bom politely asks which part of Spain she is from. But this early sequence in the film is not important merely for the incongruity it suggests between bodily function and social convention. It also sets up a triangular structure that will operate throughout this lesbian comedy: the relationship between housewife Luci and punk singer Bom (the only one that will last the length of the film) is mediated for the viewer by Carmen Maura's Pepi, who serves both as an identification figure (we see most of the action through her eyes) and as a proxy for our voyeurism. Pepi does not take part in the sex action, but is shown to initiate it and to take pleasure in watching her friends. This triangular structure ("top," "bottom," and mediating voyeur) raises particular problems for the heterosexual male spectator, whose quest for pleasure in the pornographic scene is continually disrupted by banal, material detail (knitting needles and polite conversation).[4]

Pepi, Luci, Bom, Almodóvar's first feature, was shot over a period of eighteen months (1979–1980) on a minuscule budget (Plate 3). The coarseness of the image (16 mm blown up to 35) and the muddiness of the sound track are immediately apparent. One problem with discussing this film, then, is the extent to which its cinematic qualities result from deliberate technique or financial necessity. In his interview with *Contracampo*,[5] Almodóvar claimed that he adapted the material to suit the budget: for example, he could not afford a lighting engineer, so he wrote the project in such a way that the quality of the image was not important.

On its release *Pepi, Luci, Bom* was praised for its "spontaneity" and "freshness" by such influential critics as Diego Galán.[6] However, if we look at the opening scenes (which take place just before the urination scene examined above), we can see that this effect is by no means natural and is rather the result (conscious or otherwise) of a deviation from the norms of continuity editing. Thus, in the first sequence, Pepi—played incongruously by Carmen Maura as the schoolgirl nymphette—is raped in her flat by a policeman (Félix Rotaeta). But in the next, she has changed into black leather trousers and a rhinestone top, as she paces up and down, plotting revenge. Immediately afterward (with no signal that story time has elapsed) she visits the room where Bom's punk group is rehearsing. Now she wears jeans and a pink satin jacket. The lack of attention to continuity extends from clothing to characterization: Pepi's rape changes her instantaneously from a lewd child to a scheming woman. As the punks, on Pepi's instructions, beat up the man they believe to be the policeman (it is in fact his identical twin brother), they are dressed in nineteenth-century costume as if "for the *verbena* [street festival] of San Isidro" (script, p. 9). The beating (which Pepi watches with conspicuous pleasure) inexplicably takes place to the sound of music from the *zarzuela* (Spanish operetta) *La revoltosa.*

Without taking this sequence overseriously, I would suggest that it demonstrates to the audience from the start of the film that the virtues of classical cinema (plausibility, psychology) will be subverted by anti-naturalistic techniques (incongruity of sound and image, discontinuity of character). The film would thus seem to place itself generically as a "crazy comedy," one in which anarchic humor derives from a subversion of the cinematic mechanism itself.[7] However, I will suggest that as *Pepi, Luci, Bom* continues, it also draws on the equally canonic genre of "situation comedy," which relies on the disturbance of social hierarchies plausibly represented to the viewer. Thus we must believe in the possibility of the ill-fated lesbian romance between Luci and Bom if we are to respond to its subversive and comic properties. Lesbian desire thus serves as the trouble in representation, the element that makes the film hesitate between two mutually exclusive comic modes.[8]

The grainy look and informal narrative of *Pepi, Luci, Bom* give the impression of *cinéma vérité*: sequences at a party, in a nightclub, and in a concert hall seem improvised, although in fact they often correspond closely to the original script. In his review in *Contracampo*, Alberto Fernández Torres criticizes the film for the way it relies on the spectator's knowledge of an actual referent (the Madrid "new wave" *demimonde*) that lies "beyond the camera."[9] Fernández argues that Almodóvar's attempted rupture with the formal logic of cinematic discourse (his reduction of narrative to a "disconnected babble") is itself an artificial device, no less mannered than the self-conscious minimalism of another first feature released in 1980, Fernando Trueba's *Opera prima* (*A Cousin in Opera*/*First Works*). Fernández takes it for granted that *Pepi, Luci, Bom* has no "message" or "analysis" beyond the surface of its anecdotal narrative. I would suggest, however, that in its representation of lesbianism, as elsewhere, it carries an implicit social commentary that transcends the film's undeniable concern with modish documentation.

Indeed, *Pepi, Luci, Bom*'s dialogue is thick with references to contemporary history and politics. Félix Rotaeta's policeman (rapist of Pepi, abandoned husband of Luci) is a caricature Fascist, complete with dark glasses, who complains over breakfast that he doesn't know what the country is coming to "with so much democracy." When Luci walks out on him for Bom, she claims to be a victim of "the wave of eroticism sweeping Spain." The problem with such references is that they are, of course, parodic, clichés stripped of their normal context. Like Pepi's pornographic provocations ("What do you think of my saucy little rabbit?"), political discourse in the film is shown to be secondhand, an empty repetition of propositions that have lost any claim to truth-value that they may once have had. In this (loosely postmodern) mode Almodóvar coincides with Richard Dyer's account of gay underground cinema in the United States; and *Pepi, Luci, Bom*'s explicit references to North America (the use of English-language pop music on the sound track; the appear-

ance of a drag queen claiming—implausibly—to be from New York) suggest we should look more closely at the relationship between gay cinema
in the two countries.

For Dyer, underground film is defined not so much by its formal properties (which vary from one *cinéaste* to another) as by its marginal relation to mainstream production and distribution networks and its tendency to break down social (and particularly sexual) taboos.[10] From the
forties to the sixties (from Kenneth Anger to Andy Warhol), gay underground film in the United States moved from a celebration of the filmmaker as subject to an impersonal style, in which authenticity and fidelity
of representation gave way to a desire for the inauthentic, the cult of
plastic.[11] Like pop art, the camp sensibility of the time may have been
morally and politically neutral, but it was "not socially inexpressive."[12]
While assertions of a lesbian or gay identity are dependent on an "illusory
unified sense of self," the films of the underground offered, in contrast,
"fragments and surfaces, authenticity [mixed with] theatricality"—in
short, a "fiction of identity" that questioned whether selfhood was even
compatible with cinema.[13]

In spite of the transparent differences between the films of Warhol and
Almodóvar, I would argue that *Pepi, Luci, Bom* shares an underground
ethos similar to that which flourished in New York in the sixties. Thus
the film was produced (like Almodóvar's previous Super-8 shorts) under
unorthodox conditions: shooting took place when the director had the
time and the money left over from his day job at the Telefónica. Unlike
Warhol's films, however, it achieved immediate commercial distribution
and was not subject to censorship, except by local authorities.[14] We have
seen that the breaking of sexual taboos is a constant in the film, as is the
matter-of-factness with which (porno)graphic material is presented to the
audience. More specifically, Almodóvar and Warhol share an interest in
figures whom Dyer claims as the epitomes of the underground: male
prostitutes and drag queens. And while Almodóvar's personality already
seems to dominate *Pepi, Luci, Bom* (and he makes his most extended
screen appearance as the master of ceremonies in a penis-size competition), the film does not present itself either as the authentic expression
of the *auteur* who has produced it or as the faithful representation of a
social reality it claims to reflect. Rather, it manifests a cult of the surface
and of the artificial, juxtaposing images and sounds from a bewildering
range of secondhand popular culture: *zarzuela*, comics, and television
advertising. Traditional Spanish motifs collide with transitional youth culture, as when Bom combines a Spanish fan and *peineta* [ornamental
comb]) with a lurex microdress.

The final question posed by Dyer is that of lesbian or gay identity,
which he claims is problematized by (North American) underground cinema. To see if this is also applicable to *Pepi, Luci, Bom*, we must look

more closely at the central relationship between the punkette and the housewife. After leaving her husband, Luci moves into the flat Bom shares with two gay painters (Enrique Naya and Juan Carrero). The paintings that hang on the walls of their flat (of classical Spanish ladies complete with mantillas) suggest both the postmodern cult of the ready-made and the underground crossover of painting, music, and film. The script tells us that Luci has knitted covers for Bom's punchball and weight-training equipment, "a deliciously feminine touch" (p. 57).

In a long and poorly framed take, broken only by a disorienting cut to a mirror reflection, Pepi visits the lesbian couple, offers them cocaine, and informs them that she has decided to make a film based on their story. As Luci fetches drinks in a properly submissive manner, Pepi explains excitedly that "representation is always somewhat artificial." For example, she has seen Luci peed on and beaten as if it were perfectly natural *(como si nada)*; she has seen her eat Bom's snot "as if it were a piece of bread." In cinema, this is impossible; the spectator requires proof of (woman's) pleasure: if she doesn't moan in ecstasy, then people won't believe she's enjoying it, even if she really is. Everything must be exaggerated a little. What's fun about the women's relationship is that one is the forty-year-old wife of a policeman and the other a seventeen-year-old pop singer. It is thus necessary for Bom to act up her perversion: Pepi knows Bom is a true sadist, but at first sight she simply looks unsympathetic.

There are multiple levels of irony here. For example, the monotonous performance of Bom (played by the nonprofessional actor and real-life singer Alaska) does indeed give the impression of antipathy rather than sadism, however much she drags Luci round on a dog collar. Alaska's limited acting skills thus deny us those touches of exaggeration that Pepi claims are necessary in film, if the cast is to convince the (male?) audience that the female desire represented on the screen is authentic.[15] The male, heterosexual viewer is thus deprived of those filmic signs that represent female *jouissance* to him. On the other hand, a relationship between two such mismatched characters is already wholly incongruous; the frisson of the film comes (as Alberto Fernández Torres suggests) from the combination of outrageous situations and resolutely naturalistic dialogue: the lesbian ménage of punk and housewife seems perfectly natural, even within the master-and-slave role-playing. But this perceived "naturalness" raises an important problem: if lesbian love is taken wholly for granted, then its specific relationship to social reality will be erased. There is only one point at which the affair is not taken for granted: when a "flamenco rock" singer laughs on being told that Luci is Bom's girlfriend *(novia)*. The main characters' reactions, however, show that this faux pas is clearly an aberration.

The relationship between the two women remains, nonetheless, the

most sympathetic element in the film. Luci quite literally lets down her
hair and gains in self-confidence, until she is tempted back to her husband by his superior expertise in sadism. And one formal technique in
Pepi, Luci, Bom noted by John Hopewell (the absence of establishing
shots)[16] also tends to work against the ironic, dissociative devices and to
draw attention toward the characters and away from the highly colored
environment they inhabit. There seems little doubt that the audience is
encouraged to identify with Pepi, Luci, and Bom in a way they are not
with the men in the film, who are generally presented as sadistic or voyeuristic caricatures.

Without denying the comic tone of the film, it is worth considering
what some lesbians have said about sadomasochism and role-playing,
which have in recent years been the subject of intense debate.[17] Thus
Margaret Hunt has suggested that in its attempt to root out the "victimization" thought to be inherent in S/M, revolutionary feminism has de-
eroticized women's liberation; moreover, it is not possible to make a
clean, binary divide between lesbians who practice S/M and those who
do not.[18] Cherry Smyth appraises butch/top and femme/bottom sex in
lesbian pornography: even with a dildo, this practice need not "replicate
static and predictable male-female interaction"; rather, it "signifies the
lack of fixity of gender . . . [the] potential split between the sexual object
and the object of desire."[19] Diane Hamer cites Parveen Adams's argument
that S/M denotes "an erotic plasticity and movement . . . a play with identity and a play with genitality"; as in butch/femme relations, "lesbian
desire turns on a relationship to difference [in which] different positions
are taken up in relation to another's desire; and while the positions may
be fixed . . . the individuals who occupy them are not necessarily fixed."[20]
All of these women stress the fluidity of sadomasochistic role-playing, the
way in which it offers a plurality of positions from which pleasure can be
taken.

Clearly such views are controversial among lesbian women. And they
are made in the context of a debate on pornography produced by and
for women. But I would suggest that the central relationship in *Pepi,
Luci, Bom* can also be read not as a mere reproduction (repetition) of
heterosexual power structures but rather as a liberating adoption of
erotic roles that are at once constrictive and mobile. The extreme diver-
gence between the two partners (age, class, and profession) suggests in
parodic form those differences between lesbians that many women now
seek to embrace;[21] and the fluidity of the lovers' roles (Luci abandons
Bom when the latter becomes too kind to her) suggests the critique of
homosexual identity that Richard Dyer associates with underground filmmakers such as Warhol. When all social and erotic life is surface or role-
playing, then there can be no stable position from which to affirm one's
sense of self. Lesbian (or gay) identity thus becomes a "fiction," albeit a

necessary one.[22] This does not, however, mean that we (men) can allow ourselves pleasure in scenes such as that in which an ecstatic Luci is beaten half to death by her jealous husband. Her confession to Bom from the hospital bed ("I'm more of a bitch than you thought I was"), delivered with quiet sobriety, also remains disturbing. The representation of role-playing (in this case, bottom or femme) does not dissolve ethical dilemmas. Rather, it requires the viewer to meditate on the power structures inherent in all sexual relations.

Toward the end of the film, Pepi invites the lovelorn Bom back to her flat for a meal. We first see the two women from outside, framed in separate window panes. The camera then moves inside the kitchen for a sequence of not-quite-symmetrical reverse-angle shots (perhaps determined by the limited space of the location). Once more, the sequence has an air of improvisation, which is not in fact the case: the dialogue figures in the original script. Bom is lamenting that she will never find a woman as good in bed as Luci. Pepi reassures her and goes on to talk once more about the film she is planning to make: in one ending Luci and Bom get married in white, and as a wedding present Pepi gives them the child she conceived after being raped by the policeman. This is appropriate, now that the two women have formed a home. But Bom has another ending: she and Pepi will settle down together as lovers. To the sound of a romantic tune, the camera cuts to an extreme close-up of the dish on the stove (salt cod, *bacalao*), an image that, according to the script (p. 88), takes on an "ambiguous character."

This is the only sequence in the film in which the extradiegetic (incidental) music serves to reinforce the image rather than to undermine or subvert it. It is a highly engaging scene in which both the ever-animated Maura and the normally stolid Alaska smile and gaze at each other with what seems to be genuine affection. And it is the scene on which the film ended in the original script: with a freeze frame "like a hake." I would suggest that such scenes of domestic, female intimacy (which occur throughout Almodóvar's oeuvre) are more significant than they might appear. They imply not only a sense of continuing community among women from which men are inevitably and unthinkingly excluded but also a possibility for new kinds of female relationship when the twin pleasures of cinematic narrative and lesbian role-playing coincide. It is a conjunction that will be explored at greater length in *Entre tinieblas* (*Dark Habits*).

DARK HABITS: WOMEN IN CHAINS

The scene is the dressing room in a night club: "like all dressing rooms it is reminiscent of a chapel."[23] Yolanda (Cristina S. Pascual: "pretty worn out in spite of her youth," p. 2) is looking at herself in the mirror. Sud-

denly her reflection is joined by those of two nuns requesting an autograph. Yolanda turns to face them, and the Mother Superior (Julieta
Serrano) moves into shot on the right. She looks up at a photograph of
two people on the wall. In extreme close-up, Yolanda's red-nailed hand
cuts her boyfriend from the photograph and signs her own image for the
Mother Superior. There follows a medium shot of the three women together: the Mother Superior standing in the top left of the frame; Sor
Estiércol (Sister Manure, Marisa Paredes) in the top right; Yolanda sitting
center bottom between the two nuns, who look at one another over her
head with enigmatic complicity. A poster of Mick Jagger is prominent
behind them. The Mother Superior gives Yolanda the address of their
order (The Humble Redeemers), insisting she get in contact if ever she
is in trouble.

This early sequence from *Dark Habits* is emblematic for a number of
reasons. First, it suggests that this will be a film in which men play no
part: Yolanda's boyfriend is quite literally cut out of the picture and,
indeed, is shortly to die of a drug overdose. Second, it suggests erotic
exchange within a world of women: Yolanda offers her signature and is
given in return the chance of a refuge she will shortly take up; there will
also be a rivalry among the nuns for her affection. Finally, it points to
the role of mirroring or reproduction in the film: although Almodóvar
insists on the differences between women (between a singer and a nun),
the narrative will suggest a merging of the two: the Mother Superior is
so fascinated by fallen women that she herself becomes indistinguishable
from them, exclaiming at one point, "I am the same as them."

Dark Habits (Almodóvar's third feature) has higher production values
than *Pepi, Luci, Bom*, and at least one critic[24] has commented on the
technical accomplishment of its cinematography. Indeed, the very first
scenes (which we see before the autograph scene above, although they
occur chronologically later) reveal a newly mobile frame and stylish mise-
en-scène. The film begins with the camera tracking Yolanda as she walks
down the Madrid street where she lives, then cuts to a tilt down the face
of her building before following her up the stairs to her flat. This location
is shot from low angles and in muted blues and grays that contrast with
Yolanda's blood-red trousers (a chromatic association maintained
throughout the film). When Yolanda's boyfriend dies suddenly (the event
that precipitates her flight to the convent), an extreme close-up of his
head lying on the floor is framed so as to show her face reflected in a
mirrored surface at the other side of the room. In *Dark Habits*, the aesthetic quality of the image, in particular the careful use of framing, will
have a weight of significance that will often transcend the anecdotal subject matter. I shall argue that one particular visual technique (the use of
frontality, or placing of the camera at an angle of ninety degrees to the
action) has a particular effect on our identification with the characters,

who are (superficially at least) as implausible as any in Almodóvar's oeuvre.

Yolanda, suspected of murdering her junkie boyfriend, is forced to flee to the convent. Her arrival is presented as an Annunciation, eloquently exploiting the expressive potential of light: as the nuns prepare for mass in an extreme long shot of the darkened chapel, the doors behind them are flung open to reveal Yolanda, framed by a halo of brilliant light. In a rare crane shot, the camera rises as the Mother Superior advances up a path of light to welcome the lost sheep to the convent. The eloquence of the image is thus reinforced by reference to Christian iconography: Yolanda is blonde like an angel. However, at this point in the film it is not yet clear whether such references are to be taken parodically, as a subversion of Catholic dogma, or seriously, as a secularization of divine love.

The problem recurs in a subsequent sequence in which Yolanda takes her first meal in the convent, dressed incongruously in the strapless red lurex dress in which she performs in the nightclub. Here the setup is reminiscent of the Last Supper, with the five nuns and Yolanda ranged on one side of extended tables as they eat (Plate 7). But already there have been touches of unmotivated "crazy comedy" similar to those in *Pepi, Luci, Bom*. We have learned that Sor Perdida (Sister Sinner: Carmen Maura) has a cleaning fetish and a tiger called Niño (Baby); that Sor Estiércol (Sister Manure: Marisa Paredes) is prone to LSD-inspired visions; Sor Rata (Sister Rat: Chus Lampreave) will prove to be the author of best-selling sleazy novels. But as always in Almodóvar, these eccentricities are quite taken for granted: when Yolanda recoils on catching a glimpse of the tiger, Sor Rata explains, "It's logical for her to be frightened; it's the first time she's seen a tiger in a convent." The humor relies (as so often in *Pepi, Luci, Bom*) on the contrast between that which is natural to the narrative's insiders and unnatural to the voyeur or observer figure, who stands in for (represents) the spectator on the scene of perversity. In spite of the "crazy comedy" (of the intermittent disruption of the codes denoting filmic verisimilitude), then, performances remain restrained. For example, the benevolent and sentimental Sor Perdida (Maura) would not seem out of place in *The Sound of Music* (were it not for her cleaning fetish and menagerie). Almodóvar thus rejects the easy anticlerical option of Buñuel, and is far indeed from the (heteroerotic) convent fantasies of Walerian Borowczyk.

On its release, critics gave widely different accounts of *Dark Habits*. These variations arose from their perceptions of the film's register; of its relation to established genres; and of its direction of sympathy or identification toward the central character, Julieta Serrano's amorous Mother Superior. As we shall see, the question of their response to the lesbian theme of the narrative (which generally goes unmentioned) is vital here.

There seems little doubt that the film was scandalous to many: there was a bomb scare at the Madrid opening,[25] and the Italian press was hostile when it was shown (out of competition) at the Venice festival.[26] More characteristic of what was to come was the press coverage of the Barcelona premiere, which featured pictures of gay men in the audience who came dressed as nuns.[27] The film was thus a site of conflicting ideological interpretation even before it was seen: between traditionalists and *progres*, heterosexual and homosexual audiences. J. A. Mahieu wrote in *Fotogramas* that the Mother Superior represented "the contradictions, fanaticisms, and repressions of traditional Spanish religious culture" but claimed that the director observed her with "an amused, distanced look."[28] However, Francisco Marinero in *Diario 16* wrote that the film was characterized by "crazy humor" (*humor disparatado*) that is treated "curiously enough . . . almost seriously."[29] Angeles Maso in *La vanguardia* singled out Julieta Serrano's Mother Superior as the one character not presented "in a parodic context," and claimed that Almodóvar's "innocent" fantasies were directed to the new Spanish consumer society.[30] Perhaps the most interesting account in the dailies was from José Luis Guarner in *El periódico*. Guarner claimed that the film (an impossible hybrid of a Mexican novelette, a Douglas Sirk melodrama, and an underground comic) is neither scandalous nor anticlerical. Rather, it reveals a certain affection for its characters and for the religious symbols it treats with respectful irony, "as if trying to recuperate them through a happy, pagan sensuality."[31]

None of these reviewers uses the word "lesbian." One who does, however, is José Luis Téllez in *Contracampo*.[32] Téllez does not like the film: its generic mixture leaves it paralyzed between comedy and tragedy. According to Téllez, the spiraling implausibility of the plot (the Mother Superior is not only a lesbian but also a drug addict and a blackmailer) renders audience identification impossible. Almodóvar is afraid to commit himself and thus produces a text emptied of all meaning, a "simulacrum." Téllez makes one exception here: the scenes in which Yolanda confronts the Mother Superior deserve to be "rescued in [the viewer's] memory"; here a certain distance between event and representation (*acontecimiento, relato*) leads to a pertinent tension that is later frittered away in farcical mayhem.

Téllez's point is slightly obscure: his position is not that of the plain man arguing for naturalistic cinema; rather, he demands a cinema that uses identification to provoke thought in its audience and to prevent films from being consumed like any other capitalist commodity. But what is interesting for our purpose is that Téllez locates the fruitful tension between image and referent (representation and object) in the scenes of lesbian desire. We shall now look at the most lyrical of those scenes before attempting to relate *Dark Habits'* challenging images of lesbianism to Richard Dyer's analysis of "confrontational politics" in lesbian and gay film outside Spain.

Yolanda has been staying in the convent for some time. She enters the Mother Superior's office dressed in a red blouse, with the top buttons provocatively undone. Almodóvar cuts back and forth between Yolanda and the Mother Superior: the former walks across the room, her face marked by the crisscross shadows cast by the lattice windows; the latter remains seated at her desk. Both are miming alternately the words to a bolero sung by Lucho Gatica: it tells of a love that is torture (*martirio*), a love that would better be forgotten. As the sequence continues, the reverse angles become more frontal, until both actors are singing directly to camera (directly to the other woman). In this highly stylized and emotionally charged sequence the audience is addressed directly as a participant in lesbian seduction.

Yolanda sits next to the Mother Superior, who says that she adores music like the bolero, which speaks of human feelings. Yolanda replies that this music tells the truth about life: everyone knows what love and disappointment are like. The Mother Superior compliments Yolanda on her appearance, elegantly wasted by drugs: there is a great beauty in physical deterioration. Yolanda looks at the wall behind the Mother Superior, on which female pinups are displayed as if in an altarpiece: Marilyn Monroe is prominent among the images.[33] The Mother Superior explains that she loves great sinners, for it is in imperfect creatures that God's greatness is to found: Jesus died on the cross not to save the holy but to redeem sinners. Julieta Serrano speaks her lines with quiet seriousness, entirely lacking in irony.

What we find in this sequence is the lesbian mirroring I first noted in the dressing room sequence. The camera position and editing suggest a direct confrontation between the two actors in which their very different images (scarlet woman and black-garbed nun) are reflected symmetrically in one another. Indeed, the last words of the bolero are "one facing the other, that is all there is" (*frente a frente, nada más*). But this is no facile synthesis or narcissism. Rather, the erotic charge of the scene derives from the continuing differences (of age, profession, and appearance) between the two women.

Moreover, the sequence suggests a lesbian appropriation of ready-made (heterosexual) images found in popular culture: thus each woman in turn mouths to the other words originally sung by a man to a woman. Popular music may voice universal feelings, as Yolanda suggests, but its use in this context marks a rare and specifically lesbian redirection of imagery generally naturalized as heterosexual.[34] If, in the title of the song, the two lovers are "chained" together (*encadenados/as*), then the nature of that amorous bond is quite specific to this lesbian narrative. Yolanda remains the recipient of the Mother Superior's advances only because she is obliged to remain in the convent as a refuge from the police.

The altarlike disposition of the images on the office wall is another example of the lesbian rearticulation of dominant (heterosexist) culture. The Mother Superior's praise of great sinners must ring ironically in the ears of viewers aware of her passion for Yolanda: the image of Monroe, previously caught in the unproblematic gaze of a heterosexual man, is here reduplicated, redirected, exposed to the unaccustomed look of the lesbian woman. Like the S/M role-playing of *Pepi, Luci, Bom*, the popular and religious iconography of *Dark Habits* forms a medium in which women can act out their fantasies to and for one another.

In spite of the formal mirroring of the bolero scene, then, the relationship between Yolanda and the Mother Superior is asymmetrical in two ways: the younger woman is dependent on the older one, who could give her up to the police; the older is dependent on the younger for the reciprocation of her love. This disequilibrium is reinforced in a scene where the two women confront one another once more, this time in the garden: Yolanda uses the formal address *usted*; the Mother Superior, the informal *tú*. But it is Yolanda who ends the discussion by saying she is only using her lover as a tool (*instrumento*) to get what she wants.

The situation is repeated a little later when Merche (Cecilia Roth), the youthful ex-lover of the Mother Superior, arrives at the convent, on the run from the police. When Merche says she loves the Mother Superior, the latter exclaims, "You don't love me; you need me." It is perhaps not overserious to see this scene as another pointer to an important theme in the film: the instrumental use of human beings in affective and sexual relationships, a tendency from which lesbian relationships are not exempt. The Mother Superior gravely replaces the shoes on Merche's feet as she is led away by the police.

Dark Habits is a separatist narrative in which men have no place: the convent is funded by a Marquesa whose husband has died; Sor Rata has a venomous sister outside the convent (Eva Siva, in a very different role from the submissive Luci) but no visible male relations. The only significant male role is that of the chaplain, who reveals an unexpected knowledge of and interest in Cecil Beaton's costumes for *My Fair Lady*.[35] In addition to the separatist echoes, the film coincides with strains in cultural feminism: the investigation of traditional material (such as the religious) historically gendered as feminine.[36] If we seek a lesbian/gay context for *Dark Habits*' fearless provocations, however, we are more likely to find it in the confrontational cinema of the seventies. In Richard Dyer's account, the aim of confrontational politics was to "zap" the (heterosexual) public, to shock it into raised consciousness.[37] For Dyer, the central contradiction of confrontational politics was an unresolved conflict between vanguardism and libertarianism: the first involved taking the lead in telling people the truth about lesbian and gay life; the second involved refusing to have a position, and letting people think what they wished.[38] I would suggest that this is also a problem with Almodóvar's representation of lesbianism in *Dark Habits*: on the one hand, the logic of the narrative requires that heterosexual audiences accept the representativeness of homosexual desire (there is no romance between women and men with which they can identify); on the other hand, the film refuses to offer an unambiguous direction of sympathy toward Julieta Serrano's luminous (but also obsessive and deluded) Mother Superior. When she and Yolanda decide to withdraw from heroin together, they are shown in a striking image that recalls the shot before the cooking scene in *Pepi, Luci, Bom*: the women are seen from outside the building, each framed by a different window. They are at once together (in the same cinematic frame, in the same room) and apart (separated by the composition within the frame). It is a fitting image of the intermittent identification with and withdrawal from the lesbian woman that (as critics testify) must problematize audience response to the film. Confronted by a passionate but destructive lesbian affair, with no explicit prompting from the film as to which position they are to adopt, spectators may well be amused.

At the end of the film, the nuns give a party for the Mother Superior. The mise-en-scène is gaudy: golden leaves and multicolored flowers strung on cellophane. Yolanda, dressed in a metallic cloak and matching gown, delivers a song direct to the camera (direct to Mother Superior, watching in the center of the front row). It is called "I Left Because I Left" and speaks of a "forbidden love" (Plate 8). Once more the camera positions and editing reinforce the sense of mirroring between the two women (of reflection and difference). After the party Yolanda does indeed leave, to form a spontaneous new grouping of women with the Marquesa and Sor Rata, a further example of Almodóvar's many same-sex "pretended families." When the Mother Superior discovers Yolanda has gone, she lets out what the script calls a "cry of impotence, [a] terrible lament [which] pierces the convent walls" (p. 64). As the camera tracks back to leave her once more framed within a window, the bolero she had mimed with Yolanda plays one final time on the sound track.

It is perhaps significant that in the original script there is a coda in which the Mother Superior is sent to prison for drug trafficking and Yolanda joins up with the Marquesa's grandson, who (for reasons too complex to explain here) is Tarzan. Almodóvar chose rather to end his film with the unambiguously tragic image of the abandoned lesbian lover, even though this meant leaving diverse narrative strands unresolved. Attention is thus directed emphatically to this single focus of the drama, which must be taken as preeminent. If *Pepi, Luci, Bom* is a lesbian comedy (lurching between "crazy" gags and social humor), *Dark Habits* is a lesbian tragedy, but one whose pathos is compromised by the film's oscillating register and stylized cinematic form. As Richard Dyer says, like much gay filmmaking it has the capacity to be very serious about something while treating it as if it were trivial.[39] The credits roll on the freeze-frame of Julieta Serrano behind the window: the shadows of palm fronds (hardly typical of Madrid) are cast on the wall, matching the tropical sound of Lucho Gatica's melancholy bolero. Lesbian desire is here aestheticized and distanced, but not ironized or belittled. It is a tricky sleight of hand that Almodóvar will also attempt to achieve in the all-male romance of *La ley del deseo* (*Law of Desire*).

NOTES

1. "Pepi, Luci, Bom y otras chicas del montón," original script (Madrid, 28 November 1981), 12. Further references will be within parentheses in the text.

2. For urination and sadomasochism, see the account by Antoine de Baecque of a sequence parodying television commercials, " 'Pipi [*sic*], Luci, Bom': Pedro Almodóvar joue avec les signes de la pub[licité] sur fond d'instruction sadomaso," *Cahiers du cinéma* 437 (1990): 88–89; see also reviews on the French release of this film by Philippe Royer, *Positif* 358 (1900): 79; and Jacques Valot, *Revue du cinéma* 465 (1990): 28. Neither of these reviewers mentions the lesbian theme of the film.

3. *Guía del ocio*, 3 November 1980, 4.

4. See Andrew Ross, *No Respect* (New York: Routledge, 1989), 188, for the multiple and complex reception of pornographic images. For lesbian S/M, see SAMOIS ed., *Coming to Power: Writings and Graphics on Lesbian S/M* (Boston: Alyson Publications 1982).

5. Juan I. Francia and Julio Pérez Perucha, "Primera película: Pedro Almodóvar," *Contracampo* 23 (September 1981): 5–7.

6. *El país*, 30 October 1980. See also Noam Ciusqui, "Pedro Almodóvar: Sexo y ganas de divertirse," *Diario de Barcelona*, 2 November 1980.

7. Steve Neale, *Genre* (London: British Film Institute, 1987), 24.

8. Cf. Teresa de Lauretis, "Sexual Indifference and Lesbian Representation," *Theater Journal* 40 (May 1988): 155–177.

9. In *Contracampo* 18 (January 1981): 73.

10. Richard Dyer, *Now You See It: Studies on Lesbian and Gay Films* (London: Routledge, 1990), 102.

11. Dyer, 103, 154.

12. Dyer, 144.

13. Dyer, 173.

14. See Francia and Pérez.

15. For the gender position of cinema audiences, see Laura Mulvey's influential "Visual Pleasure and Narrative Cinema," *Screen* 16.3 (1975): 6–18; for a critique of sexual difference from a lesbian perspective, see Jackie Stacey, "Desperately Seeking Difference," *Screen* 28.1 (1987): 48–61; and Teresa de Lauretis, *Technologies of Gender* (Bloomington: Indiana University Press, 1987).

16. John Hopewell, "Introducción" to María Antonia García de León and Teresa Maldonado, *Pedro Almodóvar, la otra España cañi* (Ciudad Real: Biblioteca de Temas y Autores Manchegos, 1989), 16–17.

17. See the special issue of *Feminist Review*, "Perverse Politics: Lesbian Issues" 34 (1990).

18. Margaret Hunt, "The De-eroticization of Women's Liberation: Social Purity Movement and the Revolutionary Feminism of Sheila Jeffreys," *Feminist Review* 34 (1990): 23–46.

19. Cherry Smyth, "The Pleasure Threshold: Looking at Lesbian Pornography on Film," *Feminist Review* 34 (1990): 152–159.

20. Diane Hamer, "Significant Others: Lesbianism and Psychoanalytic Theory," *Feminist Review* 34 (1990): 134–151.

21. For the erotic and deconstructive potential of differences between women, see Judith Butler's account of butch/femme identities in *Gender Trouble* (New York: Routledge 1990), 122–124; cf. Sue Ellen Case, "Towards a Butch-Femme Aesthetic," *Discourse* 11.1 (Fall–Winter 1988–1989): 55–73.

22. Dyer, 285.

23. "Entre tinieblas: Guión original de Pedro Almodóvar" (Madrid, 1982). Further references will be in parentheses within the text.

24. J. Batlle Caminal, in *El país*, 31 October 1983.

25. See the review by Francisco Marinero in *Diario 16*, 8 October 1983.

26. See Miguel Angel Trenas, "Con Pedro Almodóvar llegó el escándalo," *La vanguardia*, 29 October 1983.

27. *Correo catalán*, 12 October 1983.

28. J. A. Mahieu, *Fotogramas*, 15 October 1983.

29. Marinero.

30. Angeles Maso, *La vanguardia*, 23 October 1983.

31. José Luis Guarner, *El periódico*, 28 October 1983.

32. José Luis Téllez, *Contracampo* 36 (Summer 1984): 108–110.

33. French reviews also ignore the lesbian theme and attack the intermittence and artifice of the film: Jacques Valot, *Revue du cinéma* 445 (1989): 28–29; Paul Louis Thirard, *Positif* 336 (1989): 50–51.

34. For the redeployment of heterosexual popular culture by lesbians and gay men, see Ross, 157.

35. It is typical of Almodóvar's hostility to stereotype that this character (played by the hirsute Manuel Zarzo) proves to be heterosexual and marries Sor Víbora (Lina Canalejas) at the end of the film.

36. Dyer, 178–179.

37. For confrontational politics in Great Britain, see Jeffrey Weeks, *Coming Out: Homosexual Politics in Britain from the Nineteenth Century to the Present* (London: Quartet, 1977), 185–206. There is no comparable study for Spain.

38. Dyer, 222.

39. Dyer, 144.

Sense and Sensibility, or Latent Heterosexuality and *Labyrinth of Passions*

James Mandrell

BIRDS OF A FEATHER

Pedro Almodóvar's international renown and the spectacular commercial success of his later films are due in no small part to careful marketing and the cultivation of the international gay community. Particularly in the United States, articles about Almodóvar and his films, interviews with the filmmaker, and reviews of the films appearing in gay and straight publications alike have highlighted the gay content and, more important, the gay "sensibility" of the films. Writing in the mainstream *Film Comment*, gay critic Vito Russo claims with respect to *Women on the Verge of a Nervous Breakdown* that it is "a film that probably couldn't have been made by a director who happens to be heterosexual. The opening credits bring back *Funny Face*. The decor and fashions echo Frank Tashlin. The performances recall *Twentieth Century*."[1] Russo's comment is illustrative both of the sense of gay cinema history found in Almodóvar's imitation of high-Hollywood films and of the esteem in which he is held by the gay community and presented to the straight filmgoing public. More often than not, Almodóvar's genius is tied to his sexuality in a way that sooner or later leads to the critical creation of a specifically gay perspective that is adopted, if not endorsed, by his viewers, gay and straight alike. Ultimately, Almodóvar's renown and his films' success suggest the queering of the American film audience in the creation (through identification) of the ideal "gay" (even if heterosexual) spectator.

Almodóvar has given ample encouragement for this type of interest in his work, as evidenced by interviews both with the gay and lesbian press and with gay film critics.[2] There is, however, an equally powerful case to be made for his ambivalence toward gays and gay culture. Enrique Fernández quotes Almodóvar as saying apropos of *La ley del deseo* (*Law of Desire*), "My films are the exact opposite of films aimed at a gay public. *Law of Desire* is the most popular film in Spain today, and its greatest public is female. After a while you forget that the triangle of lovers is all men."[3] Similarly, in an interview with Lola Díaz, he remarks, "I have very obvious homosexual expressions. I mean that I don't like things made with gay sensibility at all."[4] As for his relationship with the tradition of gay cinema, Almodóvar is reported as saying to David Leavitt regarding George Cukor's *The Women*, in Leavitt's virtual homage to the Spanish filmmaker: "I love *The Women* and I love Cukor, but for me it's a film that has a very gay sensibility implied. This isn't to say that I'm not gay, or that I don't think *The Women* is a wonderful film, only that I take a different approach."[5]

This outright repudiation of an open interest in gay culture on the part of Almodóvar is confirmed anecdotally by Michael Musto in the *Village Voice* (although the latter's bons mots must be taken with a large grain of salt, since they seem motivated by personal animosity). In the first of three columns, Musto deals with a disappointing night out with the Spanish director during which Musto commented on Almodóvar's openness about his homosexuality. Musto notes that "Pedro was irritable," which was initially attributed to problems with the X rating received by *Tie Me Up! Tie Me Down!* Musto then asks, "Did I break some new law of desire with the sexuality issue? Pedro, mi amor, don't let success turn you into the thing you so loathe."[6] The second column goes into greater detail but breaks no new ground,[7] leaving Almodóvar to fire the next salvo in this encounter in his *Advocate* interview with Ryan Murphy. When Murphy asks about the "recent run-in with Michael Musto," Almodóvar huffs, "There's a type of attitude in gay journalists that I hate, and Michael has that. He doesn't have an inkling of sensitivity for others. It's not enough to be bitchy. You also need talent. Truman Capote wasn't just a queen; he knew how to write. But Michael is just a queen. He didn't respect my privacy."[8] Predictably, Musto refuses to let Almodóvar's remarks pass, once again attributing much of the misunderstanding to the fact that Almodóvar is "reputed to be so open."[9]

If Almodóvar is coy about his sexuality and the significance of gay culture to his work, it is nevertheless important to recognize that his ambivalence is somewhat more complex than it appears at first blush. In the interview with Díaz, Almodóvar goes on to explain in a way that anticipates his remarks to Murphy: "*In Cold Blood*, for example, is a novel written by a homosexual who is Truman Capote. Yet it's not a homosexual novel. And I could say the same of things by Genet or by Gore Vidal."[10] This position approximates, of course, those of artists, writers, and filmmakers who refuse or find problematic the representation of a par-

ticular gender or sexuality or entire group of individuals. Georgia O'Keeffe and Helen Frankenthaler, for example, claim to be artists, not women artists, and filmmaker Gus van Sant has a markedly ambivalent relationship to gay culture or gay sensibility, one reminiscent of, if not identical to, that of Almodóvar.[11] Thus, Almodóvar's sexuality—or gender—ought to be virtually irrelevant when it comes to the making—if not the marketing—of a film. As he says in the interview with Murphy, "I may be gay, but my films are not."[12]

What are we to make, then, of Almodóvar, a gay filmmaker whose works have been assiduously marketed to, by, and through the gay community and press but who takes umbrage when identified too closely with gay culture and sensibility? By way of an answer, it might be useful to consider in this context an early movie, *Laberinto de pasiones* (*Labyrinth of Passions*; 1982), a film that can be read as an allegory of Almodóvar's cinematic career and aspirations. To be fair, I should admit that my own take on Almodóvar and his relationship to what might be called gay culture is highly skeptical and that it derives to some degree from Almodóvar's relationship to the press but also from my reading of *Labyrinth of Passions*. In *Labyrinth of Passions*, I believe, we find an outline of the trajectory of Almodóvar's career from films that openly deal with gays and lesbians to films that are supposedly straight in their interests and intent. We find traces of what I would refer to as Almodóvar's professional latent heterosexuality. In fact, a close reading of this movie confirms Almodóvar's apparently ambivalent relationship to gay culture; it produces a narrative that runs counter to critical clichés that find in Almodóvar some version of a gay visionary.

Such a reading also helps to make sense of a film that has been peculiarly resistant to interpretation and that has, consequently, been dismissed as insignificant. Lawrence O'Toole is typical of critics who leave *Labyrinth of Passions* to one side when he avers that "Almodóvar's playful but puerile and otherwise forgettable *Labyrinth of Passion* [*sic*] . . . is about nothing so much as itself."[13] As I shall demonstrate in what follows, *Labyrinth of Passions* is most pointedly not about itself. To the contrary. It addresses issues of the psychosexual development of the individual in Western culture—and therefore of homosexuality—even as it charts what will become Almodóvar's professional trajectory. As for the trajectory of my own argument, I shall begin by outlining the action of *Labyrinth of Passions* as well as its conventional nature. I shall then continue with Almodóvar's gloss on individual development. Finally, my conclusion will point to ways in which the allegorical aspects of *Labyrinth of Passions* mitigate the parodic gloss on accounts of sexual development and thereby undercut the possibility of an unquestioned or unproblematic gay subjectivity as found in Almodóvar.

This is probably as good a time as any to address the pertinence of

psychoanalysis and psychoanalytic theories in this discussion of Almodóvar and *Labyrinth of Passions*. While it is possible to argue for the
centrality of psychoanalysis as a theoretical and critical tool in film studies, more persuasive in the present context is the foregrounding of psychoanalysis in *Labyrinth of Passions* itself. This foregrounding occurs
especially in the character of a Lacanian psychoanalyst from Argentina
who, Almodóvar suggests, is there because "Madrid was full of Argentinian psychologists and I liked it as a topic." But the plot itself, like much
of Hitchcock's work, is based in and depends on psychoanalytic theory.
Again, this is intentional. Almodóvar claims that during the filming of
Labyrinth of Passions, "the Oedipus complex was something that I had
in my head and I was looking for a father and I was looking for him in
the people around me"; and of a scene involving the female protagonist,
he says: "The moment at which she remembers the trauma in the psy-
chologist's home is very Hitchcockian. There is music by Bela Bartok to
make it even more Hitchcockian. This stuff about traumas has always
been a bit of a joke for me, but it constitutes a genre all its own in film.
In life, you can't explain everything with traumas, but in a comedy, yes,
they justify it all."[14] Psychoanalysis thus becomes a necessary discourse
for understanding the film and what is at work there; it also is useful for
understanding the broader cultural implications of Almodóvar's particular kind of humor.

FIRST THINGS FIRST, OR A DETOUR

Perhaps the easiest entry into the logic of Almodóvar's world in *Labyrinth of Passions* is not the opening sequence of the film, to which we
will return, but a key scene toward the end. At this point, the director
begins the lengthy process of drawing the disparate threads of his story
together and of trying to tie them into a more or less tight knot. The
Argentinian Susana Díaz (Ofelia Angélica), a self-proclaimed Lacanian psychoanalyst treating the orgiastic nymphomania of Sexilia de la Peña (Cecilia Roth), chases Dr. Roberto de la Peña (Fernando Vivanco), Sexi's
father and a renowned specialist in artificial insemination, down a Madrid
street. When Susana breathlessly catches up with him, Roberto exclaims,
"Hello, Susana. What a coincidence," to which the psychoanalyst knowingly replies, "Nonsense! What coincidence? Don't be silly. I came to
speak with you."

This brief exchange could serve as a description of Almodóvar's modus
operandi not only in *Labyrinth of Passions* but in all of his cinematic
endeavors. What appears to be coincidental is the consequence of living
in a world where everyone, not coincidentally, knows, is related to, is
involved with, desires, or despises everyone else; in which the actions of
one person, not coincidentally, set in motion a series of perhaps unex-

pected but not coincidental repercussions. Almodóvar's cinematic world almost always asks the viewer to respond to the action of a particular film in the same way that Dr. Roberto de la Peña reacts upon meeting Susana Díaz, with a startled, but not entirely convincing, "What a coincidence," to which the filmmaker would have no choice but to answer, "Nonsense!"

The emphasis in Almodóvar's films on the not-coincidental is responsible to a large extent for the highly stylized and "fictionalized" nature of his work. Almodóvar consistently uses a variety of cinematic and narrative techniques to disorient the viewer, which, as he notes, produces a "crazy comedy" and eventually requires the viewer to accept this view of the world on the film's own terms.[15] Given the necessary complicity of the audience in Almodóvar's world, it is no coincidence that his exploration of the labyrinth of passions should be presented so openly and explicitly, if parodically, in terms of the modern narrative of the convoluted nature of sexual desire, namely, psychoanalysis. Likewise, it is no coincidence that the logic of overdetermination found in psychoanalysis implicates itself in Almodóvar's version of Madrid.

Because of the importance of psychoanalysis for the plot and logic of *Labyrinth of Passions*, childhood traumas are found to lie at the root of what are presented as aspects of mature sexual dysfunctions. Sexilia, the shamelessly unrepentant nymphomaniac, flees from exposure to the sun only to find true love in the arms of Riza Niro (Imanol Arias), the son of the deposed emperor of Tirán, who not coincidentally spirits her away to the sun-bathed tropical island of Contadora. Riza himself will be shown to be a potential clinical case, since he is in Madrid to explore Europe's most explosive gay playground. Still, he is cured, since, when he meets Sexi, she so deeply affects him that he is made to recognize his latent heterosexuality, which was arrested by an abortive sexual encounter with his pseudo- or stepmother, Toraya (Helga Liné). Toraya, also known as the Principessa, is the ex-empress of Tirán and an obsessively anxious patient of Dr. de la Peña bent on providing her ex-husband with an heir.

For his part, Roberto de la Peña confesses to the voluptuous psychoanalyst, Susana, that his interest in artificial insemination stems from his distaste for the sexual act. He, too, is brought to his senses; Queti (Marta Fernández-Muro), the woman that Sexi has crafted to take her place so that she can slip away unnoticed to Contadora, teaches him the delights and sexual pleasures associated with filial devotion to a parent's libido. Finally, Queti's dutiful devotion to her new father is the result of a peculiar encounter with her real father (Luis Ciges), who, confused by the disappearance of his unfaithful wife, insists that his daughter is, in fact, his spouse. Apparently convinced that Queti possesses two personalities (daughter and wife), the father seduces Queti, ties her to her bed, and forces her to have sex with him. Although Queti escapes from her father, she enters into a structurally similar relationship when she seduces her new father, Dr. de la Peña, only this time it is, for her at least, merely acting and therefore not perverse.

The fact that most of the principal characters, that is, the straight characters, end up happy in *Labyrinth of Passions*, despite or even because of the convoluted nature of desire, leads one to suspect that Almodóvar is offering a pointed if humorous critique of Freudian theories of psychosexual development. This is particularly true since the two exceptions to the generally positive resolution of the action are the psychoanalyst, Susana, and the ex-empress, Toraya, who have recourse to the scientific worlds of psychoanalysis and artificial insemination, respectively, but who, as women, bear the burden of guilt for—yet derive little pleasure from—the problematic status of desire in the film. The implication, of course, is that science, be it psychoanalysis or the science of reproduction, cannot but fail to deal with the complex directness of desire. The labyrinthine conventions of psychoanalytic and scientific explanations of the labyrinths of passions supposedly are inherently flawed—indeed, unable to follow the path of what is here presented as the not coincidentally straightforward path of sexual desire.

However, issues of homosexuality and incest and its setting in the cultural milieu of Madrid's *Movida* aside, Almodóvar's *Labyrinth of Passions* is an almost totally conventional film of the boy-meets-girl-boy-gets-girl variety. As a kind of campy bildungsroman or narrative of development, it glosses even as it lapses into many of the truisms of Lacanian and Freudian theories of psychosexual development, which means that film functions as a critique as well as a recuperation of these same psychoanalytic theories. Although a crazy comedy, then, although a labyrinth that seeks to expose the fallacies of Freudian thought, this film follows in the Hollywood tradition of romance, with melodramatic overtones. Almodóvar himself says that *Labyrinth of Passions* is "a parody of the romantic comedies of adolescent love";[16] it works out or toward the resolution of a problem between two lovers or brings two individuals together so as to fulfill their romantic destiny. In this sense, *Labyrinth of Passions* shows how Sexi and Riza can be brought together; it works out the obstacles that would keep them apart.

STAR-CROSSED LOVERS

In a manner reminiscent of Hitchcock's *Strangers on a Train*, *Labyrinth of Passions* begins by having the two principal characters cross paths. The film opens with an establishing shot of Madrid's Rastro, the flea market, and cuts immediately to a medium shot of Sexi on the prowl. While the credits appear superimposed on the scenes of the Rastro, identifying the actors playing the two protagonists, the camera cuts back and forth, from Sexi to Riza, who is disguised in a curly dark wig and sunglasses. In turn, the depictions of the two stars are interspersed with glimpses of the objects of their gaze, male crotches and buttocks. We see Sexi strolling from the left of the frame to the right. Cut to Riza trying on sunglasses. Cut to a close-up of Sexi, lips sensuously parted. Cut to a man's crotch, back to Sexi, then to another man's crotch and buttocks. Cut to Riza as he looks around, seemingly frustrated. Cut to a man's crotch. And so it continues until this sequence closes with another slightly aerial shot of the Rastro. Credits complete, the film segues, typically for Almodóvar, into a scene in a café, with no indication of the passage of time or the relationship of the opening scene to the one that follows.

In the café, a seated Riza reads the Madrid daily *El país*, in which two significant stories are juxtaposed on the front page, further entangling the histories of the two protagonists. The first story has to do with Sexi's father; the headline reads, "The Spanish Biogynecologist Dr. de la Peña Achieves the Asexual Reproduction of Six Genetically Identical Parakeets." The second concerns Riza's father and proclaims that the "Emperor of Tirán flees the U.S. to the Island of Contadora." While still in the café, Riza is picked up by the elaborately effeminate Fabio (Fany McNamara), who later turns out to be a porno star. As Riza and his newfound friend leave the café, we overhear Sexi arranging an orgy at which she will be the only woman.

The scenes in the Rastro and the café suggest several things. Clearly, the stories and lives of the still unidentified Sexi and Riza will, somehow, be brought together; their paths will cross. Yet there is a practical problem. Both are searching for the same thing: a man or, in Sexi's case, a group of men. This, then, becomes the issue to be worked out by the film: how Sexi's interest in groups of men can be brought to bear on one man, Riza, who is himself fixated on other men. Likewise, the family histories of Sexi and Riza are important for understanding the how and why of their present orientations and problems. In Sexi's case, her father's obsession with asexual reproduction can be read as the cause of or an extreme reaction to his daughter's nymphomania, while Riza's homosexuality is linked to structural incest with the Principessa followed immediately by a homosexual encounter. And, of course, one of the principal subtexts of the film is the relationship between a parent and child and the question of sexual pleasure.[17]

There is, however, an important difference in the presentation of the two protagonists. To return to the opening sequence, we first see Sexi as she walks through the Rastro. In contrast, we first see Riza reflected in the rows of sunglasses that he is perusing. On the one hand, then, we look at Sexi looking; it is as if she were both the object of and an analogue for the spectator in the film. On the other, we see multiple and distorted reflections of Riza. This series of glimpses and reflections mirrors the situations of the two protagonists: Sexi likes groups of men, hence the many Rizas; and the disguised Riza is many different people to those around him. Moreover, the opening sequence is set up so that it seems as if Riza is the object of Sexi's obsessive gaze. Only in the subsequent cutting back and forth do we realize that Sexi and Riza are searching for the same thing; that, in Freudian terms, Sexi has externalized her object choice in the form of an attachment to the opposite sex while Riza has internalized his as a form of narcissism.[18] The opening scenes tease the viewer with the stories of Sexi and Riza and their possible conjunction. But it is Riza who is shown to be the object of the film's—that is, Sexi's and our—interest: Riza and his problematic narcissism, his fixation on himself, which is acted out in his homosexuality.

FATHER "NO"'S BEST

Sexi and Riza are, in fact, victims of the same scenario of seduction, which took place on a sunny beach on the Costa del Sol some fifteen years earlier. Our first inkling as to the importance of this moment occurs when Doctor de la Peña, in the flush of restoring the Principessa's fertility, tells her about meeting the now-deposed Emperor. In a flashback, we see the Emperor seated with his small retinue on the beach. Roberto recalls that the Emperor is an aficionado of gynecology and that he, Roberto, had just published a controversial article on artificial insemination that the Emperor had read and wanted to discuss with him. Later in the film, Sexi returns to the same moment at two different points: first, during Riza's performance as the singer "Johnny," and second, in a flash of recognition stimulated by the reflected glare from the mirror in the Principessa's compact, which is as strong as the dreaded sun. Fleeing the realization of her fiancé's infidelity with the Principessa—his first sexual experience with a woman—Sexi runs to Susana.

Susana senses the possibility of a therapeutic breakthrough and induces in Sexi a sort of hypnotic state that returns her to the moment fifteen years earlier when she played with Riza on a beach. Sexi, buried in the sand with only her head exposed, asks Riza to make a small hole through which she might breathe. (Curiously, he takes his finger and penetrates the sand at the approximate point where the nubile Sexi's genitalia might be.) The Principessa appears from behind some shrubbery, approaches the children, and, after tossing sand in Sexi's eyes, coaxes Riza to follow her back into the bushes by suggesting that the three of them play hide-and-seek. As if awakening from a deep sleep and seemingly unconcerned by what has happened, Sexi walks toward the underbrush and overhears the Principessa imploring Riza, "Why are you so cruel? Just like your father. Don't push me away, too. Don't you like me? Riza, you know you could have been my son." As she comes closer, Sexi sees the Principessa caressing Riza. Sexi then asks Riza to come play with her.

When the Principessa manages to detain Riza yet again, Sexi exclaims, "He prefers her!" and runs to her father. She reaches him at the precise moment that he is going to speak to the Emperor, and he pushes her away. Rejected by both Riza and her father, Sexi goes to play with a group of five boys, one of whom suggests that they play house ("Husbands and Wives"), to which Sexi responds, "I'll be everyone's wife." At this point, Riza escapes the Principessa and her ambiguous protestations of love and returns to the group, which is now beginning its play. One of the boys leaves the group and, after whispering something to Riza, leads him back to the bushes, where, we are to infer, he has his first homosexual experience.

Although this scene, played as a melodrama and underscored by tortured music, is risible in its implications, it nevertheless serves within the logic of the film to explain the origins of the psychosexual development of the two protagonists and to draw them even closer together.[19] Sexi's nymphomania stems from her rejection by her father (a possible result of his aversion to the sexual act) and by Riza; moreover, the Principessa's implied rejection of Sexi in favor of Riza suggests the importance of Sexi's absent mother, a topic never addressed by the film. Riza's homosexuality arises from the juxtaposition of the structurally incestuous relationship proposed by the Principessa and the subsequent homosexual encounter with one of his friends. By linking the psychosexual neuroses of the two protagonists in this way, Almodóvar explains—even as he explains away—the strange bond between Riza and Sexi and the reasons for their present situation.

It is somewhat easier to understand Sexi's predicament in these terms than that of Riza. Yet it is important to note that, in this scenario, Riza flees from the Principessa to his homosexual encounter. As Freud comments, "We have frequently found that alleged inverts have been by no means insusceptible to the charms of women, but have continually transposed the excitation aroused by women on to a male object. They have thus repeated all through their lives the mechanism by which their inversion arose. Their compulsive longing for men has turned out to be determined by their ceaseless flight from women."[20] Riza's homosexuality can therefore be viewed as a necessary response to the incest taboo, as the result of avoiding the overpowering love of the Principessa. His initial rejection of her and the subsequent homosexual experience are repeated until he once again meets Sexi.

MIRROR, MIRROR, ON THE WALL

Let's return to the narcissism with which the film so plainly begins. After his second homosexual encounter in the film, Riza confronts himself in a mirror as he washes his genitals in a sink. While adjusting his own disguise, his wig, he notices a photograph placed alongside the mirror, which turns out to be the feminized image of his lover. Sadec (Antonio Banderas)—who, not coincidentally, Riza picks up while the Principessa makes a call from a nearby public telephone, reinforcing the notion of Riza's flight from women in general and from this one woman in particular—is also from Tirán, so, in a sense and without even realizing it, Riza enacts his narcissism by making love to himself, by taking as his object "what he himself is." Moreover, Riza appears in these scenes to be a reluctant lover, one who views sex as dirty—hence the emphasis on post-coital washing—and merely an intermittent dalliance.[21]

This scene is important for a number of reasons, but particularly because it exemplifies the ways in which stock elements of Hollywood cinema lead in Almodóvar's films to other, more fundamental questions of sexual and national identity. When Riza spots the photo of what appears to be a woman in a *chador*, he is obviously responding to his own disguised image and to the feminine aspects of his culture. Struck by the photo, Riza asks Sadec, who has entered the bathroom and stands beside his now nervous lover, who the woman is, to which Sadec replies, "It's me, at a party, dressed like the women of my country." Riza is clearly shaken by Sadec's response, since he is fleeing all contact with people from Tirán, not just his family.

In response to this standard device in thrillers, he beats a hasty retreat and goes in search of a new identity. After Fabio gives him a new, pseudo-punk disguise and takes him to a nightclub where he makes his debut as "Johnny," the lead singer of Them, Riza/Johnny sees and is in turn seen by Sexi (Plate 5). Riza's apparent confusion and ambivalence, the sense that he is up for grabs (fully expressed in the song he sings with Them, "Great Bargain") resolves itself in the discovery of Sexi. To make a long story short, Riza and Sexi fall in love across the crowded room of the club. Riza's search has begun to end because he is, in fact, searching for Sexi; the story that is being told has to do with the way that Riza grows up and grows into being the man for this specific woman. In other words, the plot of the film has to do with Riza's progression from homosexuality to heterosexuality.

This series of encounters is similar to that of Riza's fateful first homosexual experience when he flees from the Principessa at the beach. Escaping from his family in Contadora and from Toraya, who stalks him on the streets of Madrid, Riza becomes involved with a man who ineluctably leads him back to a confrontation with his culture. In the process, Riza sees how easily his male lover can be made to appear female, that his own identity could be similarly ambiguous, that he could be either male or female, or that his homosexuality might conceal a latent heterosexuality awaiting fuller exploration. Thus Riza must run *to* Sexi, must run *away from* the homosexual experiences of his youth, in order to become an adult heterosexual. The brief narcissistic moment in Sadec's bathroom hints at the myriad issues at stake here. It is not merely a question of homosexuality but includes narcissism and femininity as well as socially constructed roles as culturally determined.

THE GREATEST STORY EVER TOLD

Labyrinth of Passions in its entirety reflects traditional—that is, Freudian—notions of the nature of psychosexual development. As a parodic psychosexual bildungsroman, Riza's story is one of flight and refuge until he takes the ultimate refuge in his attachment to Sexi. In this scenario, homosexuality becomes a stage and only a stage in Riza's development, a developmental process that culminates as Riza and Sexi flee to Contadora. With the plane safely airborne, the two consummate their relationship as the closing credits appear onscreen. Sexi's search as portrayed in the opening scenes of the film comes to an end and Riza's frustrated homosexuality, which only occasionally seems to bring him pleasure, gives way to the urge and urgent needs of being straight and of going straight home.

How seriously are we to take the action of and conclusion to *Labyrinth of Passions*? Probably not all that seriously. But probably more seriously than we would like to admit. The dominant note of the film is, of course, that of parody, which for Freud achieves "the degradation of something exalted";[22] and what is being parodied is, not coincidentally, traditional explanations of the genesis of heterosexuality. In "Jokes and Their Relation to the Unconscious," Freud explains the importance of humor in terms of speaking the unspeakable:

A joke will allow us to exploit something ridiculous in our enemy which we could not, on account of obstacles in the way, bring forward openly or consciously; once again, then, a joke will evade restrictions and open sources of pleasure that have become inaccessible. It will further bribe the hearer with its yield of pleasure into taking sides with us without any very close investigation, just as on other occasions we ourselves have been bribed by an innocent joke into overestimating the substance of a statement expressed jokingly.[23]

In this view of things, Almodóvar creates an elaborate joke by constructing a parody of a dominant theory of human sexuality. His strategy is to seduce the spectator—Freud's "hearer"—into taking the filmmaker's side by admitting to the folly of these farfetched ideas. The issue of jokes is not, however, as inconsequential as it might initially seem. Once the seduction of the spectator is under way, once Freud's explanations are seen to be equivocal, even humorous in their implications, the spectator must continue with the logic of the film and embrace Almodóvar's own view of the natural ambivalence of all desire. The extension of this view includes the fact that the spectator could, as in *Labyrinth of Passions*, live in the world "as if" he were Fabio or Sadec, that he could, in fact, as easily be gay as straight. Almodóvar's case for the inconsequentiality of psychoanalytic explanations of the development of heterosexuality ends up drawing the spectator into the polymorphous perversity for which at least a cinematic case is being made in the topsy-turvy world of Almodóvar's Madrid.

Almodóvar's presentation of desire in *Labyrinth of Passions* and his parody of Freudian theories of development thus appear to suggest that sex, gender, and sexuality are the result of the performance of an identity. If the film presents us with an array of characters performing or attempting to perform a specific identity, it is Queti, remade as Sexi, who most openly demonstrates the extent to which one's personal and even familial (and therefore biological) identities are up for grabs and amenable to self-fashioning. Jacques Lacan implicitly makes this point in "The Meaning of the Phallus" when he claims that "the ideal or typical manifestations of behavior in both sexes, up to and including the act of sexual copulation, are entirely propelled into *comedy*."[24]

Likewise, Freud adduces a sexual implication in the telling of jokes, but there it is the notion of jokes as the staging of a seduction that is key. For Freud, jokes "make possible the satisfaction of an instinct (whether lustful or hostile) in the face of an obstacle that stands in its way"; the obstacle is "nothing other than women's incapacity to tolerate undisguised sexuality, an incapacity correspondingly increased with a rise in the educational and social level."[25]

Obscene or "smutty" jokes are originally directed towards women and may be equated with attempts at seduction. If a man in a company of men enjoys telling or listening to smut, the original situation, which owing to social inhibitions cannot be realized, is at the same time imagined. A person who laughs at the smut he hears is laughing as though he were the spectator of an act of sexual aggression.[26]

The performative nature of gender and the joke in *Labyrinth of Passions* obviously goes far beyond the "merely" feminine in that it has little or nothing to do with "women's incapacity to tolerate undisguised sexuality." Instead, the social marginalization ascribed to women by Freud in his formulation of the scenario pertaining to smut is reascribed to homosexuality in Almodóvar's cinema. In this new context, it has to do not simply with the cultural marginalization of women and the role that humor plays in that ongoing process but, rather, with a cultural myopia regarding homosexuality and with various attempts at explaining gayness and gay subculture as important to something beyond the gay self and beyond personal pleasure.

And yet, to claim for *Labyrinth of Passions* some "meaning" or social importance works against Almodóvar's seductive parody of gay as opposed to straight coupling and its presentation as an inconsequential farce, an apolitical burlesque. As a burlesque, the film is no longer threatening to heterosexuals because it is all in good fun. With respect to gays, the message is somewhat more oblique, although Almodóvar would probably point out that we are dealing with nothing more than a good time.

In fact, Almodóvar wants us to believe, I think, that what is at stake here is a set of outmoded values, that *Labyrinth of Passions* represents a fun form of nostalgia or a charming diversion. In this context, the Freudian joke that allows the unsayable to be said and brings about the return of the repressed, the joke that allows sex to rear its ugly head in polite society, permits Almodóvar's films to naturalize the experiences of gays and lesbians via the identification of the spectator with one or more characters. As a kind of joke, homosexuality is drawn into dominant cultural arenas along with more or less neutral presentations of gay and lesbian experiences. But *Labyrinth of Passions*—with its parody of psychoanalytic explanations of psychosexual development—actually stages the return of the repressed, which is not some type of polymorphous perversity or even homosexuality but, in fact, heterosexuality itself. In other words, the joke of the film is not about those theories of desire that claim homosexuality *as a stage* in the development of the healthy heterosexual but, rather, about a homosexuality that claims to be anything *more than a stage* en route to a mature heterosexuality.

THE END OF MODERNITY, OR LATENT HETEROSEXUALITY

In fact, it is no coincidence that Almodóvar's second feature-length film can be read as an allegory of his career. Beginning with the lesbian scenarios of *Pepi, Luci, Bom y las otras chicas del montón* (*Pepi, Luci, Bom, and Other Ordinary Girls*; 1980) and continuing with *Labyrinth of Passions*, Almodóvar's films deal with homosexuality both implicitly and explicitly—as in *Entre tinieblas* (*Dark Habits*; 1983), *¿Qué he hecho yo para merecer esto?* (*What Have I Done to Deserve This?*; 1984), and *La ley del deseo* (*The Law of Desire*; 1987)—but there is an increasingly apparent rejection of gay and lesbian topics that turns up, for example, not only in *Labyrinth of Passions* but also in *Matador* (1986), again in *Mujeres al borde de un ataque de nervios* (*Women on the Verge of a*

Nervous Breakdown; 1988), and again in *¡Atame!* (*Tie Me Up! Tie Me Down!*; 1990).

However tempting it is to think that Almodóvar has been able to draw the gay, lesbian, transvestite, and transsexual subculture into the world of international cinema and Hollywood's vision of mass culture, we ought not to fool ourselves. As in *Labyrinth of Passions*, the gay sexual acts never come off; we see only the beginnings and the endings of the gay liaisons and never the consummation of homosexual desire. In the first instance, we see nothing but the pickup scene. In the second, we see before and after, clumsy gropings and postcoital cleansing. The third time, Riza can't get an erection for his male lover because he is dreaming of Sexi. Only the heterosexual encounters produce pleasure for Riza, for example, when Sexi and he join the Mile-High Club en route to Contadora and they audibly consummate their relationship. In *Labyrinth of Passions*, homosexuality remains unseeable, unknowable, and, ultimately, inexplicable.

It therefore seems clear that Almodóvar suffers from a case of latent heterosexual professionalism, which may be so evident to everybody else that it's not worth mentioning. Michael Bronski, for example, has a similar reading of Almodóvar's career moves, but he gives the filmmaker the benefit of the doubt and ends up with a more positive interpretation. Bronski admits that "the reason for his [Almodóvar's] acceptance and promotion by film distributors and U.S. audiences is not simply that *Women on the Verge of a Nervous Breakdown* contains none of the outré or shockingly provocative sexuality of the earlier films, but rather a change of genre on the part of the filmmaker and the cold hard facts of economics."[27] But Jay Carr, a film reviewer for the *Boston Globe*, is more typical, as when he comments of Almodóvar's *Tacones lejanos* (*High Heels*; 1991): "In *High Heels* Pedro Almodóvar plays it straighter than ever before, virtually making the kind of melodrama he has hitherto satirized with high exuberance and campy fizz." Almodóvar finally makes a straight funny film, since straight sells, or at least straight versions of anything that is bent. More to the point, only straight sex is productive, reproductive, or capable of engendering something new. Whereas the gay sensibility would logically and necessarily peter out, turn back on itself in much the same way that some critics have claimed that *Labyrinth of Passions* is self-reflexive, or give rise to monstrously aberrant offspring, heterosexual conventions, even when expressed through structurally incestuous relationships, represent the fulfillment of creative filiation if not dynastic continuity. For this reason, Almodóvar's relationship to what has been identified as gay culture is much more problematic—politically and cinematically—than is commonly supposed. And this not coincidentally means that we ought to consider the sense of his films and his putative gay sensibility with a degree of caution, if not outright skepticism.

This brings us full circle to the subject with which we began—Almodóvar's renown and the commercial success of his films—and it broaches a topic central to discussions of gay and lesbian film. Paul Julian Smith, citing Richard Dyer's seminal work on gay cinema, comments:

Richard Dyer asks whether it is possible to represent homosexuality as "incidental" in film without condemning it to marginality (Dyer 166). And this is the fundamental problem in examining the lesbian and gay interest in Almodóvar's cinema. It is possible that the "as if" places the spectator in a position of indifference or disinterest with regard to homosexuality within the film, without necessarily challenging her or his attitudes toward the subject outside the cinema.[28]

And with respect to his own treatment of Almodóvar, Smith remarks in a note, "It is thus not my aim to argue that Almodóvar's representations of homosexuality (whether as everyday reality or exotic spectacle) are inherently progressive."[29] As read here, *Labyrinth of Passions* argues against a view of Almodóvar's films as progressive. To present as incidental or coincidental something as central to the narrative and the cinematic logic of that film as the male protagonist's gayness allows the social and cultural stigmatization of homosexuality to intrude. That is, the latent or even explicit heterosexuality of film as a form of narration and as a spectacle militates in this and most, if not all, films against the putative creation of an ideal "gay" spectator and even against the ambivalent cultural gayness of Almodóvar himself. It ought to come as no surprise, then, that the sense and sensibility of *Labyrinth of Passions* narrates this central cultural truth even as it leads us through a parodic labyrinth of passions toward a humorous understanding of its social viability and necessity. So much for coincidence and nonsense.

NOTES

1. Vito Russo, "Man of La Mania: Pedro Almodóvar on the Verge . . . ," *Film Comment* 24.6 (November 1988): 14.
2. In addition to the interview with Russo, see, for example, Michael Bronski, "Almodóvar: Post-Franco American?" *Zeta Magazine* 2.4 (April 1989): 64–67; and Ryan Murphy, "A Spanish Fly in the Hollywood Ointment: Gay Director Pedro Almodóvar Refuses to Be Tied Up by Censorship," *The Advocate*, 19 June 1990, 37–40.
3. Enrique Fernández, "Off-screen: The Lawyer of Desire," *Village Voice* 7 April 1987, 54.
4. Lola Díaz, "Entrevista a Pedro Almodóvar," *Cambio 16*, 18 April 1988, 129.
5. David Leavitt, "Almodóvar on the Verge," *New York Times Magazine*, 22 April 1990, 40.
6. Michael Musto, "La Dolce Musto," *Village Voice*, 24 April 1990, 43.
7. Musto, "La Dolce Musto," *Village Voice*, 15 May 1990, 47.

8. Murphy, 39.

9. Musto, "La Dolce Musto," *Village Voice*, 19 June 1990, 56.

10. Díaz, 129.

11. See Michelangelo Signorile's scathing commentary on Van Sant in "Absolutely Queer," *The Advocate*, 19 November 1991, 35. Signorile refers to two interviews appearing in *The Advocate*: Gary Indiana's "Saint Gus: From Portland to Hollywood, the Director and His Camera Remain Candid," *The Advocate*, 1 October 1991, 57, 62, 64; and Adam Block's "Interview: Inside Outsider Gus Van Sant," *The Advocate*, 24 September 1991, 80–84. In this regard, see also David Ehrenstein's positive assessment of Van Sant's status as a gay filmmaker in "Talking Pictures: Gus Van Sant Is an Exception Among Gay Filmmakers," *The Advocate*, 24 September 1991, 85; and J. Hoberman's curiously ambiguous review of *My Own Private Idaho* in "Lowlife of the Mind: *My Own Private Idaho*," *The Advocate*, 1 October 1991, 60.

12. Murphy, 40.

13. Lawrence O'Toole, "Almodóvar in Bondage," *Sight and Sound* 59.4 (1990): 271. A refreshing exception is Marcia Pally, who notes, while missing the more problematic aspects of the film, "*Labyrinth of Passion* [sic] sends up psychiatry's efforts to cure 'abnormalities.' " See Marcia Pally, "The Politics of Passion: Pedro Almodóvar and the Camp Esthetic," *Cineaste* 18.1 (1990): 34.

14. Nuria Vidal, *El cine de Pedro Almodóvar* (Madrid: Instituto de la Cinematografía y las Artes Audiovisuales/Ministerio de Cultura, 1988), 48.

15. Vidal, 36.

16. Vidal, 36.

17. The primary example of the film's engagement with the problematic relationship between parents and their children is to be found in the "monstrous" test-tube baby, whose mother detests her. With respect to reproduction and sexual pleasure, consider the parakeets, who are listless and refuse to sing until Queti/Sexi spices their diet with the same potion that she uses to perk up her pseudo father.

18. See Freud's "On Narcissism: An Introduction," in *The Standard Edition of the Complete Psychological Works of Sigmund Freud*, ed. and trans. James Strachey in collaboration with Anna Freud, vol. 14 (London: Hogarth, 1957), 67–102.

19. Susana at least initially explains Sexi's nymphomania in terms that anticipate this recollection: "You hate the sun, which you identify with him [your father]. You're in love with him. Very much so. You screw any living thing to make him take some notice of you. But your father is blind, totally blind. He doesn't see your happiness depends on him. Yours . . . and mine. . . . Why hide it? I want to screw your father."

20. Sigmund Freud, "Three Essays on Sexuality," in *The Standard Edition*, vol. 7 (1953), 145n.

21. Not coincidentally, when Riza and Sexi finally consummate their relationship during the flight to Contadora, Riza wonders whether they should not be doing it in the bathroom, where they would not disturb the other passengers.

22. Freud, "Jokes and Their Relation to the Unconscious," in *The Standard Edition*, vol. 8 (1960), 201.

23. Freud, "Jokes," 103.

24. Jacques Lacan, "The Meaning of the Phallus," trans. Jacqueline Rose, in

Feminine Sexuality, ed. Juliet Mitchell and Jacqueline Rose (New York: Norton, 1982), 84 (my emphasis).

25. Freud, "Jokes," 101.

26. Freud, "Jokes," 97.

27. Bronski, 64.

28. Paul Julian Smith, *Laws of Desire: Questions of Homosexuality in Spanish Writing and Film, 1960–1990* (Oxford: Oxford University Press, 1992), 168–169. See also Richard Dyer, *Now You See It: Studies on Lesbian and Gay Film* (New York: Routledge, 1990).

29. Smith, 169 n15.

Melodrama Against Itself: Pedro Almodóvar's *What Have I Done to Deserve This?*

Kathleen M. Vernon

Central to what might be called the purposeful eclecticism of Pedro Almodóvar's cinematic universe is the model of American film melodrama, a source the Spanish director has appropriated to notably effective and often unexpected ends. Indeed, the presence of American film culture is palpable throughout his work, from the photographs of Ava Gardner and Elizabeth Taylor among the "greatest sinners of the world" in the personal devotions of Mother Superior (Julieta Serrano) in *Entre tinieblas* (*Dark Habits*) to the inclusion of film clips from three well-known Hollywood films—Elia Kazan's *Splendor in the Grass*, King Vidor's *Duel in the Sun*, and Nicholas Ray's *Johnny Guitar*—in *¿Qué he hecho yo para merecer esto?* (*What Have I Done to Deserve This?*), *Matador*, and *Mujeres al borde de un ataque de nervios* (*Women on the Verge of a Nervous Breakdown*), respectively.

American melodrama holds multiple attractions for Almodóvar. On the one hand, American film has provided him with a vehicle for articulating his distance from the themes and style of a recent Spanish film tradition obsessed with the country's tragic past.[1] Frequently quoted to the effect that he wished to make films as if Franco never existed—"I never speak of Franco; I hardly acknowledge his existence. I start *after* Franco. . . . The stories unfold as if he had never existed"[2]—Almodóvar can be said to have turned to Hollywood, the quintessential storyteller for a nation characterized by historical amnesia, for an alternate source of cultural and personal references (in that respect not unlike the function of Hollywood films in the novels of Manuel Puig). However, Almodóvar's borrowings from American film do not represent an unquestioning endorsement of the ideological underpinnings of Hollywood cinema. In-

stead, his intertextual and international network of references serves to
question the role of film itself, not only in reflecting the ideologies and
values of the society in which and for which it is created, but also film's
complicity in perpetuating those societal structures. Specifically, his im-
portation of *American* melodrama into *Spanish* film casts the light of
suspicion on the way both film industries have mythified the representation of historically contingent categories such as gender and socioeconomic class as natural, essential "identities" in their implicit construction
of a larger, national self-identity.

Similarly, melodrama has allowed Almodóvar to articulate a moment
of rupture in Spanish history, not merely imagining a Spain in which
Franco never existed but constructing a repertory of stories and images
for a post-Franco Spain that is perhaps yet to be. Peter Brooks, in his
influential study *The Melodramatic Imagination*, goes beyond thematic
definitions of the genre to identify melodrama as "a mode of conception
and expression . . . a certain fictional system for making sense of experience,"[3] whose historical roots he traces to late eighteenth-century France:

The origins of melodrama can be accurately located within the context of the
French Revolution and its aftermath. This is the epistemological moment which
it illustrates and to which it contributes: The moment that symbolically, and really,
marks the final liquidation of the traditional Sacred and its representative institutions (Church and Monarch), the shattering of the myth of Christendom, the
dissolution of an organic and hierarchically cohesive society, and the invalidation
of the literary forms—tragedy, comedy of manners—that depend on such a society.[4]

In melodrama, then, Almodóvar also finds a "new" fictional system for
conceiving and representing Spanish society in the aftermath of its own
ancien régime. The death of Franco, the politically and psychically repressive patriarch, "Caudillo por la Gracia de Dios," also marks the final
passing of Spain's hierarchically conceived "organic democracy" and the
institutional identification of church and state. Melodrama provides the
mode for exploring the breakdown of old hierarchies and the resultant
dissolution of barriers and boundaries in a postpatriarchal, postreligious
Spain.[5]

It is nevertheless ironic that melodrama should play this role in Almodóvar's films. Grounded in a moral and thematic Manichaeanism,
melodrama has often been read as constructing a fictional world of unambiguous absolutes, of villains vs. victims, shadow vs. light. In his 1989
study *American Film Melodrama*, Robert Lang observes that the universe
of melodrama depends on "clearly legible differences on all levels. It is
a world of binary structures: men and women, masculine and feminine,

the 'right' side and the 'wrong' side of the tracks . . . brother and sister, work and love, material wealth and poverty."[6] Indeed, much of the appeal of melodrama for students of film lies in this symptomatic overdetermination of societal and gender roles.

In the seventies, feminist film critics turned to the domestic melodrama as a privileged area of investigation, a "woman's genre," where the representation of women on the screen and the (primarily female) audience's response are foregrounded and hence more accessible to and demanding of analysis. What they found for the most part was a series of paradigmatic examples of the way "classic narrative cinema" works, and works on, the spectator. They identified narrative structures and thematics which are not simply reflective of the hierarchical patriarchal society in which they are produced; their very functioning as signifying practices and sources of pleasure and entertainment depends on the perpetuation—indeed, the polarization—of differences and boundaries.

More recent studies have moved beyond this somewhat monolithic and generally ahistorical view to acknowledge the continuing attraction and fascination of film melodrama as a source of visual and affective pleasure and even to examine its function in creating a space for resistance against the very societal structures and values it would seem to represent.[7] It is this provocative ambivalence in the melodramatic imagination, understood here as a mode of spectatorial response, that Almodóvar has exploited so skillfully in his films, using melodrama in some sense against itself. My aim in this essay, then, will be to show how the director has appropriated the language of Hollywood melodrama as a mediating structure that would allow him to have it both ways: to opt out of the binarism apparently inherent in classic narrative film as well as in many contemporary analyses of such cinema. I contend in my discussion of *What Have I Done to Deserve This?* that while, through its self-reflexive character, the film lays bare the material reality of filmic practice, the technological, economic, and institutional apparatus behind the illusion, while it acknowledges the complicity of narrative cinema in constructing images of feminity, in Laura Mulvey's words, "cut to the measure of [masculine] desire," its aim is not exclusively deconstructive.[8] Rather, the film holds out the possibility of rescuing an alternative, subversive visual pleasure that does not depend on an enunciatory structure grounded in sexual difference and, more particularly, in the repression of the feminine in favor of the masculine.

The initial sequences of *What Have I Done to Deserve This?*, the director's fourth feature film and his first international success, situate it as a cinematically mediated tale of frustrated feminine desire. The opening shot surveys a film crew on location in a Madrid square, closing in on the image of a woman crossing the plaza, followed by a man holding a sound boom. The music on the sound track evokes the movie scores

written by Nino Rota for numerous Italian neorealist films. Our awareness
of the filmic frame is further reinforced by the juxtaposition of the film's
title and credits intercut with the images. The camera follows the woman
(Carmen Maura) into a karate studio, cutting to rows of men dressed in
monklike robes who practice the martial art of kendo by delivering grunt-
ing blows in the air with five-foot-long sticks. As Maura goes about her
chores as a cleaning woman, the class ends and the studio empties out.
But while she finishes up in a mirrored dressing room in the foreground
of the shot, a naked man steps into a shower stall just beyond her on
the right side of the frame. Maura's character's unabashed gaze at the
spectacle of the male body is reflected and framed for the spectator by
the mirror on the wall. Sensing her presence, the man turns and beckons
her into the shower. However, any erotic promise in the encounter for
either characters or film audience is soon undercut. Their sexual clinch
beneath the streaming shower head responds neither to the horrific
connotations of the Hitchcockesque shower scene—explicitly evoked in
one shot—nor to the fantasy of instant sexual gratification in spontaneous, anonymous sex. The act itself is unsatisfyingly brief, especially for
the woman, who then acts out her frustration by taking up a stick left by
one of the kendo students. The sequence ends with her striking furiously
at the air as the man slinks guiltily out of the building.

Through its privileging of feminine desire, coupled with the assumption of the look by the female protoganist, Almodóvar's film from the
outset issues an implicit challenge to the patriarchal structures of both
power and pleasure inherent in the dominant cinema tradition as theorized by Laura Mulvey and subsequent feminist critics. According to Mulvey, narrative cinema is complicit with a scopophilic regime of pleasure
whereby the male spectator "possesses"—with its dual connotations of
sexual and physical control or power—the female through the look—or,
rather, the relay of looks created by the camera, the male actor's gaze,
and the male spectator who identifies with both.[9] In *What Have I Done?*,
Almodóvar seeks to opt out of the societal and filmic system that would
exclude the feminine except as a projection of male desire.

Even before his fourth film, Almodóvar had earned a reputation as a
man at home cinematically in a feminine universe. Both his first and third
films, *Pepi, Luci, Bom y otras chicas del montón* (*Pepi, Luci, Bom and
Other Ordinary Girls*) and *Dark Habits*, are set in the womanly worlds
of unhappy housewives, *porteras*, punk rock singers, and unconventional
convents. While such a focus has been notably rare among Spanish filmmakers, for decades American studios cultivated women audiences
through the popular subgenre known as "women's pictures." Starring
well-known actresses and concentrating on women's problems and specifically domestic issues, such films have been a staple of commercial
melodrama.[10] But as Anglo-American feminist film critics have demon-

strated, while "woman's pictures" provide a privileged locus for the analysis of representations of women on the film screen, these films have tended to offer only further variations on the Hollywood repertory of repression that reduces women to images reassuring to the male viewer. In contrast to the image of the glamorous star as fetishistic projection of phallic sexuality, the "weepie," in its address to a primarily female audience who would identify with the trials of the heroine, serves up a de-eroticized image of the woman as victim, often as mother or mental patient.[11] Such portrayals literally deflate the threat of feminine sexuality even as they channel the female viewer toward a masochistic overidentification—hence the tears—with the female protagonist.

Almodóvar would seem, at least initially, to have pursued that latter path in his characterization of the desperate housewife, Gloria. Trapped in a cramped apartment with her thoughtless, taxi driver husband, Antonio; her dotty, diabetic mother-in-law, addicted to sweet *magdalena* cakes and Catalán mineral water; and her two semidelinquent sons (one sells drugs and the other sells his body to his friends' fathers), Gloria's life is a series of never ending days propped up by the pills she acquires illegally from her neighborhood pharmacy. The look of the film and its heroine is unrelentingly miserable, and the actress herself speaks of the effects of playing such a decidedly unglamorous role: "During the shooting . . . I felt terribly depressed, as I'd imagined all women with a life like hers must feel. With hair like that, all messy, with those housecoats . . . I gradually became more and more miserable and then I also got very weepy."[12] Maura's reactions are particularly revealing with regard to the affective axis of the film, established through the requisite identification between protagonist and audience. Far from an extension of her performance, the feelings the actress describes are not reflected in her portrayal of the hapless Gloria, whose emotional register is characterized more by lack of affect (due perhaps to drugs or lack of sleep) than by emotional excess (Plate 9). Instead they testify to a process of interiorization of the spectator's role that surfaces at key moments of the film.

While the "woman's picture" can be said to function as the dominant model of spectatorial response for the film, the cultural meaning of the film as a whole accrues through a process of "semiotic layering" that operates through the juxtaposition of nationally and historically diverse film sources.[13] I have already alluded, for example, to the references to Italian neorealism in the musical score. But the plot and mise-en-scène owe much more to a specifically Spanish tradition of black comedies from the fifties and early sixties. Grounded in the socioeconomic conditions of the period, these films focused on the plight of urban dwellers struggling to survive in a city unable to provide jobs and housing to a population swollen by recent arrivals from the economically even more desperate provinces. Films like Marco Ferreri's *El pisito* (*The Little Apart-*

ment, 1958), José Antonio Nieves Conde's *El inquilino* (*The Tenant*, 1958), and particularly Luis Berlanga's *El verdugo* (*The Executioner*, 1961) anticipate the plight of Gloria and her family in their modern, cement-block, urban high rise overlooking Madrid's M-30 superhighway.[14] Seen in this context, Almodóvar's social criticism appears all the more devastating in that it reveals the lack of fundamental change despite the intervening years, years of the so-called economic miracle and the end of Francoism. Contrary to the director's declarations about making films as if Franco never existed, this is a world created by the urban nonplanning of the Franco years, growing out of a policy that actively sought, by passive neglect of urban social services, to discourage immigration to the "corrupt" cities.[15] Like the characters from those earlier films, both Gloria and her husband have come from the *pueblo*, the *pueblo* to which her mother-in-law and oldest son, Toni, will return at the end of the film. The post-Franco city has failed them, as it does Gloria, despite their apparently greater material well-being in a world of time-saving home appliances, the "consumer paradise" of contemporary Spain.

Still, that criticism is tempered, or at least rendered deeply ambivalent, through the persons and story of Toni and his grandmother, with their nostalgic longing for a return to the countryside. In their flight from the city they reenact the ending of the founding film of Spanish neorealism, José Antonio Nieves Conde's 1950 picture *Surcos* (*Furrows*). Hailed as "the first glance at reality in a cinema of paper-maché"[16] for its serious treatment of the problem of the rural exodus to the cities, the film—in the hands of Falangist Nieves Conde—also served as a cautionary tale regarding the moral corruption and destruction of family structures that awaited immigrants to the city. The film's conclusion, rewritten by the Spanish censors, projects the family's chastened return to the fields they never should have left. Almodóvar's film can in fact be read as an ironic rewriting of Nieves Conde's.

As in the earlier film, in *What Have I Done?* paternal authority is reduced or absent, and a harried mother overly preoccupied with material survival neglects her children's moral education. But Almodóvar's treatment of the subject takes the moral absolutes of *Surcos* and uses them against the value system they purport to represent. American film culture, decried well into the fifties as the devilish tool of a foreign, materialist ideology by the regime's guardians of Spanish moral and ethnic purity, paradoxically provides the instrument whereby Toni and his grandmother are able to articulate their discontent with contemporary urban Spanish reality.[17] Sitting with his grandmother in a darkened movie theater watching Elia Kazan's double-edged pastoral, *Splendor in the Grass* (1961), Toni voices his identification with Bud Stamper's (Warren Beatty) rejection of his oil-baron father's ambitions and Bud's desire to be a cattle farmer. "Maybe I'll set up a ranch in the *pueblo*," he exclaims, as his grandmother indicates her enthusiastic assent. The historical irony for the (second degree) spectator in Stamper's desire to return to a simpler age of American existence in a small Kansas town on the eve of the stock market crash underscores the untimeliness, and "unplacefulness," of Toni's dream as well. The small town is portrayed as a stifling, socially and sexually repressive place in the Kazan story, just as it is in numerous Spanish films of the same period, such as Juan Antonio Bardem's *Calle Mayor*. Furthermore, as the *Surcos/Splendor* juxtaposition reminds us, the simpler past to which grandmother and grandson would return is the past of Francoism, a past Almodóvar's films rewrite even as they seek to disavow it.

Another crucial distinction between both the Berlanga and Nieves Conde films and Almodóvar's lies in their treatment of the female protagonists, in each case a wife and mother. In the view of the earlier directors, the woman, Eve-like, draws the man into a Girardian triangle of desire with her eyes set firmly on financial gain and the acquisition of material goods. Thus the protagonist of Berlanga's film, for example, is trapped into becoming an executioner in order to provide an apartment for his wife and child-to-be. For Almodóvar, in contrast, it is the housewife who becomes a pawn in a patriarchal and capitalistic system of exchange. Obsessed by the pressures of meeting payments on the apartment, the television, the washing machine, and the refrigerator, Gloria's other desires are displaced onto those consumer goods. But those longings are also turned back against her.

Film historians and critics have long recognized the historical links between commercial cinema as entertainment and as advertisement, a complicity that situates the female addressee of the woman's picture as potential consumer of images of her self and her surroundings.[18] In *What Have I Done?*, once again, the character Gloria mirrors the spectator's role, for she, too, is being sold a bill of goods. As the director expresses it in his summary of the film: "[Gloria] would like to become a member of the consumer society, but only manages to consume herself, day by day."[19] Thus, even as she struggles to survive, she is aware of the distance that separates her life from the idealized images of women she sees in magazines in the doctor's office or in beauty shop windows. While it is the men in her life who fail to satisfy her, she interiorizes her discontent as a form of self-hatred. In a scene whose comic extremes may blind us to its incisiveness, she sells her son to a pederast dentist in order to buy a curling iron she has seen a shop window and about which she fantasizes as the instrument of her transformation.[20]

Almodóvar's films constantly foreground the topic of narrative cinema's collusion with the language and address of advertising. From *Pepi, Luci, Bom* to *Atame (Tie Me Up! Tie Me Down!)*, the director has delighted in including mock commercials within his films. *What Have I Done?* is no exception in that regard, but here the codes of television advertising spill over into the diegesis itself. In a telling sequence early in the film, Gloria has returned from her cleaning woman's job at the karate school to her kitchen, where she takes up her other full-time job. Placing her in a conventional kitchen setting, the camera portrays the protagonist in a series of reverse-angle shots, a classic editing figure in a two-character scene. But Gloria is alone in the room, bending to fill her washing machine with clothes and then to remove a pan from the oven. In both instances the camera is positioned to show the appliances, in effect, looking back at her. While this nonnaturalistic use of the reverse-angle shot is startling to the spectator, it is not entirely unfamiliar, since TV commercials for clothes washers and fried chicken recipes long ago appropriated this particular editing figure.

Framed in this way, the image of the desiring female subject of consumer society collapses into her own objectification. While foregrounding the role of the cinematic apparatus, as Charles Eckert has noted, in "fetishizing products and putting the libido in libidinally invested advertising,"[21] *What Have I Done?* once again recalls the specifically Spanish context in which it functions and consequently evokes the history of the explicit political manipulation of consumer desire under the Franco regime. Indeed, the creation of a prosperous consumer society, as theorized and promoted by archtechnocrat Gonzalo Fernández de la Mora in his 1961 book, *The Twilight of Ideologies*, was conceived as a strategy to guarantee political apathy among Spaniards. As historians of the period Raymond Carr and Juan Pablo Fusi observe: "There is nothing like the installment system to weaken the striker's resolution, nothing like relative well-being after struggle to weaken 'solidarity' as a working-class value."[22]

Thus the two initial circuits of desire remain uncompleted; they end in apparently irreversible frustration, blocked, at least in part, by history and the persistent legacy of the Franco years. Gloria will find no satisfaction, nor even relief, in sexual or material fulfillment. Instead, the film is carried to thematic and affective closure by a third circuit, the still more exclusively feminine realm of the maternal melodrama, with its rich filmic intertext. The director himself has signaled this dimension of the film:

It's a film about motherhood. . . . In it are reflected different embodiments of the maternal. Carmen Maura's character is that of the mother pure and simple, the mother who keeps the home together, who carries it all on her back. There are frustrated mothers like Cristal, who's a wonderful mother. And there's a very typically Spanish mother that appalls me, the kind who's always hitting her kids, that tense sort of mother I see in the streets of Madrid, the kind that, if the child falls down, on top of it all she beats him for it, very violent. And among all those mothers is my own. For me it's very significant: I was making a film about my own social class, about my origins and my family, a type of family I recognize, and I wanted my own mother to be there.[23]

The cultural specificity of Almodóvar's cast of mothers in the film—including, as he notes, his own, Francisca Caballero, who plays the role of the white-haired lady from the old *pueblo* whom Gloria meets in the dentist's office—distinguishes his film from the ideological traditions of the maternal melodrama as described by Linda Williams in her study of that quintessential film of maternal self-sacrifice, King Vidor's *Stella Dallas* (1937). Identifying an ethic of maternal self-abnegation as the hallmark of the genre, Williams signals the paradox in that "frequently the self-sacrificing mother must make her sacrifice that of the connection to her children—either for their or her own good."[24] This self-canceling structure, she notes, serves as "[a] device [for] devaluing and debasing the actual figure of the mother while sanctifying the institution of motherhood in general."[25]

In many ways, then, Almodóvar's film could not seem farther from the Hollywood ethic of glorified feminine masochism. First of all, in contrast to the traditional film mother, Gloria does not sublimate her sexual desires entirely into her maternal role. As we have seen, the film begins with an emphatic, if frustrated, expression of her sexuality. Second, until the very end of the film, Gloria gives little evidence of traditional motherly behavior. Her demonstrations of maternal affection are limited to her contacts with Vanessa, the telekinetic daughter of her neighbor Juani, the "bad mother" characterized in the Almodóvar quotation. Her ties to her own two sons, Toni and Miguel, in contrast, are strained by the family's dire economic circumstances (Plate 10). But if we focus more closely on her relationship with her younger son, the profile of the melodramatic movie mother may be seen to offer a more appropriate point of comparison.

In the early scenes of the film, Gloria is shown as being unable to fulfill the most archetypal of maternal functions toward Miguel: that of providing physical nourishment. When he comes home to a bare refrigerator, she is forced to send him to Cristal, the prostitute next door, for dinner and a sandwich for tomorrow's lunch. This ceding of maternal rights and responsibilities prefigures her later surrender of Miguel to the dentist. The defining gesture in the portrayal of Gloria within the circuit of maternal desire, it bears striking similarities to Stella Dallas's sacrifice of her daughter to a "better" mother, the upper-class wife of her former husband. In Gloria's case as well, the mother seeks to provide her child with the material advantages she herself cannot give her offspring. "You know how bad it is at home. I can barely feed you," she tells her son, who then bargains with the dentist for a stereo system, a VCR, and painting lessons. In the Almodóvar version, it is true, there is an ironic slippage between the altruistic act of maternal self-sacrifice in its most characteristic movie form and Gloria's more venal desire for a curling iron, but this subversion works against the sentimentalizing tendencies of the traditional maternal melodrama and its destructive idealization of motherhood. Unlike Stella's smiling apotheosis at the end of *Stella Dallas*, as a woman who has denied her very identity as mother for the daughter she loves, Gloria's act passes virtually unnoticed, even by the boy's father, who, we are later told, was never aware of his son's absence.

The conclusion of Almodóvar's film also runs a rather different course from the King Vidor classic, as ensuing events apparently intervene to liberate Gloria from her role as both wife and mother. Driven to the edge by too many demands for ironed shirts and dinner on the table, she accidentally kills her husband with a ham bone. In a sense Antonio's largely comic and narratively convenient demise only serves to confirm his estrangement, throughout the film, from the rest of the household and from the film's real-world and cinematic referents. The would-be champion of moral *decencia*, he chastizes Gloria for her work outside the home and her friendship with Cristal, and as such represents the voice of an archaic value system ill-suited to current economic and social realities.

Antonio's emotional distance from his family is conveyed through his obsessive playing of the Zarah Leander song "Nicht nur aus Liebe Weinen," for him a nostalgic token of his love affair with his former employer, Ingrid Müller, the aging chanteuse for whom he forged a series of Hitler letters while a "guest worker" in Germany. Indeed, a number of viewers and critics have complained of the tangential character of this complicated Teutonic subplot. I would argue, rather, that this element of the film is significant, in its conception if not in its execution. Drawing this time not on Hollywood melodrama but on one of its European cousins, as it were, the director plots the husband's story, the real historical drama of economic exile, against the suspect nostalgia of the so-called retro film. With its foregrounding of the Ingrid Müller/Zarah Leander figure, however, Almodóvar's version evokes R. W. Fassbinder's critical variation on the genre, *Veronika Voss* or especially *Lili Marlene*, with its basis in the life story of another Nazi star, Lale Anderson.

Whatever Antonio's role in life, his death is key to the film's denouement. For with him literally out of the picture, the other members of the family leave to pursue their separate destinies, as if acknowledging their liberation from the yoke of paternal authority. While Miguel is apparently happily ensconced with his dentist, the grandmother and older son achieve their desired departure for the *pueblo*, their bus tickets purchased with the proceeds from Toni's drug dealing. But as the director moves with characteristic verve to wrap up the remaining plot lines, a sudden change in the tone of the film provides a final twist. Gloria's good-byes to her son and mother-in-law, cued by the scene's bluesy saxophone score, evoke a surprising pathos, an emotional response blocked up to this point in this film. Upon her return to her empty house, Gloria experiences a sense of overwhelming solitude rather than relief. Looking over the balcony to the pavement below, she is drawn toward the void, until she catches sight of Miguel running up the steps. Parody converges with genuine melodrama as the film's finale stages an emotional reunion between mother and younger son.[26] Home once again, Miguel announces his decision to stay because, although the dentist was fun for a while, "I'm too young to be tied down to anyone, and besides, this house needs a man."

The affective punch of these final scenes is heightened by the autobiographical subtext to the film. In addition to his own mother, Almodóvar has included in the character of Miguel a portrait of himself as a young filmmaker-to-be. The boy's painting lessons, the Zoetrope he spins in his bedroom at night before shutting off the light, even his precocious homosexuality mark the character as a projection of the director. Thus the ending represents not simply a self-conscious restatement of classic melodramatic closure but a more broadly self-reflexive gesture that Almodóvar uses to offer a slyly open conclusion. By completing its thematic and affective circuit in the realm of the maternal, the film rewrites the traditional oedipal scenario. The playful asymmetry of the mother/son couple denies the restrictive narrative logic of the patriarchal family, both on and off the film screen. In the absence of the paternal Law, it is suggested mother and son are free to explore—and create—forms of sexuality and sexual identity impossible under traditional societal and familial structures.

In fact, the possibilities held out by this postpatriarchal society have already been hinted at quite tellingly in the concluding sequences of the film. In a touch of canny Almodovarian logic, the police detective investigating the death of Gloria's husband turns out to be the same impotent man with whom she shared the opening shower scene. When the distraught widow confesses her role in her husband's death, the detective refuses to believe her, and the case is closed. In a world where the Law has lost its potency and the power to enforce its strictures, crimes have no consequences.[27] Attacking the foundations of linear causality, the film affirms its capacity not, as one might have thought, to forget history, the past of Francoism, but to challenge the hold of that history over future stories. Thus, rather than a resolution, the ending to *What Have I Done to Deserve This?* ought really to be read as a beginning to the filmmaker's, and his audience's, ongoing task of rewriting post-Franco, postpatriarchal society.

NOTES

1. Significantly, melodrama has not been widely cultivated by the better-known oppositional filmmakers in Spain, who have preferred the elegiac mode (Victor Erice's *El espíritu de la colmena* and *El sur*), rural tragedy (Ricardo Franco's *Pascual Duarte* and Mario Camus's *Los santos inocentes*), black comedy (most of Luis Berlanga, and Carlos Saura's *El jardín de las delicias*, among many others) and the metaphorical psycho-drama (much of Saura).

2. Peter Besas, *Behind the Spanish Lens: Spanish Cinema Under Fascism and Democracy* (Denver: Arden Press, 1985), 216.

3. Peter Brooks, *The Melodramatic Imagination: Balzac, Henry James, Melodrama and the Mode of Excess* (New York: Columbia University Press, 1985), xiii.

4. Brooks, 14–15.

5. In an interview with Michael Bronski ("Almodóvar: Post-Franco American?" *Zeta Magazine* 2.4 [April 1989]: 65–66), Almodóvar speaks—apropos of *Law of Desire*—of his own secular appropriations of the sacred in his films as a reflection of a generalized practice within contemporary Spanish culture: "I think you have to realize that although there is a strong Catholic religious feeling and history in Spain, it is now viewed as a cultural tradition and not as an institution. . . . It is very common in Spanish culture to steal the religious ceremonies away from God and keep them for yourself. This is important. The ceremonies are sometimes very beautiful and many times people even forget the origin of their images or their ceremonies and use them for their own needs. I like this. It is a very pragmatic, practical use of religion. It is artistic about life."

6. Robert Lang, *American Film Melodrama* (Princeton: Princeton University Press, 1989), 163.

7. Christine Gledhill's introductory essay, "The Melodramatic Field: An Investigation," in her edited volume, *Home Is Where the Heart Is: Studies in Melodrama and the Woman's Film* (London: British Film Institute, 1987), offers a cogent critical survey of the history of recent approaches to film melodrama. Her essay, and Thomas Elsaesser's "Tales of Sound and Fury. Observations of the Family Melodrama," reprinted in her edited volume, stress the ideological ambiguity and adaptability of melodrama, which may "function either subversively or as escapism . . . relative to its given historical and social context" (47). In addition to the essays anthologized in Gledhill, important contextual studies of the uses of melodrama in Latin American and Spanish cinema, respectively, are Ana López, "The Melodrama in Latin America," *Wide Angle* 7.3 (1985): 5–13; and Marsha Kinder," An Introduction," in her *Spanish Cinema: The Politics of Family and Gender* (Los Angeles: Spanish Ministry of Culture and USC School of Cinema-Television, 1991). In the former, López notes the rejection of melodrama by the theorists and practitioners of new Latin American cinema as a form of cultural dependence and its subsequent, strategic rehabilitation within a "second wave" of new Latin American cinema. Kinder, in contrast, studies the role of melodrama in early post–Civil War Spanish cinema as "the official organizing narrative for a neo-Catholic fascist discourse" (5). Almodóvar's own appropriation of melodrama via Hollywood, as I suggest later, may profitably be read against this intertext.

8. Laura Mulvey, "Visual Pleasure and Narrative Cinema," in her *Visual and Other Pleasures* (Bloomington: Indiana University Press, 1989), 25.

9. See especially part 3, "Woman as Image, Man as Bearer of the Look," in Mulvey, 19–24.

10. The bibliography on the relation between melodrama and the "woman's picture" is extensive. Historically and theoretically significant approaches include Molly Haskell, *From Reverence to Rape: The Treatment of Women in the Movies*, 2nd ed. (Chicago: University of Chicago Press, 1987); Mary Ann Doane, *The Desire to Desire: The Woman's Film of the Forties* (Bloomington: Indiana University Press, 1987); and Gledhill's *Home Is Where the Heart Is*. This last volume includes a substantial bibliography.

11. See, in particular, chs. 2 and 3, "Clinical Eyes: The Medical Discourse" and "The Moving Image: Pathos and the Maternal," in Doane, 38–69.

12. Nuria Vidal, *The Films of Pedro Almodóvar*, trans. Linda Moore in collaboration with Victoria Hughes (Madrid: Instituto de Cine, Ministerio de Cultura, 1988), 110.

13. I adapt the concept of "semiotic layering" from Maureen Turim, "Gentlemen Consume Blonds," in *Movies and Methods*, vol. 2, ed. Bill Nichols (Berkeley: University of California Press, 1985), 377, where she defines it as "the accrual and transformations of meanings associated with an artifact as it passes through history, or as it is presented in different versions." In Almodóvar's case the process takes on a cross-cultural dimension as well.

14. Almodóvar has alluded to these antecedents in interviews. See John Hopewell, *Out of the Past: Spanish Cinema After Franco* (London: British Film Institute, 1986), 239; and Marsha Kinder, "Pleasure and the New Spanish Mentality: A Conversation with Pedro Almodóvar," *Film Quarterly* 41.1 (Fall 1987): 38–39.

15. See the discussion in Raymond Carr and Juan Pablo Fusi, "The Rural Exodus," in their *Spain: From Dictatorship to Democracy* (London: George Allen and Unwin, 1981), 66–70.

16. José García Escudero, *La historia del cine español en cien palabras*. Cited in Hopewell, 56.

17. See, for example, the discussion in Carmen Martín Gaite, *Usos amorosos de la postguerra española* (Barcelona: Anagrama, 1987), 30–34. The opinions quoted by Martín Gaite are tellingly echoed in Luis García Berlanga's brilliant reflection on the intertwining of Spanish–American cinematic and political relations in his 1952 film *Bienvenido Mr. Marshall*, in the character of the village priest who warns against Americans bearing gifts.

18. Most notably, Charles Eckert, "The Carole Lombard in Macy's Window," *Quarterly Review of Film Studies* 3.1 (1978): 1–21, repr. in *Fabrications*, ed. Jane Gaines and Charlotte Herzog (New York: Routledge, 1990), 100–121; Jeanne Thomas Allen, "The Film Viewer as Consumer," *Quarterly Review of Film Studies* 5.4 (1980): 481–499; Mary Ann Doane, "The Economy of Desire: The Commodity Form in/of the Cinema," in *The Desire to Desire*, 22–33.

19. Vidal, 113.

20. The importance of that particular scene and the director's rather unconventional solution for shooting Gloria looking/longing at the items in the store window, is discussed in Vidal, 105.

21. Eckert, 121.

22. Carr and Fusi, 35, 89.

23. Quoted by Francisco Blanco, "Boquerini," in *Pedro Almodóvar* (Madrid: Ediciones JC: 1989), 63. The translation is mine.

24. Linda Williams, " 'Something Else Besides a Mother': *Stella Dallas* and the Maternal Melodrama," in Gledhill's *Home Is Where the Heart Is*, 300.

25. Williams, 300.

26. In her interview with Almodóvar, Marsha Kinder targets exactly the affective dynamics I'm trying to evoke here: "It seems to me that what lies at the center of your unique tone . . . is that fluidity with which you move . . . from one feeling or tone to another, so that when a line is delivered, it's very funny and borders on parody . . . but at the same time . . . [it] moves us emotionally. . . . You start out by demystifying how movies work, but then by the end of the film those same dynamics still work on the audience very powerfully" (37, 40).

27. I thank Marvin D'Lugo for calling my attention to this role of the police as spectators-in-the-text, called upon, in a number of the director's films, to ratify the characters' unconventional, and once unthinkable, life choices. See his discussion in "Almodóvar's City of Desire," *Quarterly Review of Film and Video* 13.4 (1991): 47–65, also in the present volume.

Tauromachy as a Spectacle of Gender Revision in *Matador*

Leora Lev

Because to kill a noble bull as it deserves, not only must we use the sword, but also the heart.
> —Diego Montes, in Pedro Almodóvar's *Matador*

Pedro Almodóvar's 1986 film *Matador* opens with a sequence that is meant to shock: the male protagonist, bullfighter Diego Montes (Nacho Martínez), masturbates while viewing a masked slasher dismember a series of female bodies on his home video screen. As the film's diegesis and visual metonyms develop with the choreographic geometry of a bullfight (*corrida de toros*), a question arises. Why does Almodóvar, Spain's enfant terrible of cinematic postmodernism and answer to Andy Warhol, center one of his most iconoclastic films around the ultimate signifier for a socioculturally reactionary Spain?[1] For the *corrida* emblematizes the Spain of theological and imperialist demagoguery, Francoist iron-fisted rule, and their attendant policing of racial and gender identity, all of which are prime targets of Almodovarian parody.

It becomes clear that while Almodóvar enlists the *corrida* precisely so as to dismember regressive sociosexual and aesthetic politics, fragments of these hegemonies survive—albeit the worse for wear—*Matador*'s postmodernist onslaught. I shall explore this dynamic within the context of a radical slippage between the *corrida*'s sociohistorical development and its representation in Spanish and other European vanguard cultures. For historically speaking, the *corrida*, which embodies cultural, economic, religious, and psychosexual fetishisms, has been defused and recast as a social practice that cements the very gender and class hierarchies that it would most appear to parody and critique. Ironically, it has fallen to European aesthetic vanguards to chart these fetishisms—ways in which the *corrida* both proffers and defers transcendence of underclass status, both orchestrates and disavows transgressions of gender boundaries through the polymorphous perversity suggested by its overdetermined role-playing and its semiotically charged garb that begs comparison with drag.[2]

Pre-Franco experimental playwright Federico García Lorca's tauromachy (*tauromaquia*) is especially significant for *Matador*. García Lorca, like Almodóvar, deploys the *corrida* as a site of erotic interaction as well as artistic production so as to undermine essentializing constructions of gender identity. However, Almodóvar ultimately subsumes feminine difference to a masculinist model of desire and empowerment. Lorca's *corrida*, on the other hand, both hypothesizes and laments the difficulty of possible feminine and homoerotic *jouissances* that maintain themselves distinct from masculinist and heterosexist ontologies in a pre–Civil War Spain seething with latent nationalism.[3]

THE *CORRIDA*: SOCIAL DEVELOPMENT AND AESTHETIC REPRESENTATION

The eighteenth century saw a transformation in *corrida* culture whose ramifications for modern Spanish society were highly paradoxical. As Timothy Mitchell observes in his book *Blood Sport: A Social History of Spanish Bullfighting*, since the Middle Ages, the *corrida* has been split between a popular festive tradition and an urban spectacle performed by aristocrats on horseback and their liveried underlings.[4] But during the eighteenth century, as the Bourbon dynasty displaced the Hapsburgs, these city lackeys and their rustic counterparts usurped the blood sport, reappropriating popular bullfighting techniques, such as capework performed on foot, into the *corrida*.

This revolution in bullfighting culture both sustained the illusion of the underclass's empowerment and perpetuated and mirrored its disenfranchisement from any real-life political, economic, or social authority. The *corrida*'s underclass protagonists succeeded in legitimating their own culture of *majismo*, whose ideological roots dated from the epoch of the medieval hero El Cid, of impeccably Spanish, Catholic bloodline. *Majismo*, embodied by the *torero*, opposed itself to the penchant of Spanish aristocratic *petimetres* (little masters, from *petits maîtres*) for Enlightenment political, philosophical, and sartorial innovation.[5] But the *majos*, in allying themselves with, as Mitchell puts it, "monarchical fetishism, obscurantist Catholicism," Golden Age honor codes (*pundonor*), and xenophobic rejection of European social philosophies also forestalled any popular insurrection à la the American and French revolutions.

A further paradox inheres in the industry surrounding, and the staging of, the bullfight itself. The brave bulls' (*toros bravos*) "nobility," both metaphorically and metonymically signifying the noblemen who breed them, confers on the *corrida* a "democratic" tenor wherein *majo* confronts, and skewers, aristocrat.[6] Yet their very socioeconomic destitution is what spurs aspiring matadors to transcend this untenable status in the first place. And the glittering dream of *torero* prestige only masks the Roman gladiatorial tenor of a competition so frequently "rigged" that literal or figurative castration through goring of the failed *majo* is the destiny of the overwhelming majority.

Given that the *pundonor* celebrated by the *majos* in bullfighting culture is fueled by a patriarchalism dating from the Reconquest and codified in the Golden Age dramas of Spanish playwrights Calderón de la Barca, Lope de Vega, and Tirso de Molina (of Don Juan fame), it is no surprise that the *corrida* reaffirms an oppositional, heterosexist construction of gender. The basic bullfighting unit (*cuadrilla*) is a homosocial structure that defines itself in diametric opposition to both "femininity" and any homoeroticism that such male–male bonding might suggest. It is a microcosmic representation of "an archaic social cell of workers . . . with its origins among warriors and hunters . . . they seep into political parties, companies, the Church, and the Army. . . . The *cuadrilla* is an action-oriented family, strictly masculine: the other family."[7]

If the *cuadrilla* recapitulates a system of paternalistic patronage (*caciquismo*) that has resisted democratic reform throughout modern Spanish history, this correspondence between blood sport and politics is nowhere more evident than during Franco's rule following the Spanish Civil War (1936–1939). The *corrida* enacted an illusionistic drama of national identity that compensated, in the popular imagination, for the Spanish disenfranchisement from international politics wrought by Francoist isolationism, as well as for domestic socioeconomic disempowerment resulting from a virtually immutable class hierarchy.[8] Male spectator investment in the *cuadrilla*'s allegory of "testicular willpower," a cultural fantasy that situates absolute authority in the male genitals, diffused myriad anxieties through the myth that "a *torero* should be able to realize five consecutive [heterosexual] coituses, and nothing more offensive can be attributed to him than signs of homosexuality."[9] This heterosexist ideology was, ironically enough, consecrated in the *cacique*'s or *torero*'s consumption of the bull's testicles, a quasi-eucharistic fetishism in its own right.

Likewise, although scholarly glosses as well as popular ballads have cast *toro* and *torero* in both masculine and feminine roles, the *corrida* is plotted from an unequivocally masculinist position from which the male self must conquer, mutilate, or (less frequently) defend himself against a female other. At times the *torero* enacts the female role, dressed in a suit of lights (*traje de luces*) and pink stockings, with hair twisted into a short braid. "She" uses "feminine" wiles to subdue the loose cannon of masculine libido to the social good of marriage and procreation—figured, significantly, as castration and death. Alternatively, the *torero* is the male lover seducing his unruly woman to the point of penetration via his lance (*estoque*) of "her" vagina, the bloody fold between the bull's shoulder blades. Whichever way one slices it, however, these gender dynamics are plotted and lyricized as an irreducibly masculinist dialectic that, furthermore, disavows any hint of transvestism or homoeroticism.

Indeed, René Girard's model of triadic, or mediated, desire, itself a problematic schematization that inadequately theorizes ways in which its own teleology of sadomasochism is inflected by gender positionalities, may be mapped onto the *corrida* almost wholesale. For Girard, the novelistic subject desires another subject or object as a function of the latter's valorization by a third party. The subject's desire increases in proportion to the object's inaccessibility until the very impossibility of possessing the object, and the psychosexual violence entailed in its pursuit, displaces any desire for the object itself.[10]

With regard to the *corrida*, the public invests the blood sport with the sociosexual and economic authority to which the matador aspires. And ultimately the hyperbolic violence associated with conquest in the arena becomes obsessively desired in itself. Even matadors who have already achieved the financial and existential integrity of hero status valorize mutilation or death over the black hole of a *corrida*-free old age.[11]

Despite the *corrida*'s potential for radical disruption of sociocultural and gender hierarchies, the blood sport as a social ritual has only reinforced these hegemonies the more uncompromisingly. It has, thus, fallen to avant-garde artists, poets, playwrights, and filmmakers—from Pablo Picasso, Lorca, Salvador Dalí, Juan Gris, and Joan Miró to Carlos Saura and Pedro Almodóvar—to problematize and redeploy the *corrida*'s embodiment of multiple fetishisms, its simultaneous acknowledgment and disavowal of its own duplicitous relation to social hegemonies.

A noble linchpin figure for European vanguard movements, and one for whom *tauromaquia* is of prime significance, is Pablo Picasso. Picasso's *tauromaquia* becomes a site where aesthetic and psychosexual transgressions explicitly or implicitly foreground the *corrida*'s fetishism. Picasso continually reveals the *corrida*'s pageantry—which seemingly dramatizes the triumph of human intention over chance, of national identity over historical vicissitude, of virile presence over castration, mortality, and absence—as a choreography of dismemberment and undecidability. This conflictual representation recurs as childhood Málaga charcoal draw-

ings of doves and *corridas*, pre-Fauve oils of *corridas* awash in Mediterranean color, and the ludic stage-set collaborations with Jean Cocteau
and Erik Satie (*Parade* ballet, 1917), Manuel de Falla (*El sombrero de
tres picos*, 1919), and Sergei Diaghilev, give way to the darker 1930s
cubist *corridas*. These cubist geometries of pain, rendering and rending
the *corrida*'s human and animal victims, reach their most devastating
paroxysm in *Guernica* (1937).[12]

The *corrida*'s fetishisms are elaborated in a painting whose *corrida*
might be seen as a darker mirror image of *Matador: Corrida: The Death
of the Female Bullfighter* (1933). The permeability of the formal boundaries between *toro*, *torera*, and horse both constructs and denies a spec-
trum of ontological differences whose original, occulted referent is sexual
difference. A phallic bull bears a white horse whose breast is punctured
by a red wound, whose flanks leak pink entrails, and whose head twists
back over the belly of a similarly chalk-fleshed, prostrate, moribund *torera*.[13] The *torera*'s shredded *traje* reveals round breasts, naked legs
spread open over the horse's rump, fragile hands trailing against the
bull's curved horns. The two "feminine" principles seem to be reified
and specularized for masculinist consumption: they are linked through
castration imagery, with the horse's wound metonymically suggesting
both the anatomical "lack" and symbolic disempowerment of the open-
legged *torera*.

Yet a representation of gender difference along a sadistic gaze/maso-
chistic objectification dichotomy is disrupted. For the bull's bloodied
muzzle is aligned in a visual chain of signification with the horse's wound
and the *torera*'s "castration," and the implicit power of the prominent
taurine genitals is belied by a double castrating inscription of both *estoque* and *banderilla* into its nape. Picasso thus deploys the *corrida* as
a fetishistic scenario whose brightly colored affirmations—whether of virile sovereignty, national identity, or aesthetic intention—dismantle themselves during the very act of their realization in the bull ring.[14]

In a disparate but related vein, Federico García Lorca's *corridas* simultaneously hypothesize and memorialize transgressive—especially homoerotic and feminine—*jouissance* in a homeland whose history has
been marked by nationalistic purging of otherness and difference. In
"Play and Theory of the *Duende*" (1933), Lorca presents the *duende* as
a spirit proper to the bull ring, signifier for the agonistic *jouissance* that
erupts with any erotic, artistic, or mystical transcendence of self. He opposes the *duende* to both the angel, which inspires the lyrical elegies of
Keats and Gustavo Bécquer, and the muse, which "awakens the intelligence, bringing a landscape of columns and a false taste of laurels."[15] If
through the muse and angel the poet or philosopher may evade death
at a double aesthetic and intellectual remove, the *duende*

loves the rim of the wound, and draws near places where forms fuse together into a yearning superior to their visible expression. . . . In Spain, as among the peoples of the Orient, where the dance is religious expression, the *duende* has unlimited range over the bodies of the dancers of Cádiz, praised by Martial, over the breasts of singers, praised by Juvenal, and in the liturgy of the bulls, an authentic religious drama where, as in the Mass, a God is sacrificed to and adored. . . . You can have muse with the muleta [red cape] and angel with the banderillas and pass for a good bullfighter . . . but when the bull is still clean of wounds, and at the moment of the kill, you need the *duende*'s help to achieve artistic truth.[16]

Later, in the "Lament for Ignacio Sánchez Mejías" (1934), Lorca links the *corrida*, Roman blood sport, and Dionysian ritual in a mutedly homoerotic dirge. The *corrida* becomes a site where the bullfighter, of "marble torso," "handsome body," exemplary sword (*ni espada como su espada*), and lineage of Andalusian Rome, is vanquished by the "black bull of anguish."[17] Images of castration, penetration, and tragic metamorphosis chart the love duel between these two virile scions of mythical bloodlines: the bullfighter's thigh receives a "desolate horn," his "greenish groins" are shot through with "a lily-trumpet," the bull's incursions into his flesh let blood that spurts "each time with less force/that jet that illumines/the rows of seats." Finally, the *torero* assumes his opponent's traits: "death has covered him with pale sulphurs,/and has given him the head of a dark minotaur."

Lorca's identification of eros, art, and archaic ritual with the *corrida* links him to other European avant-garde figures such as Michel Leiris, Georges Bataille, Antonin Artaud, and Jean Cocteau, and even to the valorization of limit experience or *jusqu'auboutisme* of their predecessors Arthur Rimbaud and Lautréamont.[18] However, although Lorca associates the *corrida*'s violence with both artistic and erotic performance—and especially their suppression—he does not aestheticize a limb-shatteringly violent, heterosexist erotics. Rather, he situates women and, albeit more obliquely, gay men as the subjects of enunciation.

MATADOR'S "META-*CORRIDA*"

These vanguard explorations of the *corrida* are problematized and complicated in Almodóvar's *Matador*, even if the question of directorial intention is ultimately undecidable. The film's protagonists are Diego Montes, a matador who murders the female students in his bullfighting class for sexual pleasure, and María Cardenal (Assumpta Serna), the attorney assigned to the murder case, and a murderess in her own right who stabs her male lovers with a lethal hairpin (*alfiler*). Diego's student Angel (Antonio Banderas) attempts to imitate his master's prowess in and out of the bull ring, and dispel doubts about his masculinity, by raping

Diego's lover, Eva Soler (Eva Cobo). When Diego and María subsequently meet, they eng ige in a dance of seduction that both strains toward and defers a consummation of their desire, as well as a denouement of their entwined narratives, that will take the form of their murdering each other as they attain *jouissance* (Plates 12 and 13).

However, Almodóvar does not merely plot a filmic version of the *corrida*; he comments upon his own imaging of this spectacle with a self-referentiality that is part satire, part camp, and part gender-bending. This "meta-*corrida*" simultaneously seduces the spectator with its postmodernist reconfiguration and reifies itself as a cultural relic from a traditionalist Spain at the core of whose sociosexual politics is irreducible violence.

The meta-*corrida*'s central dichotomy is articulated cinematically through a series of tensions between the film's aesthetic rigor and its jarring diegesis, and between Diego and María's straining toward a Bataillean continuity that would violate all boundaries between self and other, inside and outside, and a postponement of this consummation through teasing feints and passes. The choreographed pattern of Diego and María's trysts, which mirrors the stylized confrontation of *toro* and *torero*, and thus bespeaks an aesthetics of geometric integrity, is contrasted with the sadomasochistic motif of dismemberment that organizes the diegesis. This fragmentation is imaged through the play of scarlet and black visual metonyms. María's painted lips, the blood oozing from her lovers' napes, and the roughed grimacing mouths of the corpses that Diego views on video perform a pas de deux with black hair and eyes, the bull's flanks, and the nocturnal interiors where necrophilic acts are plotted and realized.

No sooner are these tensions imagined as antagonistic, however, than they begin to blur and implode like overexposed or melted film stock. The distinctions between hunter and hunted, male aggressor and female prey, hetero- and homoeroticism, and voyeur and specularized object are de-essentialized. This dismantling critiques patriarchal constructions of gender, whose investment in such divisions is shown to be literally and figuratively necrophilic. Diego and María themselves begin to constitute unstable signifiers in a kaleidoscopic play of gender identities. Although Diego at moments exemplifies a lean and swarthy *torero* macho, close-ups of his melting eyes and pouting lips inscribe him with "feminine" cinematic features. Likewise, if María as the femme fatale applies crimson lipstick, the camera also teases out her virility. When Diego spies and pursues her, her coy flight reverses itself into ambush as, in a Lacanian visual pun, she awaits him in the men's room of a movie theater to warn him, "You shouldn't trust appearances." And with regard to the secondary characters, Angel is invested with "feminine" behavioral markers: he faints at the sight of blood, and uses psychic intuition rather than linear logic as his epistemological tool. And the androgynous Eva begins to resemble a beautiful young boy in the scene where she attempts to lure Diego back from María.

The link between essentialist policing of gender identity and a masculinist teleology of desire whose most extreme conclusion is necrophilia is further refracted in mirrored halls where appearances are indeed deceiving. Almodóvar, in the ultimate self-referential cameo, plays the director of a fashion extravaganza for which makeup artists construct the models' personas before a row of stage mirrors. Eva's face has been bruised in her skirmish with Antonio, but the director urges his makeup man to emphasize the purple gash even further, against her mother's protest, "What's this? a fashion show or an anti-aesthetic farce?" (Plate 14).

The fashion industry's complicity with the media in both mirroring and perpetuating necrophilic desire is critiqued in this *mise-en-abîme* of necrophilic pageantry. The positing of the female model—specularized object par excellence—as desirable to the extent that her beauty is inscribed with traces of death is undermined through a parodic realignment of gender roles. For the director's fashion extravaganza is a camp version of the patriarchal, marriage-tending melodrama. It is enacted by vampiric and vampirized female models and a "groom" who is both racially and sexually other to a Spanish, heterosexual self: a black dancer who whirls his cape in a homosexually encoded flourish. As Almodóvar prances through his array of mannequins, a reporter asks him if he still believes in marriage, and he replies, "Sure, marriage is necessary, else there'd be no wedding dresses." The director-within-a-director thus reduces marriage to its most superficial sartorial signifier, erasing depth in favor of surface, a postmodernist zero point from which reactionary referents have been banished. And as María and Diego leave the pageant scene, they must thread their way through a traditional folk dance in order to meet: the rustic organ grinder music and its superannuated dance steps must be left behind in order for a new sociosexual stage to be mounted on a bridge overlooking a post-Franco Madrid.

Almodóvar thus articulates ways in which the policing of gender identity is enacted by such dictatorial politics as that of Francoist Spain, and attempts to cancel out these constructions by casting them into the void of *mise-en-abîme*. Further, he endows María with the weaponry and skill with which to perform the taurine ballet on equal footing with Diego. However, the difficulty with this postmodernist bullfight is precisely that it requires María to acquire a matador's lance (or what Michel Leiris calls an exploding sword thrust) of her own. This problematic becomes particularly clear in a scene that deserves to be viewed through a close-up lens.

María, Diego, Angel, Angel's counselor (Carmen Maura), and the detective (Eusebio Poncela) observe the unearthing of two female corpses from Diego's property. Although Angel has confessed to the crimes to save his maestro, the film viewer and María know that Diego is the murderer. This realization arouses María; lips quivering and eyes flashing, she informs Diego that she has "something to show him." She then drives him through a forest, leads him over a bridge, and, instructing him to cover his eyes, ushers him into a dark building. Diego removes his hands to see a museum of his own bullfighting fetishes. The camera slowly circles at medium range as María observes Diego's apprehension of each fetish: a seamstress's dummy dressed in his *traje de luces*; a glass cabinet containing personal items that María has bribed Diego's maid to steal; bullfight posters sporting his image; a voluminous cape spread out on the floor.

The camera's circular motion is arrested by Diego's and María's mutual confession: he acknowledges that he killed the two women because "to stop killing was to stop living." María rejoins that her willingness to exceed the role of silent fetishist to enact that of lover was contingent upon proof that he had not stopped murdering. She explains, "men think that killing is a crime. But women don't see it that way." During this entire exchange, she fingers her semiotically charged *alfiler*, signifier for the erasure of difference between herself and Diego.

This scene images a series of gazes that disrupt traditionally gendered visual positionalities constructed by the mise-en-scène of the classic Hollywood film. In *Matador*'s initial sequence, as we saw, Diego inhabits the position of male voyeur pleasuring himself to the spectacle of the dismembered female body via the splatter film. Almodóvar equates Diego's pleasure, as well as that of the masked slasher himself, with extreme versions of the sadism implicit in the male-centered visual aesthetic that organizes Hollywood cinema, whether the classic western *Duel in the Sun* (scenes of which are spliced into *Matador*) or the contemporary slasher.[19]

However, María comes to occupy this male-identified cinematic position when she derives pleasure at the spectacle of Diego's bloodletting, and mutilation, in the bull ring, and subsequently murders her lovers with her *alfiler* as a means of discharging this blood lust. The essentialist alignment of masculine and feminine libido along the dichotomy aggression/passivity is dismantled when Diego's voyeuristic sadism and necrophilia are perfectly reproduced in María, the female subject. Or, as the two characters themselves put it:

Diego: Every murderer has a part that's feminine.

María: Every murderess has a part that's masculine.

Almodóvar, as a consummate postmodernist *bricoleur*, thus decontextualizes clips from the male-centered cinematic tradition so as to dislodge their equation of sadistic gaze with masculinity and specularized object with femininity. But although María penetrates the ranks of masculine empowerment and Diego finally meets his match, María must become a clone of Diego in order to fight him at his own game. Still, the rules of the game themselves do not change, do not free themselves from the Bataillean and Leirisian celebration of eros and art with a gaze fixated upon violence, conquest, and the body dismembered. Erasure of inequality seems necessarily to imply occultation of feminine difference in a cinematic gesture whose simultaneous acknowledgment and disavowal of the woman's phallus is irreducibly fetishistic.

Placing *Matador* in the context of other daring revisions of gender roles, the claim could be made that Almodóvar plots his campy reversals in the simultaneously refreshing and problematic manner of, mutatis mutandis, that late-eighteenth-century enfant terrible of French letters, the Marquis de Sade. Despite his penning of misogynist scenarios, Sade is, as Angela Carter observes in her book *The Sadeian Woman*, one of the first male authors to argue for women the same right to *jouissance* as that enjoyed by men.[20] In *La philosophie dans le boudoir* (1795) he has the *instituteurs* or libertine–instructors dismantle essentialist gender ideologies while literally stripping their young charge, Eugènie, as well as each other, of sartorial signifiers of difference and erecting in their place recombinatory sexual tableaux.

However, Sade seems able to free women in his erotic dystopia only by literally or figuratively phallicizing them. The women who succeed are predators for whom libidinal and monetary satisfaction are paramount. These women fetishize the phallus, in the double sense of Lacanian transcendental signifier standing in for the empowerment to which every subject presumably aspires, and of male member itself.

Although Almodóvar's work is far less problematic than that of the eighteenth-century libertine-gone-awry, *Matador* does not succeed any more than does Sade in imaging difference dialogically. However much Almodóvar may satirize masculinist desire, his screen remains cluttered with the strangled, drowned, decapitated, and impaled bodies of women whose death has heightened male *jouissance*. Turning the tables by having María perform necrophilic acts on her male victims is no less fetishistic a gender-revisionist gesture than the Marquis de Sade's granting to Juliette and her sister soldier, Clairwil, the dismembered phallus of the friar they had accosted in *Les prosperités du vice* (1797).

If Almodóvar's postmodernist *corrida* subsumes feminine difference, Lorca's *corrida* in *El público* critiques essentializing gender ideologies, and the eroticizing of violence, while simultaneously hypothesizing homoerotic and feminine difference. Here, Lorca opposes two types of theater: the "open-air theater," which suppresses the histories of marginalized homoerotic and female bodies, and "the true theater, the theater beneath the sand," a transgressive spectacle linked to the *corrida*. One of the virile characters, or *Hombres*, counters the open-air theater Director's assumption that Romeo and Juliet is about "a man and a woman who fall in love."[21] He suggests more protean possibilities for the two protagonists of the love scene: "Romeo could be a bird and Juliet could be a stone. Romeo could be a grain of salt and Juliet could be a map" (4). Indeed, Juliet is clad in self-dismantling signifiers for femininity, such as a white opera gown revealing pink celluloid breasts. "She" rejects the two essentialist patriarchal representations of femininity: voiceless, martyrized love object ("I'm not a slave just so they can pierce my breasts with scented punches," 25) and unknowable sphinx ("nor an oracle for those trembling with love at the edge of the cities," 25).

This aspect of Lorca's critique coincides with Almodóvar's. However, *Matador* then celebrates an erotics of sadomasochism as a leveler of gender inequities that would permit women the same necrophilic *jouissance* as men. *El público*'s sadomasochism, on the other hand, registers the cruelty of a regressive sociopolitical machine that polices gender identity. This distinction between pre-Franco and post-Franco script becomes clear in *El público*'s association of *corridas*, Roman blood sport, and anal eroticism. Unlike Almodóvar's fashion pageant director, Lorca's Director fears that unveiling the "theater beneath the sand" will incite the homophobic vengeance of youths who "rammed large balls of thrown-away newspapers up his [a homosexual man's] rear with bloodied pickaxes" (5). This and other of *El público*'s angst-ridden explorations of the homoeroticism inherent in the *corrida*–blood fest's rituals poignantly contrasts with Almodóvar's ludic cinematic depiction of the same dynamic. *Matador*'s camera weaves a metonymic chain of close-ups of aspiring *toreros*' sharp *estoques*, bulls' horns, and male buttocks and crotches outlined in exercise pants; the fetishistic heterosexism of "testicular willpower" is jauntily subverted here.

In traversing the route from Lorca to Almodóvar, then, both theatrical and cinematic mise-en-scènes enlist the *corrida* to critique an ideological fetishism that furtively enacts, while simultaneously purporting to suppress, transgressive *jouissance* and gender identity slippage. Lorca and Almodóvar develop a vanguard aesthetic that exploits, while remaining irreducible to, the bullfight's *mise-en-jeu* of the marginal spectacles of parodic drag performance, or feminine hysteria, as alternative discourses through which taboo desires may be spoken. Lorca's critique indirectly alludes to a pre–Civil War rallying of conservative forces in Spain, while Almodóvar attempts a radical dissociation from, via dismembering of, nationalist hegemonies institutionalized under Franco.

However, Lorca negotiates a balance between the positions of radical anti-essentialism, which distrusts any notion of gender difference as a patriarchal construct, and a feminist gender essentialism that would reinscribe "femininity" as a privileged category whose degraded, vampirized other would then be "masculinity." Almodóvar, cinematographer of the post–Franco cultural expansion, is freer to exploit the *corrida* as iconoclastic demystification of gender stereotypes. However, this exploration of links between sexuality and power in public and private spheres reenacts the very fetishism that it would parodically dismantle. For it ultimately erases all signs of feminine difference at the level of semiotic, if not literal and biological, visual cue. Despite his exuberant choreography of gender-bending thrusts, parries, and counterthrusts, the possibility of a dialogic *jouissance* is left untapped and uncharted, and his self-referential mating ballet remains a *danse macabre*.

NOTES

1. In the campy pseudo autobiography of Patty Diphusa, actress and "sex-symbol internacional," Almodóvar associates himself with Warhol: "In those first years of the eighties we lived in a perpetual Warhol factory . . . certain Madrid circles were identical to certain New York circles. . . . My films are also populated by transvestites and drug addicts." *Patty Diphusa y otros textos* (Barcelona: Anagrama, 1991), 8–9 (translation mine).

2. Indeed, the cover of Almodóvar's *Patty Diphusa y otros textos* sports a photograph of Almodóvar in *torero* drag: garbed in an ornate suit of lights, a blood-red carnation in his hair, draped in the black lace mantilla worn by Spanish *majas* on festive occasions, eyes lined in kohl, he chomps on a thick cigar that dangles coyly from the side of his mouth.

3. Betsy Wing and Sandra M. Gilbert's discussion of *jouissance*, a term central to French psychoanalytic, philosophical, and economic theory, as it is elaborated by Hélène Cixous in *The Newly Born Woman*, elucidates its multifaceted connotations: "It is a word with simultaneously sexual, political, and economic overtones. Total access, total participation, as well as total ecstasy are implied. . . . On the phonic level, one can hear: *jouissance*: *j'ouïs sens*: I hear meaning. So, yet another level of activity is implied here, one in which the word is all-important." Hélène Cixous, *The Newly Born Woman*, trans. Betsy Wing, ed. Sandra M. Gilbert (Minneapolis: University of Minnesota Press, 1986), 165.

4. The rural taurine fiestas encompassed such practices as bullbaiting, the setting of bulls' horns on fire, and local peasants and clergymen running before bulls. Timothy Mitchell, *Blood Sport: A Social History of Spanish Bullfighting* (Philadelphia: University of Pennsylvania Press, 1991), 46–74.

5. The contamination of Spanishness by these decadent Gauls and their godless *Encyclopédie* was, evidently, signified by the courtly dances wherein dangerous liaisons were choreographed as a prelude to their consummation. Mitchell, 65.

6. Mitchell, 91.

7. José Carlos Arévalo and José Antonio de Moral, *Nacido para morir*, 2nd ed. (Madrid: Espasa Calpe, 1985), 172. Cited in Mitchell, 139; translation his.

8. Mitchell, 152.

9. Manuel Delgado Ruiz, *De la muerte de un dios: La fiesta de los toros en el universo simbólico de la cultura popular* (Barcelona: Península, 1986), 105; translation mine. Mitchell discusses Stanley Brandes's notion of "testicular will-power," elaborated in Brandes's *Metaphors of Masculinity: Sex and Status in Andalusian Folklore* (Philadelphia: University of Pennsylvania Press, 1986).

10. René Girard, *Desire, Deceit and the Novel*, trans. Yvonne Freccero (Baltimore: Johns Hopkins University Press, 1965).

11. Mitchell, 162.

12. Alvaro Martínez-Novillo, *El pintor y la tauromaquia* (Madrid: Turner, 1988), 160–179.

13. The drama enacted by this series of formal correspondences is elucidated by Picasso himself, who told Juan Larrea that he "identified with the bull, a noble animal, but one that involuntarily wounds and causes pain to humans, and the white horse, [he associated] with the woman, his victim." Martínez-Novillo, 172.

14. Another fetishistic figure central to Picasso's *tauromaquia* is the Minotaur, whose overdetermined phallic signifiers, such as massive head, knife, and staff, are disavowed by symbolic castrations, such as being wounded (*Minotauro vencido*, 1933), dying (*Minotauro moribundo*, 1933), or blinded and led by a young girl (*Minotauro ciego guiado por una niña en la noche*, 1934).

15. Federico García Lorca, *Deep Song and Other Prose*, ed. and trans. Christopher Maurer (New York: New Directions, 1980), 50.

16. García Lorca, 50–51.

17. Federico García Lorca. *Romancero Gitano, Poema del cante jondo, Llanto por Ignacio Sánchez Mejías, Diván del Tamarit, Poemas póstumos*. 10th ed. (Buenos Aires: Losada, 1961), 143–153 (translation mine).

18. The French vanguard, however, reappropriates the *corrida* back into its own tradition—honed to entrail-wrenching efficacy by the Marquis de Sade—of blaspheming an enlightened, bourgeois–capitalist status quo with a pornographic explicitness unthinkable in pre-Franco and Francoist Spain. Space does not permit a comprehensive exploration of the French vanguard's use of *tauromachie*, but Michel Leiris and Georges Bataille do deserve special mention en passant. For Leiris, poetic and erotic *jouissance* are "pure and upright as the shaft of light that pierces the poet's brain or the exploding sword-thrust through which the matador fells his adversary." *L'âge d'homme* (Paris: Gallimard, 1939), 198, translation mine. Georges Bataille theorizes the *corrida* as a Dionysian clash between discontinuity, or the subject's psychically and corporeally autonomous being-in-the-world, and continuity, or the violent interpenetration of self, other, and universe. *L'Erotisme* (Paris: Minuit, 1957), 90.

19. Laura Mulvey's classic analysis of the intersection of gender politics, cinematography, and spectatorship with regard to the Hollywood film may be invoked here: "Women in representation can signify castration, and activate voyeuristic or fetishistic mechanisms to circumvent this threat . . . cinema builds the way she is to be looked at into the spectacle itself. Playing on the tension between film as controlling the dimension of time (editing, narrative) and film as controlling the dimension of space (changes in distance, editing), cinematic codes create a gaze, a world and an object, thereby producing an illusion cut to the measure of desire . . . the two looks materially present in time and space are obsessively subordi-

nated to the neurotic needs of the male ego." *Visual and Other Pleasures* (Bloomington: Indiana University Press, 1989), 26.

20. Angela Carter, *The Sadeian Woman and the Ideology of Pornography* (New York: Pantheon, 1978), 13.

21. *The Public and Play Without a Title*, trans. Carlos Bauer (New York: New Directions, 1983), 4. Further references will be included in parentheses within the text.

Almodóvar's Laws of Subjectivity and Desire

Barbara Morris

What has been called Pedro Almodóvar's "post-punk dadaism" in a series of films capturing fractured representations of postmodern subjectivity has fascinated critics and audiences on an international scale.[1] Almodóvar's films speak from the context of contemporary Spain, a country that since the seventies has undergone and continues to experience profound political and social transitions. While the young democracy has largely embraced the consumer-capitalist configuration of the individual defined through the excess of materialism, it maintains, if only temporarily and perhaps fleetingly, ties to more traditional social institutions, such as family and the church.

The juxtapositions of old, new, and hybrid forms that characterize Spanish postmodernism's transitional stage are depicted brilliantly in films such as *Entre tinieblas* (*Dark Habits*, 1983), *¿Qué he hecho yo para merecer esto?* (*What Have I Done to Deserve This?*, 1984), *Matador* (1986), and *La ley del deseo* (*Law of Desire*, 1987). Almodóvar de/reconstructs heavily codified myths and institutions of Spanish culture—the nunnery, the working-class family and motherhood, the tragic love triangle, and the bullfight—revered in Francoism's exalted iconography. Through diverse processes of recontextualization the filmmaker positions once-dominant religious, social, and romantic iconology in an ex-centric relationship to the gender-bending, camp, and self-consciously melodramatic strategies of pop culture. Filtered through the lens of the filmmaker's self-reflexivity and advertised by the Almodovarian commercial persona, these films chronicle the self-questioning and self-promotion that have marked Spain's transition, illuminating a series of cultural displacements in terms of the personal. Yet, Almodóvar's exploration of the topical belies a more complex vision than the glittering surfaces of his pop imagery and the playfulness of metafictional pretense reveal at first glance.

SUTURING *DESIRE*

In *Desire* Almodóvar conducts a parodic cinematic dialogue with the Hollywood woman's film popular in the forties and fifties, articulated through a highly personal film language. The film sustains melodrama's family focus, yet bifurcates and genders narrative dynamics between two siblings, Pablo (Eusebio Poncela) and Tina (Carmen Maura). The former, a writer and director of hip homoerotic films, and his transsexual sister, an actress, stage Jean Cocteau's *La voix humaine* (*The Human Voice*) during a steamy summer in Madrid; at the same time, Pablo's latest film has its premiere.

Desire opens abruptly with the final scenes of Pablo's film, *El paradigma del mejillón* (*The Mussel's Paradigm*). In the introductory sequence the offscreen voice of what appears to be a male voyeur directs a young man to engage in autoeroticism, asking him to repeat "Fuck me" and rub his genitals against a mirror. While the spectator might anticipate a reverse cut to a speaking subject who would confirm the expectation of a diegetic relationship between the enunciative voice and the filmed subject, Almodóvar disorients the spectator by using an unreliable point of view that explodes the dynamics of the conventional shot/reverse shot.[2] The reverse shot leads the spectator's gaze out of the implied diegesis to the talking heads of two male film dubbers. As the camera crosscuts between the filmed scenes of the actor and the film dubbers, whose moans and groans provide a humorous overlay of sound, the unfolding Cervantine metatextuality of the sequence destabilizes the spectator's position, underscoring an ever-increasing awareness of the titillating voyeurism of film spectatorship.[3] The metafictional montage recuperates homoerotic pornography's visual strategies, such as the film-within-the-film structure and the doubling and trebling of implied spectators, and through this coded structure of desire, Almodóvar sets the stage for the film's playful riffs on sexuality as performance.[4]

The sequence draws to a close in two shots in close-up: one is a take of an editor's grease mark on a film frame; it is followed by the final still of the dubbed film, a close-up collage including the money the actor has received for his sexual performance in the film-within-the-film-within-the-film. Almodóvar's visual outline of the workings of the cinematic apparatus exposes the unstable relations among the film event, narrative authority, and spectatorship, and ironically displays the monetary basis of the production and reception of cinema. The last section of the looping sequence functions as an overt critique of film production; the pleasures filmed and glimpsed may be feigned, but the economics of the art are not. The sequence sets up the laws of Almodóvar's world in which he challenges our motivations for consuming visual images by means of his own parodic self-reflexivity, drawing striking parallels between the erotic impulses of voyeurism and spectatorship and parodying the system of suture.[5]

Almodóvar configures the male body in *Desire* as one of the primary loci of scopophilic desire, and its specular display is always in visual relation to the gaze of another desiring male.[6] When Pablo's lover, Juan (Miguel Molina), leaves Madrid to spend the summer working at the beach, Pablo finds himself pursued aggressively by upper-class Antonio (Antonio Banderas), who, in a jealous rage, seeks out Juan and murders him. Antonio's need to suture over sexual instability motivates him to transform desire into narrative in the dramatic terms of seduction and violence. The sense of lack that impels his seduction of Pablo functions as a narrative mirror for the suturing of the spectator in the fiction, parodied in the introductory sequence's *mise-en-abîme*.

The climax of *Desire* recapitulates the introductory sequence, turning on the final hour that Pablo and Antonio spend together, followed by Antonio's suicide, with Tina, police, and onlookers observing and waiting in the street below. The theatrical framing staged between the areas of the personal (Tina's apartment, where the men make love) and the public (a Madrid street, where the spectators await the denouement) reflects the film's introductory sequence, in which Almodóvar's rewriting of conventional film language provocatively parodies the spectator's desire for pleasure. Thus, the film's complicated structuring of pleasure and desire suggests an analysis responsive to the dialogue between the sexual politics of the image and the aesthetics of pleasure.

GENDER INSTABILITY AND PLEASURE

Between the commercial narrative film and its audience there is an unspoken agreement that specifies pleasure in the contract. Psychoanalytic film theory has linked that pleasure to the desire to see and know: to experience voyeurism as the pleasurable consumption of visual images and narrative as the spectator's movement through the imaginary.[7] Determined by the articulation of specific cinematic codes such as the gaze, film viewing can release spectators from gender-determined responses. Since the publication of Laura Mulvey's article on visual pleasure, feminist film theory has sought alternative models of theorizing spectatorship.[8] Contemporary film theory speaks of "masquerade," "double identification," and the "transvestite" spectator—terms that seek to delineate the complexities of reading both the construction of the image and the spectator's identification with figural representation.[9]

Foregrounded on the homoerotic romantic triangle in which the male body is configured as locus of visual desire is the spectacle of the transsexual (male to female) body. From the first scene in which Tina appears silhouetted against the final shot of Pablo's film to the coke-sniffing senior detective's obsession with the dimensions of her figure, her generous proportions and dramatized femininity absorb considerable visual space and narrative subplotting (Plate 17). Even though she changed her sex in order to conform impeccably to her father's desire, Tina has since given up relations with men and become a lesbian. There is no little dramatic irony in the fact that her ex-lover, Ada's mother, is played by Bibi Andersen, the well-known transsexual actress and Spanish television personality. However, even Tina's choice of lesbianism is subject to flux, for, by film's end, she has been seduced by Antonio, who takes her hostage in order to lure Pablo to his side.

When the tearful Pablo, distraught over Juan's murder, accidentally drives his car off the road and ends up in the hospital—bandaged, limping, and with a case of amnesia—Tina rushes to his side. The hospital interlude is a gender-crossed camp of the medical discourse popular in the woman's film (*Magnificent Obsession* and *Now, Voyager*, for example) and serves as the narrative door framing this Spanish dysfunctional family through which Tina enters to tell her transgressive oedipal story to the amnesiac Pablo. (As an adolescent boy, she fell in love with their father, who took her to Morocco for a sex-change operation. Eventually abandoned by him, she returned to Madrid.) While Tina's transsexualism could be seen as Almodóvar's parodic interpretation of the oedipal narrative in which the castration threat is taken only too literally, her gender choice functions as the kind of visual transvestism described by Annette Kuhn, in which performance and sexual difference intersect, constructing a readerly desire for closure in the spectator.[10]

Tina camps an overblown version of femininity by emphasizing her physical gestures and the clothing she wears—short, tight, figure-molding clothes and stiletto heels. She is self-consciously aware of her body's amplitude; at dinner with Pablo and Ada (Manuela Velasco), she obsessively runs her fingers around the black circles of her dress that cover yet accentuate, indeed deconstruct, the form of her breasts. Conflated with her screen role as actress, Tina's performance of femininity continually brings to the surface her gender masquerade. Yet, the irresolute play of gender identifications on Tina's body runs the gamut of culturally inscribed femininity and masculinity; not only does she camp her ultrafeminine persona, but she also knocks down a police detective who insults her. The spectator's relation to the visual representation of Tina's sexuality incites his/her voyeuristic curiosity; fulfillment of pleasure comes in the street scene after the successful premiere of *The Human Voice*. In this scene Tina, suffering from the oppressive summer heat, begs a workman to douse her with water from his industrial-size hose, and, as the jets of water flow forcefully across her ample contours, she clearly delights in her carefully crafted female body.

Tina's gender instability precipitates a movement toward closure typical of melodrama. Yet, the ironic detachment with which the filmmaker revives these culturally coded "feminine" forms of pleasure, and the subversion of melodrama that he achieves by destabilizing spectatorial response, problematize any fixed determination of gender-specific male/female spectators. We simply cannot infer a strictly heterosexual, homosexual, or female-centered reading of the film, nor can we categorize it as exclusively corroborating the narrative dynamics of the woman's film. Even if the spectator demands closure to figural gender instability in the fulfillment of narrative movement, the film's aesthetic patterning contrarily impels the spectator to seek pleasure on the aesthetic rather than the narrative plane.

The play on sexual identity as masquerade in *Desire* seems to insist that sexual identifications are a "drag," not fixed but mutable, and that they depend more on the subject's mode of expressing and fulfilling desire than on core gender identity. Gender confusion, gender masquerade, excessive otherness—all reveal and revel in the instability of dominant culture's attempt to stereotype patterns of human behavior as normative, or not. Tina's "gender trouble" and the homoerotic love triangle bespeak cultural change and transition on a personal level. Although contemporary Spain's disavowal of Francoist sexual puritanism is portrayed with self-reflexive laughter by Almodóvar's camp characters, their subversions lead to tragedies that are assuaged by a return to family, albeit an excessively postmodern family. Tina's joyous physical display is introduced by a scene in which the camera frames Tina, Pablo, and Ada walking together, in one instance strategically placed under the arc of spouting water. Although the visual plotting of the nuclear family dominates one of the film's pivotal scenes, in no way is it a traditionally patriarchal family; rather, it is a parody of normativeness.

MASOCHISM'S FAMILY AFFAIR

Law of Desire is a fatherless fiction, and the narratively tangential representatives of the patriarchy—the parish priest, who was one of Tina's first loves; the pair of Civil Guard officers in the south; and the siblings' absent father—are inscribed within a subversive homoerotic context. Almodóvar's defiance of the father's law in *Desire* can be read against Gilles Deleuze's work on masochism, which provides a psychoanalytic model empowering the mother and absenting the father from its contractual discourse.[11]

Deleuze proposes that the father's functions are distributed among three types of mothers—oedipal, hetaeric, and oral—all of whom are represented in the film.[12] In *Desire*, Antonio's fascist mother corresponds to the role of the punishing oedipal mother; and Tina's ex-lover, the hetaeric mother, is associated with, if not outright prostitution, then a career supported by men. Tina, as noted, embodies the oral mother in whom father and mother coexist, a factor enhanced by her transsexual metamorphosis.[13]

Who, then, is the masochistic subject of *Desire*? While Marsha Kinder seems to suggest that Tina plays that role, she also mentions Pablo as the controlling agent of the film who reenacts his father's seduction of his brother and inspires the sacrifice of his lovers.[14] The masochist controls and dominates the pleasure/pain situation through contractual texts and disavowal, much as Pablo tries to govern the behavior of his lovers through letters, choosing a lover who abandons him, and suspensefully disavowing his final union with Antonio by means of amnesia and withdrawal. Deleuze's theory of the contractual relation of the masochistic subject to a punishing yet loving female is exploded in the film's topsy-turvy world of shifting gender identifications. Certainly, Pablo's relations with those he loves are defined by his theater and film scripts, which feed on their experiences yet demarcate the contours of their passions. In particular, the letter that is the literary catalyst of the plot functions as a negotiated attempt to linguistically determine the affection Pablo would have his young lover, Juan, demonstrate. Nonetheless, the punishing mother is subsumed in the persona of Antonio's mother, whose sadistic nature threatens the return of the banished father yet promises the hope of a rebirth, in accord with Deleuze's reading of Sacher-Masoch's pivotal figure of "the Greek," "the projection of the new man that will result from the masochistic experiment."[15] Pablo's rebirth depends on the painful loss provoked by Antonio's murder of Juan and allows him to experience the pleasure of reciprocal love, limited to the brief hour he spends as a love hostage with Antonio, who shifts from controlling sadist to suicidal masochist. And Pablo's parthenogenesis is catalyzed by the other's death as the fantasy fulfillment of his desire and, ultimately, his reunion with the idealized mother figure, as represented by Tina.

CAMP SENSIBILITY AND AESTHETIC MASOCHISM

From the self-consciousness of metafictional design, through the narrative indulgence in the twists and turns of melodramatic subplotting, to the exorbitance of Tina's visual configuration, the aesthetic mien of *Desire* is based on a surplus of pleasure derived from the roles that theatricality and artifice play in its aesthetic articulation. From the performance-oriented features of the film—its metafictional design, performing characters, and theatrical sexual posturing—I would like to draw parallels between two positions, camp and masochism, for both models rely on certain aesthetic devices in order to achieve political ends.

Masochism is both a pathology and an aesthetic paradigm, as Deleuze has argued. In the pathological dimensions of masochism the subject transgresses the social order in a pact "between mother and son to write the father out of his dominant position within both culture and masochism, and to install the mother in his place."[16] Masochism as an aesthetic model is based on the mechanisms of disavowal and fetishism that are projected in the fantasy, fetishizing the suspenseful anticipation of pleaure and thus creating elaborate and ironic structures of formal artifice in order to prolong the painful waiting for symbiotic rebirth. The aesthetic preoccupation with theatricality and artifice results from the obsessive repetition patterns, described in Freud's analysis of the *fort/da* game, which structure the suspensefully painful delay of pleasurable fulfillment.[17] The fetish of excess captured in the replaying of the scene of separation from and reunion with the mother results in formal features that emphasize the repetition of visual and aural motifs, as well as the disavowal of traditional structures of suspense in narrative, for suspense is displaced from the dramatic to the aesthetic realm.[18]

Almodóvar's aesthetically distinct and excessive visual style reveals a fondness for particular types of shots that suspend the narrative flow. A trademark in his films, the shot that either reveals an ambivalent subject of the gaze or privileges the point of view of an inanimate object, occurs frequently. In *Law of Desire* the camera shoots Pablo typing his film script from below the typewriter's keyboard, and when Pablo and Tina have decided to produce *The Human Voice*, sniffing coke to celebrate, there is a cut to a dreamlike scene in which white powder drifts across the theater program. Not only do these shots occur as repetitive visual patterns, but they also reveal the omnipotent look of the camera's pro-filmic gaze, rupture the seamlessness of illusion, and actualize the spectator's desire for suture.[19]

Conflating the camp love of hyperbolic expression with the repetitions of aesthetic masochism in a synergistic coup, the musical themes of the film's sound track function as aural fetishes that mark the aesthetic excesses of the film's emotional rhythms. The mise-en-scène of Juan's murder—on a cliff, at night, by the sea, in the moonlight—is accentuated by its musical accompaniment, "Look at the Moon" ("Guarda che luna"), which lyrically reiterates the elements of the sequence. Antonio and Pablo's lovemaking is twice ironically (dis)harmonized with the Trio Los Panchos's "I Doubt It" ("Lo dudo"). While "If You Go Away" ("Ne me quittes pas") highlights Juan's last night with Pablo, it also functions as an aesthetic leitmotif in the film, for its camp interpretation by Ada in Pablo's production diegetically recapitulates the intersection between camp humor's detachment and the surplus pleasure of masochism's aesthetics. The melodramatic finale—punctuated by suicide, fire, suspense, and the culmination of desire—is furnished a musical coda with Bolita de Nieve's "Let Me Remember" ("Déjame recordar") that serves as a meta-commentary on the action, immediately transposing the film's reception into a fantasy of memory. The surplus of visual and aural pleasures generates the supersensual encounter typical of masochism, transforming the spectator's desire for closure into a prolonged aesthetic experience.

Susan Sontag's well-known outline of camp in "Notes on Camp" delineates camp as a taste that esteems artifice and style over content.[20] Camp's aesthetic impulse is not unlike the predilections of aesthetic masochism, which also depend on the theatricality of ritualized gestures and the ironic disavowal of obsession. Sontag's conceptualization of camp, ever a taste, not a pathology, records the camp delight in artifice as never seeking to close but rather to ironically widen the gap between form and content.

Camp's fundamental metaphor of life-as-performance reverberates throughout *Desire*—from Tina's overstated histrionics as actress to the final scene in which all the players assemble for the peripeteic denouement—and the camp fondness for exaggerated aspects of femininity defines Tina's female impersonation. The camp sensibility also pays homage to a certain kind of sentimentalism that reveres the past, notwithstanding its detached posturing. Almodóvar, however, camps the passé objects and the intentions of camp. If *The Human Voice* is already camp, then Almodóvar doubles its campiness—indeed, moves it into kitsch—by over-determining its production values: Tina chops up the set and Ada sings Brel while standing on a moving camera dolly.

Law of Desire is Almodóvar's self-reflexive paean to the male body and homosexual desire (pursued with pre-AIDS sexual exuberance), and his configuration of femininity recuperates and camps the masochistic, camp, and even feminist nostalgia for a powerful female archetype. This fantasy is an attempt to remake the symbolic order by turning loss into what D. N. Rodowick has called "an erosion of phallic values," in which the film's confluence of camp and masochistic discourses is played out on a re/construction of the female body.[21] Tina has suffered the gender metamorphosis demanded by the father's law, while Almodóvar's masochistic subversion of oedipal sexuality allows the spectator the possibility of identifying with the play of gender inscribed on her body. Paradoxically, Tina's complete identification with femininity as masochistic romantic failure, motherliness, and nurturance both parodies and confirms the polarized lines along which gender differences have been traditionally drawn, despite or perhaps because of the playful conflation of gender identifications that are performed on her body. Her masquerade of femininity may not point to a radical refiguring of gender roles; it does, however, demonstrate that femininity, like masculinity, is never a fixed, essential characteristic but, rather, a socially constructed, mutable representation of gender.

CAMPING THE POSTMODERN

Almodóvar's parodic and subversive homage to Hollywood-style melodrama represents the encounter between camp's proclivity to co-opt past forms and postmodernism's critical revision of those appropriations. In his work on camp and the sixties, Andrew Ross discusses how the conflictual politics inherent in the mainstreaming of marginal groups are often camped by those very groups, in order to deflect the seriousness of the shift in power; further, Ross sees camp as "liberating the objects and discourses of the past from disdain and neglect."[22] Camp, then, works from within the structures of power in order to invest its subversion in culture's marginalia and reinvent the past. The survivor mentality imbricated in the camp sensibility creates a past that is triumphant, despite the sufferings undergone, just as Pablo elaborates and camps Tina's romantic failures in his art.

In *Desire* masochism's aesthetic model is conflated with the excesses of melodrama that function as the social externalization of interior psychic processes. While the pathology of masochism restricts itself to a private reenactment of the masochist's fantasy, melodrama, as Christine Gledhill suggests, does not work to release individual repression, but moves toward the public enactment of socially unacknowledged states in which the family is a means, not an end.[23] The subversion of the Father's Law that masochism privately points to in its rewriting of the family affair, is publicly proclaimed in cinematic melodrama. *Desire*'s closure upholds traditional values—the destructiveness of passion and the satisfying bonding in family—at the same time as it demonstrates the transitory nature of the means of expressing those values. In Almodóvar's new Spain the past's detritus—the woman's film, boleros, classic camp—is revitalized and placed in the context of a transgressive social mentality. This "law of desire" camps postmodernism's politics of complicity and critique that both acknowledges a historical continuum and parodies patriarchal representations. Thus, Almodóvar's famous dictum that he makes films as if Franco had never existed,[24] reveals a clever disavowal of history in which the Father's Law, although camped and masochistically suppressed, is not entirely forgotten.

NOTES

1. See "Women on the Verge of a Nervous Breakdown," *Lincoln Center Stagebill*, 1988 New York Film Festival (New York: B and B Publishers, 1988), 20D.

2. Kaja Silverman explicates the dynamics of the shot/reverse-shot formation as allowing the viewing subject to know whose gaze controls what it sees within the diegesis, while both limiting the viewing subject's sense of visual freedom and maintaining the cinematic illusion, in *The Subject of Semiotics* (New York: Oxford University Press, 1983), 202–204. Almodóvar offers no such comfort of illusion, for his parodic and reflexive use of the shot/reverse shot serves to unbalance the viewing subject's sense of subjectivity in relation to the image.

3. The initial sequence of *Matador* also humorously plays with the dynamics of the traditional shot/reverse-shot formation. While the film titles roll, the first scenes of the film show a televised slasher cult film that features the bloody deaths of a series of young women. As in *Desire*, the reverse shot reveals the presence of a gaze outside the diegesis of the film-within-the-film, that of the masturbating matador.

4. See Richard Dyer's work on gay pornography in "Male Gay Porn: Coming to Terms," *Jump Cut* 30 (1985): 27–29.

5. See Silverman's definition of suture as "the process whereby the inadequacy of the subject's position is exposed in order to facilitate (i.e. create the desire for) new insertions into a cultural discourse which promises to make good that lack," 231.

6. The film's visually specific homoerotic content invites not only a homosexual gaze; Susanne Moore postulates that homoerotica may also invite the gaze of some female spectators, as long as pleasure is contained within a narcissistic discourse. See Moore, "Here's Looking at You, Kid!," in *The Female Gaze: Women as Viewers of Popular Culture*, ed. Lorraine Gamman and Margaret Marshment (Seattle: Real Comet Press, 1989), 55. On the other hand, certain types of spectators could be understood as resistant, refusing the gaze and/or the desire to be sutured into the narrative.

7. See Teresa de Lauretis, *Alice Doesn't: Feminism, Semiotics, Cinema* (Bloomington: Indiana University Press, 1984), 136; and Stephen Heath, *Questions of Cinema* (Bloomington: Indiana University Press, 1981), 53.

8. Laura Mulvey, "Visual Pleasure and Narrative Cinema," *Screen* 16.3 (Autumn 1975): 6–18. See also D. N. Rodowick, who calculates the lack in Mulvey's theory as her inability to see that the male gaze could, in fact, submit to the female object if one were to carry her argument to its completion by pairing masochism with fetishistic scopophilia, in *The Difficulty of Difference: Psychoanalysis, Sexual Difference, and Film Theory* (New York: Routledge, 1991), 8–12.

9. Mary Ann Doane, "Film and the Masquerade: Theorizing the Female Spectator," *Screen* 23.3–4 (September–October 1982): 74–87; Lauretis, 141–144; and Laura Mulvey, *Visual and Other Pleasures* (Bloomington: Indiana University Press, 1989), 37.

10. Annette Kuhn, *The Power of the Image: Essays on Representation and Sexuality* (London: Routledge, 1985), 52–59.

11. Gilles Deleuze, *Masochism: Coldness and Cruelty*, with Leopold von Sacher-Masoch, *Venus in Furs*, trans. Jean McNeil (New York: Zone Books, 1989).

12. Deleuze, 55.

13. In her interview with Almodóvar, Marsha Kinder mentions that "cruel mothers" and "absent, mythified fathers" predominate in Spanish films. "Pleasure and the New Spanish Mentality: A Conversation with Pedro Almodóvar," *Film*

Quarterly 41.1 (1987): 42. Almodóvar, speaking of the mother, contends that he defended the mother in *What Have I Done to Deserve This?* but adds, in regard to the cruel mother of *Matador*, "Yes, I find this kind of mother very hateful, but there are several other mothers in that film . . . I feel very close to the mother. The idea of motherhood is very important in Spain. The father was frequently absent in Spain. It's as if the mother represents the law, the police," 42–43 (ellipses in the original). With Kinder's prompting, Almodóvar reveals the plural dimensions of empowered motherhood in its masochistic aspects that are present in *Law of Desire*.

14. Kinder, 41.

15. Deleuze, 66.

16. Kaja Silverman, "Masochism and Male Subjectivity," *Camera Obscura* 17 (Fall 1988): 57.

17. Sigmund Freud, *The Standard Edition of the Complete Psychological Works*, trans. James Strachey, vol. 18 (London: Hogarth Press, 1953), 14–15.

18. See Gaylyn Studlar, *In the Realm of Pleasure: Von Sternberg, Dietrich, and the Masochistic Aesthetic* (Urbana: University of Illinois Press, 1988), 120.

19. In her analysis of suture in *Psycho*, Silverman notes how Hitchcock privileges an inanimate object's point of view, that of the money Marion has stolen: "We enjoy our visual superiority to Marion, but at the same time we understand that the gaze of the camera—that gaze in which we participate—exceeds us, threatening not only Marion but anyone exposed to the film's spectacle." And she concludes that "suture can be made more rather than less irresistible when the field of the speaking subject is continually implied." *The Subject of Semiotics*, 208.

20. Susan Sontag, *Against Interpretation and Other Essays* (New York: Dell, 1979), 275–292. My evocation of Sontag's high-modernist essay is intentional; her work serves as a guide to Almodóvar's camp of traditional camp themes. That is, *Law of Desire* is not only a camp film, it is also a film that camps the classic camp that Sontag profiles.

21. Rodowick, 85.

22. Andrew Ross, "Uses of Camp," in his *No Respect: Intellectuals and Popular Culture* (New York: Routledge, 1989), 146–149.

23. Christine Gledhill, "The Melodramatic Field: An Investigation," in *Home Is Where the Heart Is*, ed. Christine Gledhill (London: British Film Institute, 1987), 31.

24. In Peter Besas, *Behind the Spanish Lens* (Denver: Arden Press, 1985), 216.

Plate 2. Poster for *Pepi, Luci, Bom and Other Ordinary Girls*. (Courtesy of Pedro Almodóvar)

Plate 3. Up from the underground. Filming *Pepi, Luci, Bom* with Carmen Maura, Alaska, and Eva Siva. (Courtesy of Pedro Almodóvar)

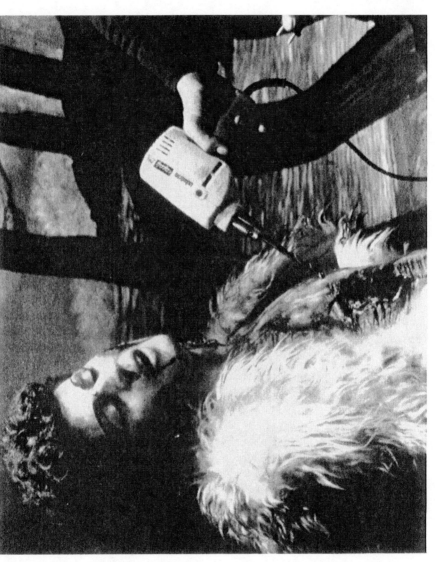

Plate 4. Fabio (Fabio de Miguel, a.k.a. Fanny McNamara) re-creates a scene from Almodóvar's porno novel *Toda tuya* in *Labyrinth of Passions*. (Courtesy of Pedro Almodóvar)

Plate 5. Riza (Imanol Arias) disguised as Johnny performs "Gran ganga." (Courtesy of Pedro Almodóvar)

Plate 6. McNamara and Almodóvar reprise their punk-glam rock duo in *Labyrinth of Passions*. (Courtesy of Pedro Almodóvar)

Plate 7. Mother Superior (Julieta Serrano) and Yolanda (Cristina S. Pascual) share a communal meal in the convent of the Humble Redeemers in *Dark Habits*. (Courtesy of Pedro Almodóvar)

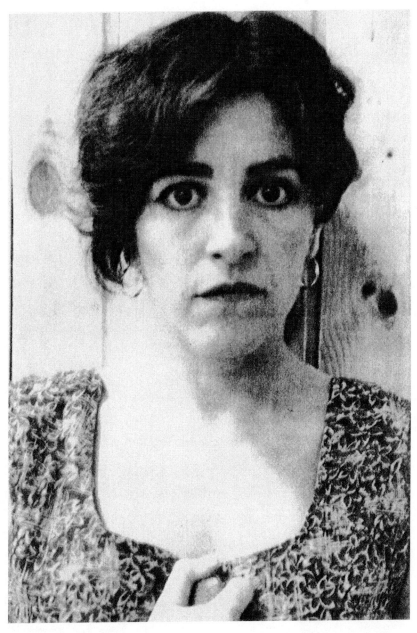

Plate 9. Head shot of Gloria (Carmen Maura), the bedraggled housewife of *What Have I Done to Deserve This?* (Courtesy of Pedro Almodóvar)

Plate 8. Melo-drama: Yolanda sings of forbidden love at the farewell party for Mother Superior. (Courtesy of Pedro Almodóvar)

Plate 10. A maternal moment? Gloria and Toni (Juan Martínez) confer over money. (Courtesy of Pedro Almodóvar)

Plate 11. Antonio (Angel de Andrés López) primps for Ingrid Müller as Gloria's frustration comes to the surface. (Courtesy of Pedro Almodóvar)

Plate 12. *Matador*'s mirror images: Diego (Nacho Martínez) in his web of desire. (Courtesy of Pedro Almodóvar)

Plate 13. María Cardenal (Assumpta Serna) murders and mates. (Courtesy of Pedro Almodóvar)

Plate 14. Modern bride. Pilar (Chus Lampreave), Eva (Eva Cobo), the reporter (Verónica Forqué), and designer Montesinos (P. Almodóvar) prepare for the fashion show "Divided Spain." (Courtesy of Pedro Almodóvar)

Plate 15. Exterior night in the city of desire. Madrid's Manila cafeteria in *Law of Desire*. (Courtesy of Pedro Almodóvar)

Plate 16. Antonio's (Antonio Banderas) and Pablo's (Eusebio Poncela) final embrace before the May altar in flames. (Courtesy of Pedro Almodóvar)

Plate 17. Spectacle and spectators. Tina (Carmen Maura) commands the foreground as the police bear witness to homosexual desire. (Courtesy of Pedro Almodóvar)

Plate 18. Pepa (Carmen Maura) dubs Joan Crawford in *Johnny Guitar* in *Women on the Verge of a Nervous Breakdown.* (Courtesy of Pedro Almodóvar)

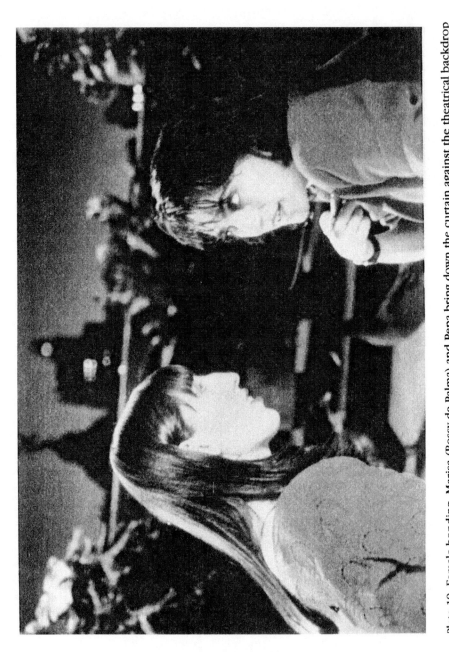

Plate 19. Female bonding. Marisa (Rossy de Palma) and Pepa bring down the curtain against the theatrical backdrop of an idealized Madrid skyline. (Courtesy of Pedro Almodóvar)

Plate 20. Marina (Victoria Abril) embraces the wounded Ricky (Antonio Banderas) before their mirror reflection in *Tie Me Up! Tie Me Down!* (Courtesy of Pedro Almodóvar)

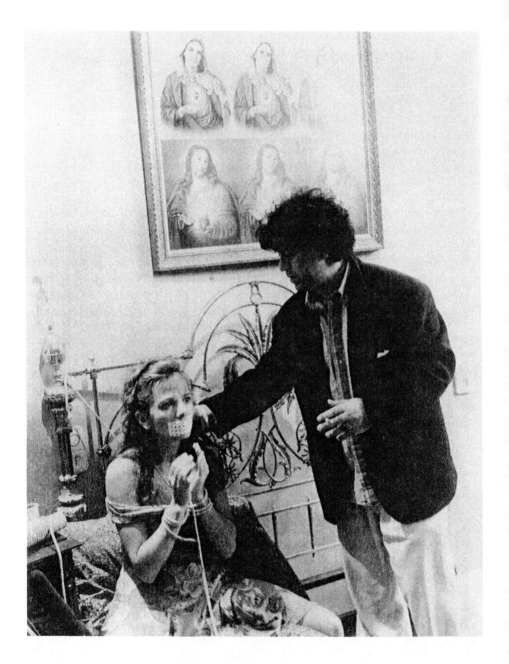

Plate 21. *Tie Me Up*'s metaphor of the heart. Almodóvar directs a bound Victoria Abril beneath an image of the Sacred Heart. (Photo by Mimmo Cattarinich, courtesy of Miramax Films Release and Pedro Almodóvar)

Plate 22. Mother and daughter reunion. Rebecca (Victoria Abril) and Becky (Marisa Paredes) in *High Heels*. (Courtesy of Miramax Films Release and Pedro Almodóvar)

Plate 23. *Cherchez la femme*. Becky's assistant (Ana Lizaran), Becky, and Rebecca react to a poster of Femme Letal. (Courtesy of Miramax Films Release and Pedro Almodóvar)

Plate 24. Poster for *Kika*. (Courtesy of Pedro Almodóvar)

Figuring Hysteria: Disorder and Desire in Three Films of Pedro Almodóvar

Brad Epps

There is something at once mad and methodical about Pedro Almodóvar's films. Frenetic, effervescent, wild, and rapturous, they are also willful, deliberate, and self-conscious. They focus on dispersion, center on
marginality, and concentrate on excess. They seem designed, almost sys-
tematically, to scandalize and trouble; they seem fixed, almost obsessively, on the movement of sexual desire. They are also, of course, framed
largely around figures of femininity and homosexuality: figures subject,
in Almodóvar's eyes, to nervous anxiety, emotional exhaustion, and flamboyant histrionics: to hysteria. Though most visibly "characterized" as
women and gay men, these figures of hysteria function on a formal level
as well, pointing to problems of stillness and mobility, placement and
displacement, continuity and discontinuity, framing and figuration. Hysteria is, as Michel Foucault puts it, "indiscriminately mobile or immobile,
fluid or dense, given to unstable vibrations or clogged by stagnant hu-
mors."[1] Rife with paradox, hysteria signifies, if anything, a quandary of
classification, "a crisis of signification."[2] As such, it is an oddly adequate
figure for Almodóvar's films, where comedy itself is open to dramatic
revision. Hysteria, then, is of critical significance for matters of gender
and sexuality, form and method, genre and style, and finally, given the
problem of classification, socioeconomic class. In fact, while hysteria figures in all of Almodóvar's films, I have chosen to examine three that
engage diverse cultural classes: transvestites, aristocrats, and terrorists in
Labyrinth of Passions; the working class of cleaning women, taxi drivers,
seamstresses, and prostitutes in *What Have I Done to Deserve This?*; and
the privileged class of professionals, psychologists, fashion models, and
commercial entertainers in *Women on the Verge of a Nervous Break-*

down. Together, and separately, these films suggest through the firm but fluid figures of hysteria, a methodical madness that I entertain as critical to Almodóvar's work.

Part of what makes hysteria so cinematically suggestive is the fact that it entails a gender- and class-coded method of acting and directing, a method virtually made for the camera. Though undeniably ancient, hysteria entered the age of modern technological control in Jean-Marie Charcot's union of (largely working-class) women and photography in late-nineteenth-century France. Photographing hysterical attacks in hypnotic, "alienated" women before an audience of doctors, students, and fashionable onlookers, Charcot transformed the lecture hall of the Salpêtrière into a showplace where entertainment at times overtook medical knowledge. All the while invoking documentary objectivity and scientific neutrality, Charcot set the stage where, as Elaine Showalter remarks, "female hysteria was perpetually presented, represented, and reproduced."[3] Representation, of course, assumes many guises; and if the first "subjects" are preserved for posterity as silent and still, Dora, under the study of Freud, is subsequently scripted as hysteria's most (in)articulate actress, oscillating between the contrasting yet connected roles of victim and heroine, object and subject, even woman and man.[4] An individual of economic privilege, Dora upstages, as it were, the poorer women of the Salpêtrière, just as Freud, the listener, prompter, and scriptor, overshadows his teacher Charcot, "the *visuel*, the seer."[5] Thus plotted, hysteria itself seems to move from the clinician's amphitheater to the analyst's study; remaining something of a spectacle, it becomes less public and more private, more intimate, more perilously seductive. The psychotheatrical metaphors I have been employing are neither entirely ornamental nor accidental: Charcot's use of performative and iconographic devices; Freud's description of the unconscious as *ein anderer Schauplatz*, "another showplace"; and Joseph Breuer's patient Anna O's representation of daydreaming and desire as a "private theater" all indicate the profoundly histrionic dimension of hysteria itself.[6] Hysteria may indeed be, as so many critics assert, a spectacular construction, an invention, and a "malady through representation";[7] but it is one in which Charcot's camera and Freud's script, the image and the word, play a crucial role. Only a principle of motion is lacking.

Motion is, after all, fundamental to hysteria. As a condition first characterized as "a pathological wandering of a restless womb," hysteria connotes instability and errancy, "unnatural" bodily movement.[8] Its incredibly diverse symptoms include enervation and hyperactivity, mutism and babbling (often in other tongues), depression, hypochondria, convulsions, fainting spells, amnesia, and an array of acts and attitudes like bisexuality, masturbation, promiscuity, abstinence, and anxious sexual morality. For Freud, not surprisingly, "[t]he symptoms of the disease are nothing else than *the patient's sexual activity*."[9] That these patients are primarily female has important ramifications for the representation of gender and sexuality in Almodóvar's films, but it is the principle of motion that I want to stress here. For if photographs and words capture a sense of hysteria, it is the art of *motion* pictures that most fully represents it. Tracking its convulsions and ramblings, its starts and stops, film captures the kinetic quality of hysteria. Film holds, however ironically, the subtle slips, the furtive quirks, the flashes and lulls of the body. It not only shows the malady but exposes it to potentially endless speculation and study. While Freud may not employ cinematic devices in his work, there is nonetheless something telling about the affinity between the (dis)continuities of hysteria and film.[10] Stanley Cavell, among others, notes the historical coincidence of psychoanalysis, born out of hysteria, and cinema, born out of photography, and further notes how both construe woman as a principal "problem" of knowledge and representation.[11] Lynne Kirby, shifting the focus from female to male disorder, also acknowledges the connections between hysteria and film. For her, the moves of the hysterical and the filmic body are symptoms of broad social change and commotion. According to Kirby, "cultural displacement as massive as nineteenth-century mechanization and urbanization . . . made of its traumatized victims something like female hysterics."[12]

This brief overview of the history of hysteria may seem beyond and beside Almodóvar. After all, from one fin de siècle to another, from modernity to postmodernity, much has changed: film has become smoother, psychoanalysis more cautious, sexuality more out in the open. Hysteria itself is now seen more as a metaphor than as a malady, more as a figure than as a fact. And yet, in Almodóvar's production of nervous, rattled women; in his depiction of passion, obsession, and repression; and in his self-reflective play with voice, body, image, and movement there lies, I believe, the historical residue of hysteria, its discourses, and its spectacles. Catherine Clément has declared that hysterics are outmoded figures, that they no longer exist,[13] but it is just this that allows them, and their condition, to be restyled and reinvested, to be revamped as postmodern cinematic camp. Fundamental to hysteria and film, motion is fundamental to the *Movida* as well.[14]

From his first full-length feature film, *Pepi, Luci, Bom and Other Ordinary Girls* (1980), Almodóvar appears to have his hand on the pulse, and later the purse, of Spanish society. Making the best of his modest beginnings as a telephone worker, he exploits the humor implicit in the exaggeration, pastiche, and collapse of boundaries known as postmodernism. He markets, with increasing success, the giddiness of Spain's fledgling democracy, its heady entry into the European community, and the artfully commercial madness of the *Movida*: in short, what he himself has called the new Spanish mentality. As he puts it in a 1989 "self-interview" in the significantly titled *El Europeo*: "I am utterly ignorant of everything pertaining to geography and history."[15] Though Almodóvar undoubtedly exaggerates his ignorance, he does so to get beyond the somber fixation on the Spanish Civil War that colored much cultural production under Franco. He asserts that he actively forgets the past in order to create in the present. Where Franco's order enforced propriety and obedience, Almodóvar's (dis)order, at least on the screen, appears to enforce nothing so much as its own dissolution.

Still, while Francoist censorship, conformity, and control seem to dissolve into something radically new and different, older constraints remain.[16] I am referring not simply to the Catholic Church, the Opus Dei, or the police force, all restyled in Almodóvar's films, but to the system of capitalist exchange that frames, and fragments, the cinema as a whole. Constraining as it is, capitalism is also the condition of possibility of the style-conscious, fashion-oriented, trend-setting vision of Almodóvar: even, if not especially, when what is in style is grungy and disgusting (*cutre, guarro, y borde*), shocking and schlocky.[17] The *Movida*, that boisterous movement of cultural and sexual experimentation in the late seventies and early eighties, is a marvel of marketing. Sex sells, particularly when repackaged according to, possibly as, the latest fad. This is not to deny the critical power of Almodóvar's work but to acknowledge the commercial power of cultural critique itself. More important, the tense movement between critique and commercialism may well be a peculiarly compelling mode of hysteria. In fact, if hysteria itself has been seen as a symptom of "the bourgeois value system of patriarchal authority and sexual asceticism,"[18] perhaps it is here, in the wake of father Franco, a symptom of the commodification of desire, its ceaseless conversion to capital. Perhaps, that is, hysteria signals not merely the law of desire but the law of the market.[19]

FABULOUS FRAMES IN *LABYRINTH OF PASSIONS*

> In these hysterical, convulsive gestures . . . it would be difficult, not to say impossible, to guess that virility lay hid.
> —Baudelaire

Labyrinth of Passions opens with a stroll through the market: Cecilia Roth as Sexilia and Imanol Arias as Riza Niro wander through the Madrid flea market, the Rastro, shopping for the fullest and most appealing crotch. Sporting sunglasses, they cross paths but do not see each other until later, in a nightclub. Lovestruck, the two renounce their erratic, erotic romps in the market of desire for heterosexual monogamy. This is "funny," that is to say, curious, because the very promiscuity and homosexuality that make this film "positively bristle with vibrant color and a wildly comic sexual energy" are plotted as pathological, as problems to be overcome.[20] Passion may be labyrinthine, but it apparently needs to be set straight.[21] This rectified coming-together of a man and a woman suggests a classical, all too classical, story; but so many comings and goings elsewhere suggest a story that is unabashedly modern. Almodóvar has called *Labyrinth of Passions* a "catalogue of modernities," a sort of initiation, or "baptism," into modern being.[22] The film is a cult classic, its modernity not limited to an amalgamation of rock music, drugs, and sexual diversity; it derives as well from what John Hopewell describes as an artful and incongruent reelaboration of tradition.[23] This is especially apparent in *What Have I Done to Deserve This?*, where the grandmother's insistent references to her village play off the equally insistent references to the urban sprawl of contemporary Madrid. In *Labyrinth of Passions*, however, the most elaborate reelaboration targets the clinic instead of the countryside. Medicine and, more important, psychoanalysis comprise the codes and traditions that Almodóvar reworks and, in many respects, ridicules. Homosexuality, nymphomania, incest, delusion, impotence, obsession, and sublimation figure prominently in the film and are related to psychic disorder, to hysterical trauma. Both Sexilia and Riza are explicitly designated as traumatized and as suffering from their passions, though Sexilia alone is highlighted as the patient to be analyzed and cured.[24] Those presumably responsible for analysis and cure—be it the self-designated Lacanian psychoanalyst, Susana Díaz, or the eminent gynecologist, father of artificial insemination and of Sexilia—are themselves plagued with problems. Everyone, it seems, has either too much or too little sexual desire; everyone participates in the bedlam.

Volatile as they are, these roles are tethered to an extensive tradition of Freudian narration and interpretation, but a tradition become hackneyed and exhausted by popularization and overuse. The resulting tension between meaningful content and its exhaustion or evacuation, between the classical and the modern, is of course the perilously hackneyed mark of postmodernism, itself forever on the verge of breaking down. According to Jean Baudrillard, "the characteristic hysteria of our time" is a collapse of scandal and spectacle, a loss of distance between the viewer and the viewed, and an overproduction of difference that issues in total indifference.[25] But hysteria is also a historical staging of scandal and spectacle, a reiteration of distance, and a classical production of difference in and against the feminine, or feminized, body. Almodóvar, professing to be ignorant of history, flirts with a rhetoric that is similar to Baudrillard's, but his dogged insistence on the sights and scenes of gender and sexual orientation keeps him from succumbing completely to it. If there is a hysteria characteristic of our time, Almodóvar sees it in fairly determinate characters and characterizations; and he does so de-

spite—or rather because of—the crisis of representation that hysteria entails. As *Labyrinth of Passions* rushes to its close, Sexilia exclaims at least
three times that she is hysterical (*histérica*). The fact that this word has
become so widespread in present-day Spain as to designate virtually any
feeling of exasperation, confusion, or impatience does not so much
empty it of content as point to a curious success. Hysteria spills over into
popular discourse, becomes trivial, banal, and common, so common that
it can characterize anyone and everyone. Still, in Almodóvar's world it
retains a special echo for women. In no way does this mean that men
are not also hysterical, or that they do not also (dis)articulate themselves
in such terms. But the male hysteric, acknowledged even by Charcot and
Freud, raises some peculiarly prickly problems: he shifts, among other
things, the matrix of speculation to include the body of the speculator
himself.[26]

The most spectacular male hysteric is not Riza but Fabio, played by
Almodóvar's one-time punk rock partner, Fanny McNamara. Shortly after
Riza and Sexilia stroll through the Rastro, Fabio, vampishly posed in the
La Bobia café, takes a long, luxurious whiff of fingernail polish, surveys
the potential pickings of desire, and exclaims to his companion: "No
money, baby. No car, no 'girl,' no drugs, no vice, no rimmel. I'm hysterical" (*¡Estoy histérica!*). Referring to himself in the feminine, Fabio takes
a popular expression—*estar histérico*—and utters it in a way that renders
its uterine origins risible, that is to say, humorous. A female malady of
"humoral imbalance," hysteria is, as we have seen, a principle of motion
with serious restrictions.[27] Fabio's mad humor, his hysteria, is thus not
simply the ecstatic sign of tolerance and openness but also the exasperating sign of the persistence, albeit in different dress, of scarcity, need,
and desire. He seems to intimate this, for he declares that he is *histérica*
only after enumerating the things he lacks: money, a car, sex, drugs, vice,
cosmetics. While the first two objects remain more elusive, the others are
all around (on and in) him. Spotting Riza at a nearby table, Fabio writes
him a note in lipstick, seals it with a kiss, and has the waiter deliver it.
The note is a lispy, idiosyncratic piece of writing where s is x, f is ph,
and that darling of gays, Elizabeth Taylor, is tacked onto the word for
happiness: "Sí me guxtaría hacerte pheliz (taylor) exta tarde" (Yes, I'd
like to make you happy this afternoon). The note is untranslatable because the style is as important as the message. In that respect it resembles
Fabio's speech, an effusive, polyglot babble of Spanish, English, and
French: "¡Qué overdose!," "lipstick," "moving on," "un shocking," "el
libro des coiffeurs, de nuit et de jour, pour les femmes," and so on. As
he walks up to Fabio's table, he addresses, again in the feminine, the
audience of his seduction: "Hi, hi, everyone. I'm here again, but not for
you." Someone in the crowd calls him *histérica*, thereby echoing what
Fabio has already announced. Coming on the heels of his declaration of

lack, need, desire, and hysteria, Fabio's seduction of Riza is flamboyant, public, and to the point.

There are, however, more subtle factors at work here. Fabio makes a spectacle of himself, but he does so in a space where consumerism remains intact (in Almodóvar's Rastro, barter is consumer kitsch). Accordingly, Fabio writes a note with borrowed lipstick, but the waiter requires that someone pay for its delivery. Fabio does not hesitate to say that Riza, the addressee, will pay; and, sure enough, he does. This is a telling moment of exchange, telling for the very reason that it seems so minor. To take a note from one table to another, the waiter charges 200 pesetas (around 2 dollars), an amount at once insignificant and exorbitant. It is exorbitant not only because the waiter could deliver the note free of charge but also because Fabio, seated only two tables away, could deliver it himself, could even forgo writing anything at all; and it is insignificant because Riza Niro is the heir to the throne of Tirán, a man accustomed to a life of "sex, luxury, and paranoia." Fabio's seduction of Riza is thus realized amid insignificance and exorbitance, scarcity and excess. Epistolary in form, it is economic in function: mediated by money, it promises a release of sexual energy, a satisfactory expenditure and exchange. It *promises* a release, but it never delivers it to the audience; we see Fabio cruise Riza, proposition him, and pick him up, but nothing more.

Something more specific than sexual discretion is involved in this refusal to show and deliver. Paul Julian Smith writes of the nagging disavowal of homosexual specificity in Almodóvar's work. Poses, propositions, and promises of gay encounters abound in this film, but nowhere does homosexual pleasure succeed in showing itself. The sex between Fabio and Riza, Sadec (Antonio Banderas) and Riza, can only be imagined, for it is not to be seen. The sex between Santi (Javier Grueso) and Riza is, in contrast, a visible failure: when we get a glimpse of homosexual pleasure, when we come close to seeing it, we must imagine instead that Riza is dreaming of Sexilia, that he cannot see himself with anyone but her. On screen, homosexuality reveals itself as desiring heterosexuality. Riza is thus not really gay, nor are his flirtations and caresses with Fabio and Sadec sufficient signs to the contrary. And although the sex between Riza and Sexi also remains offscreen, it comes through loud and clear: in the final shot, over the image of an airplane in ascent, we hear, amid sighs and moans, their orgasmic voices. In fact, the most explicit sexual scene is the rape of Queti by her father.[28] The most explicit sexual scene is, in other words, a scene of violence. In the visual economy of *Labyrinth of Passions*, incest, rape, and violence are shown to succeed while homosexuality and promiscuity are shown to fail. Thus, while Fabio coquettishly responds to Riza's description of the size of his room by saying, "better too much than too little," it appears that when it comes to showing certain things, and only certain things, less is indeed better than more.

The visual economy is based on the transactions between the seen and unseen, the scene and the ob-scene. For Jean-François Lyotard, this economy is violent not only in what it succeeds in showing but also in what it fails to show: "just as the libido must renounce its perverse overflow to propagate the species through a normal genital sexuality allowing the constitution of a 'sexual body' having that sole end, so the film produced by an artist working in a capitalist industry . . . springs from the effort to eliminate aberrant movements, useless expenditures, differences of pure consumption."[29] Tying sexual renunciation to economic restriction, repression to oppression, Lyotard questions what is at stake in such basic cinematic techniques as framing, découpage, montage, and mise-en-scène. Exclusions, effacements, and forced unifications underwrite, as Lyotard observes, cinematic production. The result is a type of enclosure, where the norms of representation dovetail the norms of social reality. Subversion and disorder may be represented, that is, but they are represented as part of a tenacious, perhaps inevitable, order of control, authorship, and direction. This is especially important in the case of a director, or *auteur*, like Almodóvar, whose films have been seen, with good reason, as "anarchic and irreverent," as part of "a fast-paced revolt that relentlessly pursues pleasure rather than power, and a postmodern erasure of all repressive boundaries and taboos."[30] Without disputing the spirit of such views, I want to focus on how the sexual exuberance of the labyrinth of passions is at the same time the effect of restriction, how pleasure is bound to power. It is here, again, that hysteria proves to be cinematically productive. Fabio's erratic movements and fitful speech designate him as a singularly hysterical subject, one who resists the established order even as he is an effect of that order. This tension between resistance and restriction is crucial to hysteria and leads to a number of violent figurations. Such is the hysteria that Lyotard figures as a quasi-lethal *jouissance* and Lacan figures as a fragmented body, as an aggressive, Bosch-like disjunction of form and fantasy.[31] Such is the hysteria that Almodóvar figures, and frames, as an instance of power.

Of all the characters who populate Almodóvar's film, Fabio is the most intemperate and intractable, the campy cock of the walk, the queen of artifice and bad taste: spectacular, scandalous, hysterical. He signifies, in Susan Sontag's terms, "the sensibility of failed seriousness," "the theatricalization of experience," and "the convertibility of 'man' and 'woman,'" and in Lyotard's terms, disorder, flippancy, and flashy, nonreproductive pleasure.[32] Enacting femininity as an aggressively masculine (im)posture and (dis)possession, Fabio signifies the persistence of a desire that does not recognize itself in the mirror of reproduction, a love that dare not see its image. And yet, it is just this image of daring

that makes Fabio so special, so much a challenge for Almodóvar. Fabio
first appears in the Rastro, negotiating sex with Riza. He next appears not
writhing in bed with Riza but writhing under a power drill and a camera,
posing for a sadomasochistic photonovel or, as he calls it, a "foto porno
sexi killer" (Plate 4). In the move from the Rastro to the photography
studio, from a scene of seduction to a scene of violence, the sexual act
is lost: offscreen, ob-scene. Or rather, the sexual act is lost as anything
but a violent simulacrum. To underscore this, Almodóvar himself enters
the picture. As he tells the photographer what to do, he shouts to Fabio,
"Enjoy it, enjoy it more, you desire this drill so much. Yeah, yeah, try to
like it. You like the way it tastes, say more: 'I deserve it.' " What Fabio
has done to deserve this is perhaps the subject of the photonovel, but
the subject of this scene is filmmaking itself. Almodóvar directs Fabio to
enact a violent ecstasy, to desire his own destruction before the camera.
He exposes the theater of hysteria as a theater of model violence.

   According to Almodóvar, "in every film there is always a moment when
something must be done and there is no one to do it. That's where I
come in. Specifically, in *Labyrinth of Passions* the scene was with Fabio."[33] The critical moment for Almodóvar, the moment when the problem of direction caroms into the problem of representation, occurs with
Fabio in the role of victim, not seducer. Fabio, Almodóvar declares, is
marvelous, but he lacks control: he (mis)places himself; he threatens to
slide off-frame and to slip offscreen; he says things that are funny and
witty, yet inessential and imprecise; he acts and forgets everything, even,
or especially, that he is acting. Against Fabio, then, comes Almodóvar, the
director, placing himself directly in the scene to ensure the proper place,
the essential speech, the precise movement, of Fabio. In-frame, onscreen,
the director controls and commands: in a word, he authorizes. And central to his authority is the centralizing pull of the camera, the force of the
frame. Faced with the possibility of an oblivious, babbling, errant actor,
and hence with the possibility of a scandalously inchoate (non)spectacle,
Almodóvar intervenes to reinforce, in his own terms, the frame or limit
that allows the show to go on.

   Almodóvar's onscreen appearances recall those of Alfred Hitchcock,
although, according to Almodóvar, his interventions are performative,
whereas Hitchcock's are merely figurative.[34] And yet, Almodóvar's role
entails nothing less than the authoritative figuration of Fabio, himself in
danger of disfiguration and disappearance, a hyperperformance that dis-
locates the scene, disregards the audience, and disrupts basic cinematic
standards. What is so ironic about this authoritative figuration of Fabio
is that it is focused on disfiguration: Almodóvar intervenes not merely to
guarantee that Fabio does not disfigure the scene, script, and film by
sliding offcamera, but also to guarantee that Fabio is himself disfigured.
The trouble with this is that the authoritative (dis)figuration of Fabio,

appealing as it does to hysterical trauma, is at one and the same time the (dis)figuration of an image of femininity and of male homosexuality. Almodóvar makes trouble, is in trouble, directs and performs it, by exposing the violent power of limits and frames. His relationship with Fabio–Fanny is in this sense critical. For insofar as Fabio plays across the boundaries of gender and sets hysteria wandering in masculinity, he evokes the dream of an unframed imagination. He evokes, that is, the explosion of the limits of representation, the ecstasy of the cinema. Of course, to evoke such ecstasy he must, paradoxically, be contained.

Just as the persistence of lack or scarcity enables desire, so the persistence of constraints enables "anarchic and irreverent" representations. Transvestism, camp, and drag, all the signs of Fabio's wildness, are as much the effects of a constraining system of gender as they are its *mise-en-critique*. "Paradoxically," writes Marjorie Garber, "the male transvestite represents the extreme limit case of 'male subjectivity,' 'proving' that he is male against extraordinary odds."[35] Camp and drag are likewise compromised, sadly relying on sexual identities even as they seem to undo them.[36] Fabio's own undoing is "sad" in part because it is played for fun: as if the only figure who could be so violently disfigured and still remain "comical" had to be hysterical, gay, and a transvestite. While this may be read as a sign of Almodóvar's complicity in a system of established representation, it may also be read as a sly exposure of the pain underlying representation itself, particularly when it comes to so-called minor and marginal subjects. In this film of happy heterosexuality, it is after all with Fabio, not with Sexi and Riza, that Almodóvar comes out as a performer, not just as a singer in a nightclub (Plate 6) but as a director. Staging hysteria in a sexually charged theater, showing it to be a spectacle under direction, and framing and cutting it as violence, Almodóvar keeps it, and his film, on the move.

DOMESTIC DUELS: *WHAT HAVE I DONE?* AND *WOMEN ON THE VERGE*

> The hysterical fit is an equivalent of coitus.
>
> —Freud

Keeping women hysterically on the move is what *What Have I Done to Deserve This?* and *Women on the Verge of a Nervous Breakdown* are all about. More centered than *Labyrinth of Passions* on heroines, homes, and work, these two films are in many respects just as hectic. Although they limit transvestites and rock musicians to advertisements on television, and banish royalty altogether, *What Have I Done?* and *Women on the Verge* buzz with everything from murder and suicide to telekinesis, burning beds, and shoot-outs. Amid all this activity, they make a compelling pair: united and separated, as dark to light, down to up, misery to luxury. What pairs these two films is not merely the figure of Carmen Maura in contemporary Madrid but a sense of frustration, entrapment, and imminent collapse. Both Gloria and Pepa, both the working-class woman from the overcrowded Barrio de la Concepción and the professional woman from the elegant Barrio de Chamberí, rush madly across the screen, working out and against the memory of men. Popping pills and brandishing everything from ham bones to telephones, Gloria, Pepa, (and Carmen) illustrate the emotional versatility of hysteria, at once funny and sad. And yet, if their nervous condition seems to make them sisters in emotional arms, they belong to different socioeconomic contexts. In other words, the signs of cinematic hysteria do not signal a feminine uniformity, or universality, beyond class difference. Even the body of Carmen Maura, functioning as an essentialist lure, as the real beneath the role, is contextually sensitive and continually othered as acted.[37] Pepa, as commercial celebrity, glamorizes Maura and markets hysteria as postmodern slapstick, while Gloria, as domestic servant, works Maura into a market where hysteria is melodramatic and glamour is always for someone else. Keeping in mind the interplay between these two films, between Pepa and Gloria, I want to examine some of the ties between economic class, the psychosexual body, and hysteria.

What Have I Done to Deserve This? is torn between confusion and exasperation. Its title in Spanish, *¿Qué he hecho yo para merecer esto!*, begins with an inverted question mark and ends with an exclamation mark. This detail is frequently overlooked in reviews and critiques of the film, particularly in English. I follow the tendency to pose the title as a question rather than as an emphatic declaration, but it is nonetheless significant that something, from the very outset, is either missed or eliminated. The difficulty of processing so many details engenders a sense of conflict, exhaustion, and loss. In *What Have I Done?* much is indeed missing and lost, much unnoticed. Antonio (Angel de Andrés López), Gloria's husband, does not notice that his son Miguel has left home; the exhibitionist does not notice that Cristal (Verónica Forqué), Gloria's prostitute friend and neighbor, has remained unmoved by his self-proclaimed sexual prowess; and the police do not notice that Gloria, her face visibly bruised, has murdered her husband. Men, in this film, seem especially— though by no means exclusively—oblivious to what is, and is not, before them. And yet, for all that, it is Gloria who is repeatedly designated as oblivious to her surroundings. When Gloria cannot find her watch or her "minilips" (pep pills), her mother-in-law (Chus Lampreave) shakes her head and says, "I don't know where you've got your head"; when she burns the chicken, her husband snaps, "Fuck, you're never where you should be" ("Joder, nunca estás en lo que estás"). Almodóvar has said that no one notices her, but that is not quite the case.[38] Others do notice her. But what they notice about Gloria, when they notice her, is that she is forgetful, unmindful, scattered, and distracted; what they find, when they find her, is a woman lost. Among the missing signs of *What Have I Done to Deserve This?* is its central character.

To the eyes of those around her, Gloria is like a blank screen. To the spectator's eyes, however, she is the figure who most visibly fills the screen, its center. This figure that fills the screen as a blank screen for other figures presents a perceptual problem. Gloria is seen, by the spectator, as a woman not seen. She therefore remains the object of the spectator's gaze, but an object that is largely missed by other objects of the gaze (i.e., the other characters). This "missing" is, furthermore, closer to pure failure than to feeling. For example, if Antonio misses Gloria, it is not because he feels her to be missing from his life. The missing that is felt, and that undergirds and motivates desire, Antonio reserves for Frau Müller (Katia Loritz), his former employer in Germany. Antonio misses Frau Müller, feels her absence, and longs for her presence; but he misses Gloria, fails to acknowledge her, let alone long for her, even when he is having sex with her. Almodóvar underscores this failure of feeling in a most economical way. As Gloria asks Antonio for money to pay the bills, he grabs her, kisses her neck, and throws her onto the bed. She continues to tell him that she needs money, and the scene cuts abruptly to a program on television: a sort of Andalusian burlesque show in which Almodóvar sings to Fanny McNamara in drag. The song he sings, or rather mouths, is Miguel Molina's "La bien pagá" ("The Well-Paid Woman"), a song whose lyrics provide an ironic commentary to the goings-on in the bedroom: "I don't owe you anything, I don't ask anything from you, forget me already . . . I don't love you, don't love me." With the song winding down, the scene cuts back to Gloria, still clothed on the bed. She is smiling, but her smile soon fades because Antonio, utterly inattentive to her pleasure, has evidently climaxed. There is yet another cut, this time to the grandmother, singing along with the television: "Well-paid, well-paid, well-paid, woman, you were." Gloria, needless to say, is not well-paid, on any account; not only does Antonio not give her the money she requests, he does not give her anything (pleasure, attention, respect) at all. Put simply, Antonio sets Gloria at naught, having sex not with her but through her. When he seems to desire her most, he misses her.

Gloria is in many respects missing from the desire of others. While the encounter with Antonio in the bedroom is quietly brutal, the most poignant instance of Gloria's disjunction from desire occurs in Cristal's apartment. There, as Cristal has sex with a man, Gloria sits by, the voyeuristic presence that Cristal's client requires for his stimulation. She is an imperfect voyeur, however, for just as she is scarcely noticed by others, here she, in turn, scarcely notices what is going on beside her. Far from being excited or disgusted, Gloria is merely exhausted. Her body slouched, her face fallen, her eyes empty, her thoughts presumably elsewhere, she appears utterly estranged from the sexual activity in which Cristal is engaged. Then again, Cristal herself appears estranged. Distant from desire, she looks at her fingernails as the man on top of her asks if she is coming. She says yes, but her tone suggests boredom, even exasperation. Cristal, of course, is acting out a routine that earns her money, not pleasure. So seen, she is as much a working woman as Gloria, but with a number of important differences. She is single; she has no children; she sets her own conditions; and she is relatively solvent, feeding Gloria's children when Gloria cannot. The putatively well-paid woman, she extends and alters the earlier bedroom scene with Gloria and Antonio. Cristal is to Gloria as prostitution is to matrimony: similar yet different. Almodóvar is indebted to such well-established topics as the whore with a heart of gold and the frustrated housewife, but he invests them with a blend of humor and sadness that keeps them from being either flip or maudlin. This is a difficult blend, to be sure, for as Gloria sits drained and distracted, more attentive to her husband's arrival than to the commotion beside her, she fiddles with a newly purchased curling iron. The phallic charge of this instrument of feminine beauty is evident, vulgarly so, and indicates that Gloria's place in the order of desire may be one of displacement but not of exemption or exteriority. With Cristal and client next to her, and a curling iron in her hands, Gloria remains in a phallic economy even as she is beside it.

The curling iron functions as a Freudian joke, undercutting Gloria's somberly detached mood. It is yet another nod to a store of psychoanalytic images and instruments whose hermeneutic force has been popularized, like hysteria itself, to the point of banality. But it also has a function that is formal. Gloria's curling iron does not merely bind together the two scenes in which it figures directly; through the play of similitude, it indirectly binds together an array of scenes. Similar objects include kendo poles, mops and brooms, a rough wooden stick (the grandmother's staff), a ham bone, and a boom microphone. The film opens with a shot of Almodóvar's camera crew in a city square. Gloria traverses this space, and as she does so a sound man follows her with a microphone on a long black boom. She turns once, twice, as if menaced by the microphone, and enters a karate studio. The titles begin to roll and are intercut with shots of men practicing kendo. They wear black gowns and masks of metal mesh, hop forcefully around a room, and lunge first at the camera and then at each other with long bamboo poles. As they lunge, they emit a series of guttural shouts, ending in a lone bloodcurdling scream. The scene then cuts to Gloria cleaning the dressing rooms. A naked man enters a shower stall, and motions to her to come. She obeys, and once she is inside the shower with him, he embraces her. As the water drenches them, they have, or seem to have, sex: seem to, because it is later revealed that the man is impotent. Straightening her hair and her dress, Gloria exits the shower. To the mounting strains of a German song, Gloria grabs a kendo pole and lashes out at the air. A cut follows, visual not auditory, to Antonio singing along to the same song that has punctuated Gloria's rendition of kendo. The song expresses Antonio's nostalgic attachment to Frau Müller as well as Gloria's sexual and emotional frustration. It is replayed several times in the course of the film, and although it is most closely connected with Antonio, it is also, as the opening scene indicates, connected with Gloria, or more precisely with Gloria in the act of striking out. Later, of course, Gloria will wield not a kendo pole but a ham bone, and she will strike not the air but Antonio. But here, already, Almodóvar has made effective use of the interplay of sound and image. Having established a link between sound and a menacing phallic object (the boom microphone dogs her here as the song does later), he underscores the link by replaying it in a growing chain of sounds and visual objects. This complex audiovisual chain is no joking matter, for when Gloria holds the curling iron, she holds not just something sexual but something violent.

The links between sex and violence in *What Have I Done?* are subtly, even elegantly, cinematic.[39] This is ironic because the story is itself rather sordid. The failed writer Lucas (Gonzalo Suárez) articulates the links between elegant form and sordid content when he tells Cristal that what he wants from her is "an elegant, sophisticated, and well-worn sadism like one sees in French movies." Cristal is unable to comply, not through any failing of her body but through a failing of her accessories. In an attempt to satisfy her client's sadomasochistic request for a thrashing with a leather whip that she does not possess, Cristal goes to Gloria. What Gloria offers her is not a whip but the grandmother's wooden stick. Taking it firmly in her hands and giving yet another powerful lunge, Gloria remarks, "you could even kill him with this." Her actions are underscored with the sound of sirens, with the insistent urban music of ambulances or police cars. The stick is in fact later examined by the police as a possible murder weapon; but here, in this prelude to sophisticated sadomasochism, Cristal takes it, rubs it, and notes with a wink how big it is. Cristal's thoughts are sexual while Gloria's are violent, and together they implicitly invest the object with the image of sexual violence.

The ramifications of such a combination are unsettling, so much so that Lucas promptly rejects the stick as too rough and rustic. Lucas's own combination of sex and violence relies on a principle of delicacy that is more in line with Roland Barthes than the Marquis de Sade. Lucas is not, as Cristal points out, a true sadist but a mime or simulator. The form of elegance he desires does not admit breaches between model (French porno films) and copy, at least when the copy is visibly modified by scarcity, when ideal whips are replaced by rough sticks. Lucas desires, that is, an elegance whose form is one of explicit correspondence, blatant mimesis: an elegance where artifice replicates artifice. That is why Lucas is a failure as an artist and, I might add, why he serves as a counterpart to Almodóvar. For unlike Lucas, Almodóvar does not make artistic subtlety depend on the occultation of scarcity, sordidness, and need; he does not make formal elegance depend on the representation of elegant objects. In fact, Almodóvar's success may well lie in his ability to communicate what others, like Lucas, find comfortably contradictory: the elegance of sordidness and the sordidness of elegance.

Sordid objects and elegant optics: *What Have I Done?* is carefully crafted neorealism. Almodóvar acknowledges the similarities between his film and the neorealist films of Roberto Rossellini, Fernando Fernán Gómez, and Marco Ferreri, but he is careful to note that the similarities are more on the level of intention than of production and mise-en-scène.[40] While he maintains that *What Have I Done?* has a clear political position typical of neorealist cinema, he stresses the film's dark humor and artificiality.[41] Eighty percent of the film is shot in a studio, not on location or in the street, as is customary with "true" neorealism. For Almodóvar, true neorealism is false insofar as it denies its technical bases and naturalizes its artifice.[42] In contrast to the neorealists, when Almodóvar takes to the street, it is to display his artistry, not to hide it. I am referring to the window-shopping scene where the curling iron first appears. It is an eminently commercial scene in which objects assume a striking ascendancy. Gloria and Juani walk along the street, passing a flower shop, a cosmetics shop, and an appliance shop. The camera follows them, but from inside the shops, not outside. Sutured so that it flows quite effortlessly, this sequence of traveling, or tracking, shots turns the tables on consumerism, showing the two shoppers to be the objects behind the glass, the consumers to be consumed.

It is in this exchange of objects and sights that Gloria and Juani consider the curling iron. "What a luxury," sighs Gloria, her eyes filled with desire for the curling iron, for the image of a more beautiful self. Gloria, as the spectator-buyer of the curling iron, sees and buys an image of herself. For John Berger, this specular, speculative dynamic is characteristic of the self in capitalism: "the publicity image steals her love of herself as she is, and offers it back to her for the price of the product."[43] For Gloria, the price of the product is her son Miguel, whom she "sells" to a dentist in order to have the money for such a necessary luxury (as well as for rent, gas, electricity, and food). The iron is thus ridiculously rich with meaning: an instrument of beauty, a symbol of the phallus, a sign of displaced violence, a replacement for her son, a lure for her "self," a reservoir of desire, and a not so simple commodity. But more than the curling iron is at stake here; it is the way Almodóvar plays with the objects of vision that makes this scene so valuable. Reversing a naturalized order, he has us see Gloria from inside the space of commerce, an object among objects. Objects are, as Almodóvar says, "the only witnesses of her life."[44] If Gloria is not noticed, it is in part because objectification no longer issues from other subjects but from other objects.

Watching Gloria through shop windows, ovens, washing machines, and refrigerators, we see her in a consumerist relation that is markedly different from that of Pepa in *Women on the Verge*. For while Pepa is a consummate consumer, impetuously disposing of material possessions, continuously changing her clothes, renting and retaining her penthouse, promoting household products on television, marketing her voice and her image, Gloria is consumed by her inability to consume. According to Almodóvar, she desires not the overturn of capitalism but its opening and expansion, its accommodating embrace.[45] Frustrated in her consumerism, she is given to a kind of nervous consumption, an exasperating depletion of energy. Pepa pops downers to help her relax; Fabio sniffs nail polish to help him cruise; Gloria pops uppers (when she can get them) and sniffs dishwashing liquid to get her through her household chores. Rushing from one unsatisfying job to another and then home, she is both overworked and underemployed. She is not, at any rate, "unemployed" or "unoccupied" in the discreetly bourgeois sense that Breuer and Freud discuss as conducive to hysteria. She may suffer from "[t]he monotonous family existence without a corresponding psychic labor for the unused excess of psychic activity and energy," but neither her monotony nor her labor is that of Breuer's and Freud's typically well-heeled patients. Gloria does not "disburden" herself "through the continuous work of her phantasy" any more than she exacerbates her nervous condition through "habitual day-dreaming."[46] In fact, far from exercising her fantasy, Gloria continuously works her body to the bone. This does not mean that she has neither the time nor the energy to be hysterical, but that hysteria itself has become, under the influence of Freud, a construction in which working-class women (and men) are in large measure missed or left unnoticed. Reversing this trend, Jan Goldstein reminds us that "the hysterics of the Salpêtrière were not bourgeois women, living within the framework of a bourgeois value system, but urban working-class women—seamstresses, laundresses, domestic servants, flower sellers."[47] Gloria, an urban working-class woman at the end of a different century, is similarly engaged, similarly seen and missed.[48] She may go routinely unnoticed by the people around her, yet when they do notice her, she seems flighty, volatile, and flustered: in a word, hysterical.

When, if, and how Gloria is noticed, or not, is not just a function of time and energy (repetition, routine, endurance, exhaustion) but also of space. Gloria occupies a space that is neither wildly orgasmic like Fabio's nor comfortably fashionable like Pepa's. Instead, for most of the film she inhabits a darkly domestic space whose closure the camera, largely stationary, emphasizes. Within such dim, claustrophobic surroundings, without payment or recognition, Gloria cooks, cleans, washes, and serves. A maid or charwoman outside her house, she is the same inside, except that she is also a wife and mother. The film deliberately shuffles these roles—mother and maid, housewife and charwoman—and in the process places work inside and outside of the house on the same footing. This is the context for Gloria's "nervous condition," a context and condition that Cristal articulates as follows: "She's a little hysterical, but the poor woman has two kids and spends her life working all day as a maid." Cristal's assessment is echoed by Gloria's mother-in-law and son, among others. When Gloria snaps at the grandmother, the latter responds: "Gloria, calm down, or you're going to have a breakdown." And when she offers her son a diet pill to stave off his hunger, he responds, "no, it makes me nervous; look how you are." In this close, dark, cold house where money is the name of a pet lizard (Dinero), Gloria moves, murders, and contemplates suicide. The murder itself is dramatically filmed, though quickly dedramatized in the "murder" of Money (the pet lizard), the bumblings of the police (the chief inspector is the impotent seducer of the early shower scene), the telekinetic remodeling of the kitchen, and the departure of Toni and the grandmother for the ironically idealized village. The most dramatic, or rather melodramatic, moment occurs at the very end, when Gloria returns to an empty, only partially remodeled house. Drained and despondent, she finds no calm liberation in solitude. Instead, approaching a state of emotional vacancy, beyond hysteria, Gloria goes out onto the balcony of her apartment, leans forward into a brighter, more open space, and signals a suicide that the return of her son Miguel prevents. In what may well be the film's most troubling line, Miguel announces: "This house needs a man." Gloria, after all she has so richly not deserved, after all she has so somberly resisted, after the violent elimination of "her" man, seems to agree. *What Have I Done?* ends where *Women on the Verge* begins.

Carmen Maura as Pepa utters her first lines in *Women on the Verge of a Nervous Breakdown* over a close-up shot of a scale-model building (a maquette), a cardboard sun, and the sound of quacking ducks. As is so often the case in this film, the voice does not accompany the image. It thereby announces, on the level of form, a split or separation that it affirms on the level of content. Pepa speaks, in the past tense and from someplace out of frame, of separation and splitting, absence and abandonment. She had been abandoned by her partner Iván (Fernando Guillén), an aging Don Juan with a golden voice. With his departure, she says, the world seemed to collapse around her. She struggled to save herself and her world, bound up as they were in her relationship, but to no avail. Feeling like a modern-day Noah, she set up a coop for ducks and chickens on the terrace of her penthouse, preparing herself, symbolically, for the loneliness of the flood. These past events are then depicted on screen—unfolded, as it were, from a point of view after the flood. The film suggests a subtle circularity, then, with the final scene of Pepa and Marisa on the terrace—talking about sex, love, virginity, maternity, and feminine independence—providing a clue as to the possible site of the film's opening enunciation. Ending with a sort of bedraggled feminist triumph (women do not need men), *Women on the Verge* nonetheless opens with a house, and a woman, in need of a man. This need and its overcoming structure the body of the filmic narrative. Centered in Pepa, it is played out in a number of other women: in Candela (María Barranco), an Andalusian model suffering from betrayal by a man who turns out to be a Shiite terrorist; in Marisa (Rossy de Palma), the brusque, domineering, virginal fiancée of a man who falls for Candela; in Lucía (Julieta Serrano), the pistol-wielding, clinically insane first wife of Iván; in Paulina (Kiti Manver), the so-called feminist lawyer who insults Pepa and is going to run off with Iván to Sweden; and finally, in Vienna (Joan Crawford), the strong-willed entrepreneur who is saved by Johnny (Sterling Hayden) in Nicholas Ray's *Johnny Guitar*. These women vary significantly: they are of different ages and professions; they are even of different realities (the *mise-en-abîme* of a film within a film). But they all have one thing in common: they are all, to varying degrees of nervousness, in need of men.

The need for a man has long been posited as crucial to hysteria. As Beret Strong styles it, "[t]he hysteric is a woman in search of a man."[49] The womb wanders, or so the story goes, but it does so in part out of unfulfilled desire, improperly channeled erotic energy, prolonged abstinence, and "amorous ardor."[50] With respect to men, hysteria is frequently associated with emasculation and symbolic castration, with the lack of, and need for, what ostensibly makes a man a man. For better and for worse, Sexilia, Riza, and Fabio in the market of desire, no less than Gloria in the market of self-image, gravitate around things phallic. While what is at stake may ultimately be more a question of need—and of course of desire—in general than of object choice in particular, heterosexual women and homosexual men do seem to be particularly susceptible to the plays of hysteria. And yet, as the reference in *What Have I Done?* to Elia Kazan's 1960's psychomelodrama, *Splendor in the Grass*, suggests, even nice straight boys like Warren Beatty can become faint and silly when they do not have what they want, what they supposedly need. Sexual repression and renunciation, those mainstays of morality, are hence deeply implicated in the nosology of hysteria. In the words of Charles Bernheimer, "the psychological understanding of hysteria was born in complicity with moral condemnation of its victims"; or in the words of

Beret Strong, "[t]he weak body appears to spread the contagion of its faulty integrity to the hysteric's morality."[51] This moral specter, mobilizing problems of agency, responsibility, guilt, and choice, haunts *What Have I Done?* in its very title.[52] In *Women on the Verge*, moral dilemmas are unquestionably less pressing (murder, forgery, prostitution, and the "education" of children are absent), but they continue in the guise of problems such as fidelity, honesty, and solidarity. In other words, the hysterical fixation on, and need for, a man in *Women on the Verge* runs up against the need for friendship and self-respect. Pepa comes back from the border of a nervous breakdown when she realizes, through a classically heroic act (she saves Iván from murder), that her needs need not be mediated through a man.

At the very end of the film, Pepa returns home to a house in shambles, steps over broken glass and a slew of sleeping bodies, goes out onto the terrace, and has a quiet conversation with Marisa. Unlike Gloria, Pepa contemplates not suicide but the beauty of the city under a starry sky. Never mind that both city and sky are a painted backdrop, that they are, as the film's final song indicates, "pure theater," Pepa is able to appreciate them anyway (Plate 19). Marisa is drowsy but luminous, and tells Pepa that she has had an intensely erotic dream in which she has lost her virginity by herself, without any real need for a man. Pepa, in turn, tells Marisa that she is pregnant, but that she will have the baby alone. Envisioning a house without a man and a child without a father, Pepa appears fatigued but content and calm. This exchange of confidences among women is indeed the calmest communication in the film. So much else is only partly communicated, or miscommunicated, or not communicated at all. Pepa and Iván play phone tag for two days, always just missing or, in Iván's case, just avoiding, the other. The telephone itself, indelibly associated with Almodóvar's job at the phone company, assumes an irksome preeminence, simultaneously denying and affirming separation. A voice in a machine is at times all that remains of human contact. In *Women on the Verge*, telephones, microphones, loudspeakers, answering machines, tape recorders, and sound tracks, far from helping people to connect, bring them apart. One of the most acutely cinematic disconnections is that of body and voice, a fact that Almodóvar exploits without marring the film's smooth Hollywood mood. Acknowledging a blend of formal experimentation and commercialism, Almodóvar has said that the film owes much to the comedies of Billy Wilder but that its origins are to be found in Jean Cocteau's *La voix humaine* (*The Human Voice*). Cocteau's piece is an experimental monologue that is performed in part by Carmen Maura, as the transsexual Tina, in *The Law of Desire*. As Pepa in *Women on the Verge*, Maura acts considerably less tortured, but here, too, she waits anxiously for the phone to ring: rushing to it, screaming at it, and at one point throwing it out the window, breaking it as she herself is breaking down. The telephone is for Pepa a curious object of desire, frustration, and anger. As such, it recalls Iván, promising communication but not delivering it. When it is repaired, it hardly matters: Pepa's conversation with Marisa is not only without a man, it is without a machine.

Communication can have hysterical consequences. Along with the convulsions, fainting spells, and swings of emotion classically tied to hysteria are problems of communication: aphasia, mutism, babble, uncontrolled polyglotism, and so on. These problems are not confined to the hysterical body, however, but to the plays and replays of desire, knowledge, and language between bodies: doctor and patient, analyst and analysand, and man and woman. Almodóvar makes effective use of these problems from early on in the film. We hear Pepa before we see her, and we hear Iván before we see him. His voice is joined not to a body but to a script. And as he says, "Pepa, darling, I don't ever want to hear you say 'I'm unhappy,' " the image on the screen is a close-up of the handwritten, multicolored gloss to the preprinted list of songs that includes the song, circled for good effect, "Soy infeliz." Writing is spoken, speech is written, but what is signified is a telling desire for silence or deafness: "I never want to *hear* you say 'I'm unhappy.' " Iván spends the greater part of the film not hearing, not wanting to hear, Pepa say that she is unhappy. When he does finally offer to listen, after Pepa has saved his life, again, as with the repaired telephone, it hardly matters: Pepa no longer cares to tell him. But before, she had cared too much, so much that Iván is the stuff of her dreams.

What follows Iván's statement of deaf desire is the only dream sequence in Almodóvar's work. The dream is entered by way of three close-ups: an alarm clock ringing, a black-and-white photograph of Pepa and Iván (their first visual appearance, colorless and static), and Pepa asleep in bed (the brightly colored fabric of her pajamas contrasting sharply with the black-and-white frame of photograph and dream). The dream itself is filmed in misty black and white, and consists of a leisurely stroll by Iván, microphone in hand, past a dazzling gallery of women: Spanish, Nordic, Arabic, African, American, Asian. Iván does not speak so much to the women as into the microphone, narcissistically absorbed in the mellowness of his own voice. His remarks are trite and trivial declarations of insincere love, as airy as the wind heard in the background. The scene ends with a woman scoffing at his claim to "accept her just the way she is." The dream lays bare a number of communicative problems, but it is when the film becomes self-referential that these problems really come to the fore.

As black and white dissolves into bright red—first a light, then something like the sun—Iván makes his first true-color appearance. He appears, significantly fragmented: an extreme close-up of his lips against a microphone. He slowly licks his lips and begins to speak. "How many men have you forgotten?" he asks, then, after a pause, "tell me something nice." He speaks in Spanish, of course, but the words are not his. For as soon as he asks to hear something nice (not something unhappy), there is a cut, not to the figure of Carmen Maura but of Joan Crawford. Iván is dubbing Sterling Hayden's part in *Johnny Guitar*, a film that enjoys almost a cult following in Spain. *Johnny Guitar* is, among other things, a campy melodrama, a western with a female lead. At its center is the story of a failed love affair and a woman's attempt at achieving success on her own. Crawford, as Vienna, plays a strong, swaggering character who nonetheless needs the real strength of a real man. Hayden, as Johnny, is that man, and he saves Vienna's life. The scene that Iván is dubbing is certainly the most successful in Ray's film, but it is also crucial to Almodóvar's. In it, in the original, a man feeds a woman lines, scripts her words to suit his pleasure. "Lie to me, tell me all these years you've waited, tell me," and then, "tell me you'd have died if I hadn't come back," and finally, "tell me you still love me like I love you." Truth, it seems, is engendered in lies and repetition, in one saying what the other wants to hear and then hearing it as one's own. Vienna reacts to Johnny's request first with violent derision, then with true confession: "Once I would have crawled at your feet to be near you. I searched for you in every man I met. I have waited for you, Johnny. What took you so long?" In *Johnny Guitar* this communicative exchange and emotional change lead to a happy Hollywood ending, to Johnny and Vienna walking off arm in arm. But in *Women on the Verge*, it is significantly altered. Iván dubs Johnny, doubles his artificiality, and exposes himself as a cinematic product. What is more, he dubs him without hearing anyone but himself. He experiences, in a sense, a troubling powerful male fantasy: Joan Crawford flashes across the screen, moves her lips, and keeps silent—a woman beautiful, desirable, mute. Pepa is not there to dub Vienna, but asleep in bed. The image of her sleeping, dreaming body cuts the dubbing scene, but Iván does not miss a beat. He does not need Pepa to do the scene; he needs only himself.

Pepa also plays the scene alone, but she is not as independent and distanced as her former partner. For when she speaks Vienna's lines (back) to Johnny, she is unhappily hearing Iván. Unlike Iván, Pepa is pictured wearing a hefty set of headphones (Plate 18). His voice surrounds her, separating her from everything else. As a guitar softly begins to play, the camera focuses on the red light of a movie projector and gradually moves back to show the black celluloid strip running through. The frontal shot changes into an aerial shot, and the camera follows the light that streams out of the projector, over the seated figure of Germán, the director of the dubbing, and toward Pepa, standing before the screen. She begins to dub, first with her voice in off, then in synchronization with Crawford's image. She tells Johnny (Iván) what he wants to hear, Vienna's truth as well as her own. She tells him that she is waiting and dying for his love. No sooner does she finish her lines and fill in the silences in the scene, than she faints. As she faints, her glasses fall beside her and before the camera, blurring her to our view. With regard to her emotional state, she remains blurred and muddled for most of the film, pausing and reflecting only to pursue Iván all the better. She does, of course, finally free herself from him, but only after much havoc (including Candela's suicide attempt, Lucía's murder attempt, and the Shiites' terrorist attempt). Continually on edge, she repeats the lines of the woman in *Johnny Guitar*, but to different effect. Here, the happy ending comes in the form of a woman without a man, a woman whose independence is communicative (witness Marisa) instead of spurious and self-absorbed (witness Iván). *Women on the Verge* is thus a revision or redoubling of *The Human Voice* and, more directly, *Johnny Guitar*. Within a deceptively conventional framework, it pushes at disjunction and desire and ends up with a woman who no longer waits for or leans on a man. But it dubs and redoubles another film as well. *Women on the Verge* takes the dark domestic needs and desires of *What Have I Done to Deserve This?* and replays them as happy, sunny, stylish slapstick, as a sort of upscale, toned-down *Labyrinth of Passions*.

This interfilmic relation need not be resolved in favor of either of the two films. It is no doubt tempting to criticize *Women on the Verge* as a falling from critical truth, as a selling out, and to celebrate *What Have I Done?* as politically committed and socially aware or, obversely, to celebrate the former as showing a woman's success (despite the figure of Paulina Morales) and to criticize the latter as showing a woman's failure. But to do so is to overlook the critical significance of tension itself. This tension is, as I have been arguing, figured here as hysteria, or at least as some postmodern simulacrum of hysteria: mad, methodical, and ever so metaphorical. Hysteria, after all, is a site of considerable tension—psychosexual, to be sure, but ethical, political, epistemological, and aesthetic as well. It involves a crisis of categories and classes, an errant diffusion of bodily signs, and a troubling generation of images that critics have denounced in terms of victimization and championed in terms of resistance. It entails the disjunctions, framings, movements, spectacles, and speculations that Almodóvar's films find as their form; and it entails the problems of language, desire, body, image, gender, and class that they find as their content. Hysteria figures the women and, at times, the men of Almodóvar's films; it does so with often uneasy humor, slipping, especially in later works, between sadness and laughter. On the whole, Almodóvar's films have been remarkably successful, commercially as well as critically, perhaps because humor is always more uneasy than we may think; perhaps because the art of histrionics is always, after a fashion, hysterical.

NOTES

1. Michel Foucault, *Madness and Civilization: A History of Insanity in the Age of Reason*, trans. Richard Howard (New York: Random House, 1965), 142.

2. Lynne Kirby, "Male Hysteria and Early Cinema," *Camera Obscura* 17 (1988): 123.

3. Elaine Showalter, *The Female Malady: Women, Madness, and English Culture, 1830–1980* (New York: Penguin, 1987), 150.

4. Beret Strong, "Foucault, Freud, and French Feminism: Theorizing Hysteria as Theorizing the Feminine," *Literature and Psychology* 35.4 (1989): 20, notes the gender ambivalence (what I call the transvestite impulse) in Freudian epistemology.

5. Sigmund Freud, "Charcot," in *Early Psychoanalytic Writings*, ed. Philip Rieff (New York: Macmillan, 1963), 14.

6. Joseph Breuer and Sigmund Freud, *Studies in Hysteria*, trans. A. A. Brill (Boston: Beacon Press, 1964), 14.

7. For the spectacle and construction of hysteria, see Georges Didi-Huberman, *Invention de l'hystérie: Charcot et l'iconographie photographique de la Salpêtrière* (Paris: Editions Macula, 1982). As J. Laplanche and J.-B. Pontalis indicate, Freud subscribes to Pierre Janet's view of hysteria as "a malady through representation." *The Language of Psychoanalysis*, trans. Donald Nicholson-Smith (New York: W. W. Norton, 1973), 195.

8. Jan Goldstein, "The Hysteria Diagnosis and the Politics of Anticlericalism in Late Nineteenth-Century France," *Journal of Modern History* 54.2 (1982): 210.

9. Sigmund Freud, *Dora: An Analysis of a Case of Hysteria*, ed. Philip Rieff (New York: Macmillan, 1963), 136; emphasis in the original.

10. Lynne Kirby links hysteria and film: "If, as is commonly asserted, the repression of discontinuity is what classical, invisible editing is all about, then perhaps we could say that continuity editing is about the control of trauma as well" (126).

11. Stanley Cavell, "Psychoanalysis and Cinema: The Melodrama of the Unknown Woman," in *The Trials of Psychoanalysis*, ed. Françoise Meltzer (Chicago: University of Chicago Press, 1987–88), 245.

12. Kirby, 124.

13. Catherine Clément and Hélène Cixous, *Le jeune née* (Paris: Union Générale d'Editions, 1975), 111.

14. The word *Movida* designates the fervent cultural movement after the death of Franco. Almodóvar notes that the *Movida* is largely a media invention, but he does acknowledge the deliberately outrageous activity and cult of the modern in Madrid from around 1977 to 1982. See Nuria Vidal, *El cine de Pedro Almodóvar* (Barcelona: Destino, 1989), 39–40; all translations from this text are mine.

15. Pedro Almodóvar, "Bordando el borde," *El Europeo* 8 (1989): 67; my translation.

16. The idea that post-Francoist Spain is "new" and "different" finds itself co-opted by such Francoist slogans as "la nueva España" and "España es diferente."

17. Paul Julian Smith notes the importance in Almodóvar's work of "such 'external' factors as press coverage, marketing, and 'style' " in his *Laws of Desire: Questions of Homosexuality in Spanish Writing and Film: 1960–1990* (Oxford: Oxford University Press, 1992), 163. Smith cites Guillermo Cabrera Infante's "rebaptism" of Almodóvar as "Almodollar." But this rebaptism is itself belated: "Almodollar" is a refashioning of "Avida Dollars," André Breton's "rebaptism" of Salvador Dalí.

18. This characterization is critically examined by Goldstein, 212.

19. My reading of hysteria and postmodernism is overshadowed by an appeal to schizophrenia as *the* postmodern condition par excellence. The proponents of postmodernity as, or in relation to, schizophrenia include Gilles Deleuze, Félix Guattari, and Fredric Jameson. Jameson, perhaps because he uses it so much, is wary of the term "schizophrenia." For him, "it is meant to be descriptive and not diagnostic." "Postmodernism and Consumer Society," in *The Anti-Aesthetic: Essays on Postmodern Culture*, ed. Hal Foster (Port Townsend, Wash.: Bay Press, 1983), 118. While I, too, am skeptical of "some culture-and-personality diagnosis of our society and its art," I do not believe that the diagnostic impulse in "schizophrenia" can be so easily dismissed. In addition, I hold that schizophrenia enjoys such high critical currency in part because it, unlike hysteria, does not necessarily entail issues of sexuality and gender.

20. Marsha Kinder, "Pleasure and the New Spanish Mentality: A Conversation with Pedro Almodóvar," *Film Quarterly* 41.1 (1987): 34.

21. Smith addresses Almodóvar's image (wild, irreverent, and gay) and the way he, or rather his work, turns away from it.

22. Vidal, 39.

23. John Hopewell, *El cine español después de Franco: 1973–1988*, trans. Carlos Laguna (Madrid: Ediciones el Arquero, 1989), 445–446.

24. Sexilia suffers from a debilitating fear of the sun and is by preference a creature of the night; furthermore, her fear of light is tied to her love of sex, and her photophobia to her pornophilia. She is, in other words, *visibly* traumatized. "Trauma" derives from the Greek for wound, itself from a form of the verb meaning "to pierce." Sexilia's trauma, strikingly suited to the cinema, is a psychological wounding of the eye, a violently symbolic piercing of vision. Freud describes hysteria as a "psychic trauma, a conflict of affects," as "a disturbance in the field of sexuality" (*Dora*, 39); but it is also, as Charcot makes clear, a disturbance in the field of visibility. Sexilia's disturbance or trauma, depicted in flashbacks to an adolescent sexual scene, is removed as it is remembered. As Breuer and Freud remind us, "the hysteric suffers mostly from reminiscences" (*Hysteria*, 4), though the "cure" also is reminiscence. Rich with paradox, hysterical trauma is also, as Almodóvar sees it, rich with humor: "I've always taken traumas as something of a joke, but they comprise a separate genre in film. In life you can't explain everything with traumas, but in a comedy you can; they justify everything" (Vidal, 59). And yet everything is not "justified" or resolved. On the one hand, the film, through the traumatic flashback, shows homosexual and nonmonogamous sex to be detours or deviations, the "unfortunate" effects of an original misperception; on the other hand, it shows monogamous heterosexuality to be a re-vision or an afterthought that closes (down) the comedy.

25. Jean Baudrillard, "The Precession of Simulacra," in *Art After Modernism:*

Rethinking Representation, ed. Brian Wallis (New York: New Museum of Contemporary Art, 1984), 268.

26. There seems to be a hysterical, transvestite impulse in psychoanalytic knowledge that threatens the sure casting of subjects in terms of masculine power and feminine powerlessness. The "threat" of epistemological exposure to the very femininity (and, by extension, homosexuality) that psychoanalysis attempts to classify and contain, has been noted in Neil Hertz, "Dora's Secrets, Freud's Techniques," in *In Dora's Case: Freud-Hysteria-Feminism*, ed. Charles Bernheimer and Claire Kahane (New York: Columbia University Press, 1985); and John Forrester, *The Seductions of Psychoanalysis: Freud, Lacan and Derrida* (Cambridge: Cambridge University Press, 1990).

27. Strong, 11.

28. Cosmetically altered to look exactly like Sexilia, Queti promptly seduces Sexilia's father as Sexilia runs off with Riza. If what traumatizes Sexilia is her apparent rejection by Riza *and* her father, she overcomes this trauma, sees it, and sets it right by *apparently* attaching herself completely to both. Appearances can be deceiving, especially when what is disturbing (incest is real) is reassuringly asserted as merely an appearance and when what is reassuring (incest is a simulacrum) is disturbingly asserted as real. This movement of reality and appearance is confusing, but it bears an uncanny resemblance to the history of hysteria. This history, at least in its modern versions, views hysterical symptoms as arising from either suggestion/simulation or actual events. Freud links hysteria to seduction, particularly the incestuous seduction of daughters and fathers, but soon abandons its real basis in favor of a constellation of psychic desires. Needless to say, what Freud finds reassuring (i.e., seduction as simulation), his women patients do not. Almodóvar himself maintains that the most disturbing scene in *Labyrinth of Passions* is not Fabio posing for the *fotonovela* but the rape of Queti (Vidal, 56).

29. Jean-François Lyotard, "Acinema," in *The Lyotard Reader*, trans. Paisley N. Livingston (Oxford: Basil Blackwell, 1989), 172.

30. Smith, 168; Kinder, 34.

31. Lyotard, 171; Jacques Lacan, *Écrits*, vol. 1 (Paris: Editions du Seuil, 1966), 94.

32. Susan Sontag, "Notes on Camp," in *A Susan Sontag Reader* (New York: Vintage Books, 1983), 109, 115; Lyotard, 172.

33. Vidal, 51.

34. Vidal, 51.

35. Marjorie Garber, "Spare Parts: The Surgical Construction of Gender," in *The Lesbian and Gay Studies Reader*, ed. Henry Abelove, Michele Aina Barale, and David M. Halperin (New York: Routledge, 1993), 324. There is a sense in which Fabio's act is a violent travesty of femininity that implicates Almodóvar's direction; as such, neither is beyond misogyny.

36. Almodóvar himself speaks of a sadness under the light tone of *Labyrinth of Passions*, something typical of comedy but also very dramatic (Vidal, 44). This sadness is an effect of the ideological entrapment and symbolic constraint that infuse what Andrew Ross calls the politics of camp; see Ross's *No Respect: Intellectuals & Popular Culture* (New York: Routledge, 1989), 161. This politics is itself "sad," not because it negates resistance and leads to catastrophe and nihil-

ism but because it conceives of resistance, and hence of some form of oppression, as interminable.

37. Smith (through Francisco Ors) also heeds the body of the star, 201.

38. Vidal, 121.

39. "The subtlety, complexity, or intelligence of a picture is not to be found in its given meanings. These qualities may be seen in its organization." V. F. Perkins, *Film as Film* (Harmondsworth, U.K.: Penguin Books, 1972), 118.

40. Vidal, 116.

41. Vidal, 117.

42. Vidal, 118.

43. John Berger, *Ways of Seeing* (London: BBC and Penguin Books, 1972), 134.

44. Vidal, 121.

45. Vidal, 122.

46. Breuer, 28.

47. Goldstein, 213.

48. Gloria, insofar as she acts out a working-class version of Freud's "housewife neurosis," is beyond the pale of established psychoanalytic discourse. Freud gives short shrift to the neurosis with which he diagnoses and dismisses Dora's mother; but many critics appear just as reluctant to re-view the condition of the housewife as other than bourgeois. Those who do examine the role of economics in hysteria include Goldstein; Forrester; and Jann Matlock, *Scenes of Seduction: Prostitution, Hysteria, and Reading Difference in Nineteenth-Century France* (New York: Columbia University Press, 1994).

49. Strong, 16.

50. Foucault, 139.

51. Charles Bernheimer, "Introduction" to *In Dora's Case*, 4–5; Strong, 14.

52. Smith proposes seeing Almodóvar's films in terms of "moral melodrama," 203.

Almodóvar's City of Desire

Marvin D'Lugo

HISTORY AND DESIRE

Madrid has figured prominently in Pedro Almodóvar's cinema, gradually coming into focus as the implicit protagonist of nearly every work. In these films, the city is regularly imaged as a cultural force, producing forms of expression and action that challenge traditional values by tearing down and rebuilding the moral institutions of Spanish life: the family, the church, and the law.

Inspired by the conventions of cinematic representation of the city in film and, most pointedly, American filmic depictions of urban space,[1] Almodóvar's cityscapes succeed in imitating the American cinema's un-self-conscious universalization of particular milieus as the natural mise-en-scène of action. In the context of a cinema such as Spain's, which has for so long been marginalized, this project needs to be recognized as a self-affirmation of a culture that no longer sees itself as marginal and intuitively reframes and recenters its characters within a broader cultural field.

This foregrounding of the city as an assertion of a vibrant Spanish cultural identity is built around a rejection of the traditions that ordered Spanish social life for four decades. While Almodóvar has long insisted that his cinema is without any connection to Franco or Francoism, textual evidence suggests the contrary.[2] An essential axis of meaning in much of his filmic work lies precisely in the ways the ideas and icons of Francoist cinema—those related to religion, the family, and sexual repression—are set up as foils to stimulate the audience to embrace a new post-Francoist cultural esthetic.

Historically, the Francoist animosity toward urban culture revealed an important conflation of politics and sexuality that would inform cultural development and particularly cinematic development decades after the end of the Civil War. Francoism constructed its own ideal of the Spanish nation against the models of social and political deviance embodied as much by the urban life-styles of Madrid and Barcelona as by the external otherness of foreign political ideologies and social customs. During the thirties and forties, a strongly folkloric cinema emerged that imaged a sanitized, provincial world of pure spiritual and moral values, implicitly opposing the milieu of moral corruption, sexual promiscuity, and heretical foreign ideas that for the regime was synonymous with urban culture.[3]

One of the most striking cinematic examples of this negative conception of the city is José Antonio Nieves Conde's 1950 film *Surcos* (*Furrows*), which chronicles the dissipation of the members of a provincial peasant family as they struggle to survive in economically depressed Madrid. The root of the family's difficulties in the big city, as that film insists, lay in the emerging dominance of female characters who usurped the traditional authority and power of the male in Spanish society. The film's mother and daughter expose the degree to which female sexuality had become a dangerous counterdiscourse to the dominant ideology of Francoism.

The technocrats who staffed key government ministries beginning in the late fifties helped modernize Spain's antiquated economic and social institutions. Their policies effectively discarded the doctrinaire anti-urban bias of earlier government officials. Yet, while the notion of urban culture as enemy receded as an official view, the opposing notion of the city as a haven from the ideological repression of the provinces seemed not only to persist but even to intensify. In Juan Antonio Bardem's 1956 film *Calle Mayor* (*Main Street*), the critique of repressive provincial life is pointedly contrasted with the lure of Madrid, where characters are not plagued by the closemindedness and intolerance of the community. Hints of a similar repudiation of the provinces and of the intense appeal of the city are central to Fernando Fernán Gómez's *El extraño viaje* (*The Strange Journey*, 1964).

Francoist antipathy to urban culture clearly shapes the critical opposition cinema of the sixties and seventies, which, in turn, establishes the bridge to Almodóvar's films of the eighties. Drawing, for instance, on the commonplace of the city as refuge from the oppression of provincial life, seventies films such as Jaime Armiñán and José Luis Borau's *Mi querida señorita* (*My Dear Young Lady*, 1971), Vincente Aranda's *Cambio de sexo* (*A Change of Sex*, 1976), and Ventura Pons's *Ocaña* (1979) repeatedly figure the city—Madrid and Barcelona—as the haven for characters whose sexual identity had been deformed by the repressive social environment of provincial life.

By the early eighties, Madrid became cinematically as well as socially the site of a generational schism chronicled in films as diverse as Gutiérrez Aragón's *Maravillas* (*Marvels*, 1980), Carlos Saura's *¡Deprisa, deprisa!* (*Hurry, Hurry!*, 1980), and Fernando Trueba's *Opera prima* (*First Work/A Cousin at Opera*, 1980). In this subgenre urban milieus were increasingly identified as the locus of a defiant youth culture that rejected the mores and morality of its parents.

To a certain extent, this emphasis on Madrid locales is the result of the centralization of much of the film industry in and around the capital, which made it financially expedient to locate certain narratives in and near the city. Whether coincidental or intentional, however, this narrative centering led to the rise in opposition cinema in the seventies of implicit "scenarios of the Spanish nation." In films such as Pedro Olea's *Pim, pam, pum . . . fuego* (*Bang, Bang, You're Dead*, 1975), Gutiérrez Aragón's *Sonámbulos* (*Sleepwalkers*, 1978), and José Luis Garci's *Asignatura pendiente* (*Pending Exam*, 1977), to name only three conspicuous examples, the narrative is situated on the symbolic national stage, the capital city, thus transforming presumably local action into broader meditations on national historical issues.[4]

Though Almodóvar's cinema represents in most ways an unequivocal stylistic rupture with nearly every Spanish filmic tradition that precedes it, the figuration of the city in his films enables us to recognize a similar pattern of reflection on Spanish cultural identity that the flashy surfaces of particular films may tend to belie. In Almodóvar's cinema, Madrid comes to be seen as the place where the oppression of the old Spain depicted by earlier filmmakers is deciphered, challenged, and, in quite surprising ways, displaced.

The final sequence of *Law of Desire* (*La ley del deseo*, 1987) dramatizes these tendencies by foregrounding the urban mise-en-scène of Madrid as the medium through which this radical reformulation of Spanish cultural values is expressed. This is a cardinal moment in Almodóvar's cinema, in that this cluster of narrative motifs is joined to a strategy of subject address that foregrounds the crucial thematics inscribed in the urban milieu. In that scene, Antonio, the murderous lover of Pablo Quintero, the film director, has been cornered by the police in the apartment of Pablo's transsexual sister, Tina, played by Carmen Maura. Antonio agrees to release Tina and a captured police detective in exchange for one hour with Pablo. Finally alone with his lover, Antonio puts on a phonograph record ("Lo dudo") that expresses the sentiments of pure, unfailing love, then proceeds to undress Pablo for their last sexual union. The camera discreetly cuts away to a shot of the street below as the assembled police and relatives look up to the window of Tina's apartment, where the homosexual love scene is taking place (Plate 17). As Marsha Kinder describes the scene: "Their faces are full of awe and envy. Even the police are softened and eroticized by the passion that they imagine is going on in the room. They become the quintessential Almodóvar spectators!"[5]

After the lovemaking scene, Antonio, understanding that he is trapped, commits suicide, shooting himself in the head and falling dead before Tina's altar of kitsch artifacts—Barbie dolls and statues of Marilyn Monroe and the Virgin Mary. Pablo rushes to his side and, in a mock re-creation of Michelangelo's *Pietà*, holds his fallen lover in his arms (Plate 16). The film thus ends with an image that daringly transposes the scene of gay love, and perhaps the entire film, into what for some audiences must appear as a surprising religious context.

The scene is constructed around an essential historical irony. Not only is a religious discourse mobilized to valorize those sexual activities that the church had traditionally suppressed within Francoist society, but the dramatized audience and presumably the authenticators of that new de-marginalization are the police, the enforcers of those repressive social and moral codes. In short, the apparatus of Francoist social and sexual repression is reinscribed into the scene to affirm the very values that historically it had blocked and suppressed.

In highlighting the traditional institutions that articulated and enforced the social discourse of the past, the scene enunciates a basic linkage between two forms of desire: Antonio's individualized passion for Pablo and the "collective" scopic desire of the assembled audience on the street below. Madrid, as the narrative attests, constitutes a privileged space in which individual desires freely circulate, inevitably transforming the urban milieu into the site of a continual spectacle. Part of that transformation is the positioning of other *madrileños* to "bear witness" to the scenario of sexual liberation of the protagonists, which in turn triggers in them a recognition of their own desires long repressed by the social institutions of the Francoist regime.

This subversive reinscription of the dominant discursive register of Francoist ideology in *Law of Desire* dramatizes what Michel Foucault called "effective history," that is, "not [history as] a decision, a treaty, a reign, or a battle, but the reversal of a relationship of forces, the usurpation of power, the appropriation of a vocabulary turned against those who had once used it, a feeble domination that poisons itself as it grows lax, the entry of a masked 'other.' "[6] The result of this effective history, as Foucault asserts, is to open up a range of discursive discontinuities, of ruptures that will, in fact, place into question the very genealogy of received cultural knowledge. Foucault thus sees effective history as a "curative science," affirming knowledge not as an absolute but rather as a perspective, "[creating] its own genealogy in the act of cognition."[7]

The notion of "effective history" as a strategy of subject address coincides with Linda Hutcheon's view of postmodern parody as a means through which "an artist [can] . . . speak to a discourse from within it, without being recuperated by it."[8] "Parody," Hutcheon says, "appears to have become, for this reason, the mode of . . . 'the excentric,' of those who are marginalized by the dominant ideology." It is, as well, a means through which "to investigate the relation of ideology and power to all our present discursive structure."[9] As the dramatization of an appropriation of a dominant discourse now turned against those who had once imposed it, the final scene of *Law of Desire* addresses its audience through a series of ironic reversals in the social authentication of sexual identity. These reversals of traditional Spanish ideology foreground a historicized spectatorship to Almodóvar's film. A broader cultural discourse, in other words, has been displaced onto a sexual discourse, and one comes to view the film not only in terms of the specific sexual alignments it recounts but also as the affirmation of a new social logic of toleration and openness.

Detailing the generational cleavage that lies at the center of his films as it mirrors the larger social picture of Spain after Franco, Almodóvar observes: "We have lost the fear of earthly power (the police), and of celestial power (the church). . . . And we have recuperated the inclination toward sensuality, something typically Mediterranean. We have become more skeptical, without losing the joy of living. We don't have confidence in the future, but we are constructing a past for ourselves because we don't like the one we have."[10]

The construction of a "new past" as dramatized in each of Almodóvar's films involves, as Foucault's effective history suggests, the appropriation of the language of the old order now turned against itself to constitute a new Spanishness. A close look at the function of the city within the narrative and visual structures that define these films reveals a coherent textual order that actively appropriates the social constructions of Francoist culture—the family, the church, the police—and mobilizes them into the emerging expression of new cultural "desires."

CITY OF DESIRE

Almodóvar's first two feature-length films, *Pepi, Luci, Bom and Other Ordinary Girls* (*Pepi, Luci, Bom, y otras chicas del montón*, 1980) and *Labyrinth of Passions* (*Laberinto de pasiones*, 1982), are, by the director's admission, products of the *Movida*, that effervescence of youthful energy in music, art, and popular culture that occurred at the end of the seventies.[11] Inspired by the movement's punk style, both films express the brash self-confidence of a newly emerging youth culture that suddenly discovers Madrid as "the center of the universe."[12] In *Labyrinth of Passions*, for instance, Toraya, the dethroned Empress of Tirán, is in search of her gay stepson, Riza. She comes to Madrid because she knows he has heard it is "the most entertaining city in the world, and so modern." The ironic displacement of the traditional centers of Western culture, New York and Paris, and the improbable centering of the culture of the periphery[13] are a source both of humor and of cultural self-affirmation.

Cityscapes in these early films tend to emphasize the concept of physical movement and social mobility underscored in the very word *Movida* (Movement). Characters like Pepi, the heroine of Almodóvar's first film, and Riza, the hero of the second, have come to Madrid looking for a freedom obviously denied them elsewhere. They are able to seek out kindred spirits in an atmosphere that, as both films assert, is socially liberating and the impetus for new artistic creativity.

Although, as Almodóvar insists, Franco doesn't exist for these characters,[14] the foils for his liberated protagonists turn out to be fathers and husbands who serve as transparent embodiments of traditionalist, patriarchal order. In *Pepi, Luci, Bom*, for instance, Pepi, the heroine, has been raped by a police detective who continually voices the tenets of old-guard Francoist ideology: law and order, misogyny, and homophobia. In seeking her revenge against the detective, Pepi befriends the latter's wife, Luci, who soon abandons her husband for a lesbian relationship with Pepi's girlfriend, Bom. The formerly laconic Luci is introduced to the emancipated atmosphere of a post-Franco Madrid populated by gays, lesbians, and transvestites, all of whom implicitly reject the phallocentric political and social order embodied by Luci's estranged husband.

In *Labyrinth of Passions*, Almodóvar distances himself from the overt marks of the old Spain but continues the assault on conventional categories of sexuality. In the opening sequence of the film we see Riza and Sexilia, the nymphomaniac daughter of a woman-hating gynecologist, cruising the Sunday morning flea market, the Rastro, in search not of bargains but of sexual partners. From the establishing shot that identifies the Rastro, the camera swiftly cuts to a chain of medium close-ups of crotches and buttocks as the protagonists vie for sexual mates. The point of the erotic spectacle is that both male and female characters are going after the same sexual partners. By casting the spectator in the role of voyeur of this sexual spectacle, the scene deploys the scopic register of cinema as a form of discursive resistance to patriarchal constructions of sexual identity; from the very first moment, the spectator is positioned to occupy a cinematic gaze that transcends the repressive categories of sexual identity and to enter into the film's "labyrinth of passions," which is synonymous with Madrid.

In this way, the credit sequence highlights the essential breaking down of the boundaries between public and private spaces that is one of the basic features of the cinematic characterization of Madrid in the early films. In that newly created space of interaction between personal and social behavior, new relations are shaped; new identities are forged. That very same message is affirmed in the opening sequence of *Pepi, Luci, Bom*. The camera poses what at first appears to be an exterior shot of apartment building facades in Madrid, only to reveal the source of that view to be inside the window of Pepi's tiny apartment. When the doorbell rings, Pepi answers it and we meet the detective who has been eyeing Pepi's marijuana plants from a window in one of the nearby buildings we have just viewed. Confusing personal desire with social desire, the detective winds up raping the girl he had come to arrest, thus setting in motion the film's intricate narrative of revenge and friendship.

The visual and narrative blurrings of interior and exterior space as the impetus for the mobilization of desires is repeated in an elaborate scene of sexual spectacle later in the film. A contest called "General Erections" is staged among the male guests at a party held in the courtyard of an apartment building. The scene is viewed by a bisexual male, situated at the window of an apartment overlooking the orgy, who observes these actions through a pair of binoculars as he makes love with his transsexual wife.

Though seemingly motivated as affirmations of a hedonistic youth culture, these scenes also operate to secure the notion, common to both films, of an urban mise-en-scène in which the tearing down of scopic and sexual barriers leads to a series of social and sexual realignments. The individual desires that surface in this environment work, in turn, to break down the mythologies of sexuality identified within the broader cultural politics of traditionalist Spain, especially those of machismo and subservient females. As a city of pure, hedonistic desire, Almodóvar's Madrid thus becomes the site of radical new social desires as well.

CITY OF WOMEN

Although, from the start, female characters assume centrality in Almodóvar's cinema, it is not until *Dark Habits* (*Entre tinieblas*, 1983) that the city is self-consciously figured as the site of female empowerment. The plot of Almodóvar's third film is set in motion by two female antagonists who represent the spiritual and material interests of Spain after Franco. Sister Julieta, a mother superior who leads a religious order of nuns, *Las Rendentoras Humilladas* (*The Humbled Redeemers*), in a Madrid convent, confronts a crisis for her order when the convent's benefactor, the Marquis, dies and his widow refuses to continue her fascist husband's support of the convent. This situation forces the order to face the harsh economic realities of the real world. Thus the Madrid of the post-Franco era is defined implicitly as a space in contention by two opposing forces, one moral, the other materialistic, and both, importantly, embodied in strong female characters. Tellingly, all views of contemporary society in the film are mediated through female characters.

The Humbled Redeemers have come from the provinces to perform charitable work by providing haven from the police for youthful drug addicts, prostitutes, and murderers. It soon becomes apparent, however, that the nuns' "good deeds" are as much a liberation for them from the oppressive cloistered atmosphere of the provinces as they are a demonstration of good samaritanism. As a critique of traditional Catholicism's lack of connection with the problems of contemporary society, *Dark Habits* also weaves the historical tension between the city and Francoism's idealized provinces. Under the impetus of the urban milieu, the nuns have been led to discover the force of their own desires. Their religious faith, at best a convenient sublimation of those desires, becomes the catalyst for each woman's self-realization.

The arrival of Yolanda Bell, the fugitive torch singer who takes haven in the convent, pointedly dramatizes the linkage of individual desire with the urban mise-en-scène. The scene begins as the nuns are in the convent chapel preparing to take communion. They sing a religious chant of devotion to God expressing the confusion between sacred and erotic passion that will shortly be enacted. As they sing, the nuns form a line in the aisle and approach the altar, where a priest awaits them. The scene is shot from the altar so that when the rear door of the chapel suddenly opens and reveals Yolanda standing in the doorway, it is as if one sees a "divine apparition."[15] Sister Julieta turns around and approaches Yolanda, inviting her to participate in the mass. Rear lighting from the street pours into the darkened chapel and thereby gives Yolanda the appearance of a saintly figure with a halo surrounding her head and body. The voices of the female chorus block out the noises of passing traffic on the street; yet the blending of the visual and auditory tracks of the convent and the city streets suggests a continuity between the religious fervor that appears to possess the nuns and the city that seems magically to have delivered Yolanda to the waiting arms of Sister Julieta. By foregrounding the mise-en-scène in this fashion, Julieta's lesbian desire for Yolanda Bell, which is the dramatic heart of the film, is defined within the play of cloistered and urban spaces that situates that melodrama within a larger context of Spanish culture in transition. Indeed, *Dark Habits* is the first of his films where Almodóvar takes aggressive control of the development of narrative space in order to develop the dramatic identity of his characters.

It is also this film where Almodóvar makes his first explicit connection between the urban milieu and moral categories, supplying us with a framework for understanding the rewriting of "celestial power" by his Humbled Redeemers. "Jesus didn't die on the cross to save saints," Sister Julieta tells Yolanda, "but to redeem sinners. . . . Soon, this house will be filled with murderers, drug addicts and prostitutes, just like in earlier times."

The principles of the religion Julieta preaches are both egalitarian and sexually liberating. On one hand, the Humbled Redeemers appear to be recuperating Catholicism's tradition of ministering to the humble and weak, while on the other, their contacts with urban life inevitably lead each of the women to realize her own inner desires. The patron saints of this religion, according to Almodóvar, are as much Jean Genet as St. John Bosco, the founder of hospices for abandoned youths.[16] Speaking of the portrayal of religion in the film, the director says:

In *Dark Habits* the important thing is the absence of religion, or rather religion understood from another point of view, with another subject and another object. That is to say, religious sentiments are provoked by something other than God. Religion is the language that human beings have invented for themselves to connect with something superior and that language contains a series of religious rituals that pass for piety. The paradox of the film is that these nuns have a religion, but not a religion inspired in God.[17]

In Almodóvar's next work, *What Have I Done to Deserve This?* (*¿Qué he hecho yo para merecer esto?*, 1984), the identification of Madrid with the liberation of the female and the attendant revision of the moral order becomes even more pronounced. Inspired in some measure by the melodramatic formulas of Italian neorealism, particularly the films of Roberto Rossellini, Cesare Zavattini, and Vittorio de Sica,[18] *What Have I Done?* is set in the recognizable working-class *barrio de la Concepción*, a neighborhood of high-rise cheap housing built in the sixties as a demonstration of Franco's modernization of living conditions in Spain. The film's setting foregrounds its neorealist intertext, suggesting to some critics an update of the opposition cinema of Bardem, Luis Berlanga, and Marco Ferreri, which also drew heavily on Italian neorealism.

That historical intertext is continually paired, however, with the obvious evidence of a dystopian present tense. Almodóvar says of his development of the film's exteriors: "The few times that we moved outside for exteriors it had to be like *Blade Runner*, with that atmosphere of an uncomfortable future that novels always tell us about, that continuous, disagreeable spitting of bad weather. But also that gothic enormity of *Blade Runner*."[19] Indeed, the frequent shots of the urban expressway vividly establish the image of modern-day Madrid as a European cognate of Los Angeles and therefore the anti-image of Francoist Spain.

Through the destinies of its two central female characters, *What Have I Done?* textualizes that cultural duality of a city hovering between a wretched past and an even more depressing future. Gloria (Carmen Maura) and her mother-in-law (Chus Lampreave) have come from the same provincial village, but the older woman cannot tolerate the city and longs to return to the provinces, while, as Gloria's family dissolves around her, she comes to understand that the city is precisely her destiny. In a certain respect, Madrid shapes and directs this duality, for it is both the place that symbolizes the schism between the old and the new, and the cultural agency of the changes that will eventually liberate Gloria.

Visually debunking the Francoist dream of high-rise modernity, the narrative also attacks the Francoist myth of the ideal Spanish family. The key to Gloria's eventual deliverance from social, sexual, and emotional imprisonment lies precisely in her extricating herself from the family, which she does by accidentally killing her brutish husband during an argument. Near the end of the film, in a moment of defiance, she admits her guilt to the detective investigating the murder, but he takes her confession to be an emotional outburst occasioned by the shock of the murder. In this way, *What Have I Done?* constructs a parable around the liberating force of the city: the family, the cultural institution that traditionally has replicated Francoist ideology on the individual level, has been shattered by the city, and the father has conveniently been eliminated. With the valorizing glance of the law, however, Gloria, the embodiment of a different kind of Spanish mother, is able to free herself from the tyranny of the old patriarchy and reconstitute the Spanish family anew with her homosexual son, Miguel, while her older son, Toni, returns with his grandmother to the provinces. The film's final reconciliation between Gloria and her gay son underscores the persistent bonding of female and gay characters throughout Almodóvar's cinema as they each recognize the city as the place of liberation from the tyrannical sexual and social codes of the patriarchy.

The identification of individual destiny with locale is foregrounded in a number of scenes in the film. One of the most pointed of these is a cinematic self-reference. Gloria's mother-in-law takes Toni to the movies to see Elia Kazan's *Splendor in the Grass.* We see the two sitting in the darkened theater as they watch the key moment when Warren Beatty tells his father that he doesn't want to go to college but, instead, prefers to run the family farm. The film-within-the-film is obviously used to prefigure part of the denouement of *What Have I Done?* as Toni and his grandmother return to their village. But on a broader, self-referential level, the use of the film-within-the-film device suggests the power of the cinematic medium, including the Almodóvar film we are viewing, to enunciate individual and collective desires.[20]

What Have I Done to Deserve This? crystallizes the multiplicity of opposing individual and collective desires that Madrid activates for Almodóvar's characters. The film uses urban space to establish a basic historical tension that, as John Hopewell observed of a later Almodóvar film, is "not a distance from the past but a sensitivity to the legacy of the past."[21]

NEW MYTHOLOGIES FOR A NEW SPAIN

While Almodóvar's early films defined the city as the embodiment of generational self-affirmation and female liberation, his next three films—*Matador* (1986), *Law of Desire* (1987), and *Women on the Verge of a Nervous Breakdown* (1988)—mythify their protagonists in order to rewrite cultural identity within the matrix of a liberated and liberating Madrid.

This rewriting of the mythologies of Spain coincides with the cinematic reimaging of the city in progressively more sensuous and evocative colors. Before *Matador*, Almodóvar's films foregrounded the unattractiveness of Madrid. In fact, in *What Have I Done to Deserve This?*, his intention was precisely to capture that external ugliness that coincided with the internal tawdriness and claustrophobia of the heroine's world.[22] Visually, *Matador* reverses that *feoista* (uglifying) tendency by giving pictorial prominence to a more cosmopolitan urban imageability.[23]

Matador situates its action in a recognizable Madrid while again playing out the ideological scenarios of otherness through the development of two mother figures: Angel's mother, Berta (Julieta Serrano), a member of the conservative Catholic lay group Opus Dei, and Pilar (Chus Lampreave), the understanding and modern-thinking mother of Eva, a popular fashion model. As Almodóvar says, these women represent two notions of Spain.[24] Yet, rather than contenting himself with what by now is the cultural platitude of the "two Spains," he stands that hoary cliché on its head when, appearing in a brief cameo as a fashion designer, he is interviewed by a reporter who asks him why he has called his fashion show "Spain Divided." He answers, "Because this country has always been divided in two." When she pushes him for a clarification, he responds, "On one side, there are the envious; on the other, the intolerant . . . I'm on both sides."

Reducing ideological conflict to a fashion show,[25] Almodóvar seems to have resolved the age-old conflicts of national identity by suggesting simply that it's all a matter of changing fashion. But tellingly, the only model we ever see actually parade in this fashion show is Pilar, who walks from the dressing area to her seat, simulating the movements of a model. Indeed, she is the ideal maternal model of the new Spain, liberated from the deforming values of its intolerant past.

As the film's title suggests, *Matador* is centered on the popular images of the bullfighter. Instead of repeating trite stereotypes, however, the film reformulates the bullfighter clichés into a new Spanish myth, one in which passion and death are given a contemporary meaning. The plot focuses on a curious triangle. Diego Montes, a retired *torero*, relives the thrill of the bullring by committing a number of murders. One of the students in Diego's bullfighting class, Angel, wracked by a sense of personal guilt instilled in him by his religious mother, confesses to the crimes. Angel is defended by a female lawyer, María Cardenal, who happens to be a murderous nymphomaniac and ardent admirer of Angel's teacher, Diego. Diego and María eventually form the perfect couple and achieve their long-sought erotic pleasure by attempting joint suicide at the moment of orgasm.

Our initial view of Madrid is, tellingly, a highly mediated one. In the first narrative sequence after the credits, we see Antonio sitting in Diego's bullfighting class and fantasizing a scene obviously triggered by Diego's description of the proper manner for killing a bull. Antonio's reverie is visualized as the scene cuts to a plaza in the city where María is seen seducing a young man for what will be her own ritual of death in the afternoon. In this way, the stereotypical bullring image of Spanish cultural space is transformed into a space of seduction in which the female, not the male, is predator. This view subsequently gives way to the image of the new Spain as a chic fashion show, and finally ends with the reworking of the matador motif into the film's final image of the two murderous lovers, draped in a bullfighter's cape, in deadly embrace before the admiring eyes of the police inspector. This final pairing of Diego and María as the ideal erotic-murderous couple, along with their shared identity as *matadores*, suggests once again an intentional blurring of the traditional, rigid lines that defined male and female identities in the old Spain.[26]

Even more reflective of the cultural logic of the new order, particularly its reframing of traditional ethics and morality, are the secondary characters Angel and Inspector del Valle, the police detective investigating the rash of murders committed by Diego and María. Angel is the critical link between the moral order of the past and the ethical identity of post-Francoism. Having so deeply absorbed conservative Catholic dogma, he believes himself guilty of the murders committed by others. In a cinematic quotation of the mushroom-picking scene from Victor Erice's *Spirit of the Beehive* (*El espíritu de la colmena*, 1973), Almodóvar has Angel caution the gardener at Diego's house not to pick "bad," poisonous mushrooms. As in Erice's film, the act of distinguishing between "good" and "bad" mushrooms is a metaphoric expression of the political and social judgments that were the foundation of the Francoist ethic. Angel's mouthing of the Manichaean distinction works to reinforce his identity as a child of Francoism who is struggling to shake loose from the grip of the old order. His dubious confession leads Inspector del Valle to witness the new cultural ideal represented by Diego and María's ritual of passionate love and death.

This notion of transforming the old into the new is given an additional moral dimension in a key scene near the beginning of the film, in which Angel's mother forces him to go to confession. After mass, Angel approaches the priest, who tells him to wait a moment while he changes his vestments. In a perfectly matched cut to maintain continuity, we see Angel walk through the church with its excessive Catholic iconography, then open a door and enter what turns out to be a police station. He walks to the reception area and says to a receptionist, "I've come to confess." The radical juxtaposition of scenes constructed by this *faux raccord* crystallizes the equally radical transformation of morality and religion that has occurred in post-Franco Spain, where a new secular morality has displaced the old tyranny of the church.

Ironically, Angel's confession is delivered to the most improbable representative of the law, Inspector del Valle. As Almodóvar describes the del Valle character: "The detective is secretly in love with Angel. . . . This is a surprising kind of police detective, subtle, sensitive, ingenious, and well-dressed, qualities which one doesn't usually attribute to a Spanish police officer. But Spain has changed a lot, and I want to believe that so have its police officials."[27] Adding other crucial details to the conception of the detective, the director says, "He is more of a criminologist than a policeman. Justice doesn't interest him and he lacks any sense of morality."[28] Out of such a character, who outwardly embodies the forms of continuity with the past but inwardly disavows its stern judgmental posturings, *Matador* seeks to rewrite the mythologies of Spanish cultural identity.

In Almodóvar's next film, *Law of Desire*, Madrid once again shapes a tale about characters who, like del Valle, embody the shifting value system that has transformed the cultural fabric of Spanish society. Almodóvar's vision of the city by night in *Law of Desire*[29] implicitly imparts a libidinous connotation to much of the action (Plate 15). Urban space pointedly serves as a frame for a continuous erotic spectacle that the filmic narrative persistently chronicles. Speaking of the film's mise-en-scène, which reveals a number of buildings and plazas in the city that are under renovation (including Tina's apartment building, the site of the film's final image), the director further notes: "Madrid is an old and an experienced city, but full of life. . . . Its restoration, which seems interminable, represents this city's desire to live. Like my characters, Madrid is a spent place for which it isn't enough just to have a past because the future keeps on exciting it."[30]

Perhaps the most explicit marker of this erotic textualizing of the city comes in the scene on a street at night, near Tina's apartment, when she asks a sanitation worker to hose her down, with all the erotic visual symbolism that action implies. The onscreen audience of the transsexual's erotic spectacle are Tina's gay brother, Pablo, a popular filmmaker, and her young ward, Ada, the daughter of her former lesbian lover. In other words, the performer and audience of this erotic spectacle foreground the identification of the city as the place of a persistent breakdown of the traditional categories of sexual identity in Spanish society. That meaning is overdetermined by the centering of the scene on the transsexual's body as it signifies the dramatic collapse of sexual difference: male/female; gay/lesbian, heterosexual/homosexual. As we watch Tina's ecstatic response to the thrust of water on her body, we unconsciously bear witness to the power of the city as the agency of the individual's release from the constraints of the social suppression of body and mind.

Marsha Kinder notes the similarity between the hosing scene and the precredit sequence of *Law of Desire* in which a young man is auditioning for Pablo's gay porno film, *The Mussel's Paradigm*. The actor's delivery of the script line, "Fóllame, fóllame!" ("Fuck me, fuck me!") will later be echoed in Tina's words to the sanitation worker, "Riégueme riégueme!" ("Hose me, hose me!").[31] That textual similarity retrospectively establishes the film's underlying equation between the urban mise-en-scène and the cinematic institution, that is, between social praxis and cinematic praxis. In both, scopic energies, previously institutionalized by social conventions, are rechanneled through erotic rituals of the body that effectively undermine the viewer's socially constructed responses. The two prompters who serve as the onscreen audience of the audition momentarily lose themselves and discover, as Almodóvar says, "their relation to their own erotic desire."[32] In the same way, the scene of Tina's sensuous release and abandon before her staged audience suggests that the spectacle triggers in those who view it a liberating sense of abandon from socially controlled responses to the city.

Almodóvar recognizes the implicit "sexual danger" in the film's opening scene.[33] That danger is rooted in the historically repressive notions of sexuality as defined by authoritarian society. The underlying textual desire that appears to inform *Law of Desire* is one that seduces the viewing subject, as in both of those scenes of erotic spectacle, and engages that subject in the process of breaking down the differences related to sexuality as part of a more expansive revision of his or her identity within a social community.

This effort to subvert the power of traditional categories of sexual difference is part of the larger project of *Law of Desire*, the rewriting of the mythology of the city around the liberation of desires. The film's action centers on the intricate sexual complications in the life of a successful screenwriter and director, Pablo Quintero. Pablo tries literally to "write" the desires of his lover, Juan, by sending him a letter that he wants Juan to mail back to him. The letter is eventually read and misinterpreted by Antonio, the third member of the film's love triangle. For his part, Antonio wants Pablo to write him letters signed with a woman's name to cover up the true nature of their gay love affair. These intricate narrative twists serve to deemphasize the fact of gay love as a social issue in the fictional world and to define the film's center of gravity as the struggle of individuals to achieve their own desires.

The final sequence of *Law of Desire* connects these questions of personal desire with the shaping of the larger community's desire by staging the realization of Pablo and Antonio's final union as a "public" event that self-consciously constructs as its audience a community that did not exist previously. Individual desire as it operates in that final scene works as a magnet, bringing together members of the community and thereby setting in motion a series of collective desires that function as resistances to the traditional patterns of Spanish societal order, such as those conventionally represented by the police and the church.

The focus on religious iconography in the final sequence of *Law of Desire* is linked to earlier actions by Tina and her young ward, Ada. When Tina reencounters Father Constantino, the priest who had seduced her as a child, he shuns her, telling her to find God in another house. "God is everywhere," he says. So Tina builds a chapel in her apartment, a pagan altar with the kitsch paraphernalia of contemporary pop culture, mixing popular religion with the adoration of movie stars. "The altar is the symbol of a pagan religion," one critic has noted. "It serves to ask for things. The Virgin Ada adopts is like the fairy godmother of a children's story who grants the protagonist three wishes. Ada asks this Virgin to help Tina land the job in Pablo's new play; to have Pablo return after he and Tina have had an argument; finally, to have Pablo resuscitate after Tina has announced that he has died."[34]

Tina describes Father Constantino as one of the two men she ever loved, the other being her father. In her chance meeting with the priest, she introduces Ada as her daughter. As the film progresses, it becomes increasingly apparent that Tina associates the concepts of religion and family with the episodes from her youth related to seduction and abandonment by her two "fathers." Her actions in the present are efforts to reconstitute both family and religion in terms that will construct for her a utopian world. Indeed, the trajectory of *Law of Desire* appears to be centered precisely on the figure of Tina as the embodiment of Almodóvar's thesis of the contemporary Spaniard being dissatisfied with the past and therefore constructing a new one. The key to Tina's identity is inextricably tied to the destiny of the city as the site of transformation of traditional patriarchal values into a new cultural order as emblemized in the film's final scene of "adoration."

In *Women on the Verge of a Nervous Breakdown (Mujeres al borde de un ataque de nervios,* 1988), the spectacle of the city is once more identified with the project of rewriting cultural mythology for the Spaniard. The film again focuses intensely on the status of women, this time, however, in the context of a society that, from all perspectives, has already

undergone radical transformaticn, yet in which the female is still emotionally tied to the archaic phallocentric order.

Religion and history are figured in a prominent discursive move that
addresses the spectator at the film's beginning. Pepa speaks the film's
opening lines in a voice-over as the screen reveals a close-up of an improvised farmyard showing chickens in a caged area on what will soon
be identified as the terrace of her Madrid apartment:[35] "It had been
months since I moved into this penthouse with Iván. The world was
drowning around me. I felt like Noah; I wanted to save myself and the
world." The explicit biblical intertext invites us to read the ensuing action
as the narrative of a new social and moral order authored by the female
and constituting a rewriting of the relations of domination between men
and women in Spanish society.

Pepa's struggle to locate the womanizing Iván to inform him of her
pregnancy serves as the starting point of an intricate chain of narrative
moves that organizes the film's plot. Significantly, Pepa is continually
identified with places in the city (her penthouse apartment, the various
locales she goes to in search of the elusive Iván), and is further characterized as an outwardly mobile woman. As the action progresses, it becomes increasingly apparent that her mobility is merely the illusion of
freedom as long as she is emotionally tied to Iván. The symbol of the
female's false liberation is embodied in the person of Paulina Morales,
the feminist lawyer who is indifferent to the plight of women and, as it
turns out, is Iván's latest conquest. Like the city with whose destiny she
is intimately identified, Pepa needs to achieve more than the outward
trappings of liberation; she needs an inner spiritual emancipation.

After the use of urban settings as the mise-en-scène of a more expansive
scenario of the nation in *Matador* and *Law of Desire*, *Women on the
Verge* appears at first to be caught up in a very localist vision of Madrid,
marked by the continuing narrative device of situating actions at specific
street addresses in the city (Almagro 38, Montalbán 7, Castellana 34). But
such details only reinforce the notion that the character, despite her outward liberation, is still confined within the recognizable spaces of the old
city. As the film suggests, Pepa's full liberation will come only from a self-
distancing from patriarchal traps. That distancing is ironically embodied
in the space of Pepa's penthouse, a space that situates her far above the
city and provides her with an idealized view of the Madrid skyline.

In reality, such a view does not exist. Almodóvar has simply constructed
a studio set that invents a fantasized Madrid skyline to prefigure the eventual fulfillment of Pepa's desires. From its initial appearance as a view
from Pepa's terrace, this idealized Madrid flaunts its artifice,[36] recalling
the cinematic constructions of highly legible New York and Paris cityscapes as the backdrops to fantasized cultural scenarios in American films.

Indeed, the strategy of *Women on the Verge* is to use such artifices to lead Pepa to her own self-distanced lucidity.

In that context, the use of cinematic self-reference becomes a critical move. When Pepa sits on a bench across the street from Iván's apartment, she sees a female dancer rehearsing in an apartment on the first floor. She then notices a young man pining on a terrace on one of the upper floors. The scene recalls details of Hitchcock's urban thriller *Rear Window*, and pointedly places Pepa in the androgynous role that merges the functions of the James Stewart and Grace Kelly characters. That is to say, she is able to view the problems of romantic coupling at a distance, as the Stewart character does, and, by virtue of a mobility identified with the Kelly character, can effect the changes that are denied the Stewart character throughout Hitchcock's film.

A more ostentatious cinematic self-reference is presented in the narrative device of having Pepa and Iván working as dubbers involved in voicing the lines from the famous "Tell me lies" dialogue of Nicholas Ray's *Johnny Guitar*. Once again cinema self-consciously writes the heroine's destiny, as it did in *Matador*. Foregrounding the cynical identity of Joan Crawford's forceful character, Vienna, Pepa speaks the lines that perfectly prefigure her own eventual disengagement from her sentimental entrapment in a masochistic relationship with the egotistical and deceitful Iván (Plate 18).

The narrative follows the heroine's emotional itinerary from dependency upon the male, expressed in the opening scenes in her apartment, through the various locations in the city, back to that apartment, where, after definitively breaking with Iván, she is able to announce her pregnancy without concern for the father. With the "Annunciation" of a new generation, presumably one that is unfettered by the archaic patriarchy, Pepa will effectively assume the position of matriarch for the new city and the new cultural order. In one of the last lines of the film, she claims she is not going to sublet her apartment because she "loves the view."

LAW AND DESIRE

As the denouement of *Women on the Verge* suggests, the city in Almodóvar's films is increasingly aligned with the imaging of a new moral order. The surface impression of a hedonistic world of immediate sensual gratification that was at the heart of the early films has gradually ceded to a fairly constant framing of actions within a more tolerant moral system. This new moral matrix serves to center a group of characters who, within the culture of the dictatorship and in the immediate post-Franco period, were viewed as marginal types.

The increasing focus on characters who represent "earthly power," as Almodóvar calls the law and the police, becomes a parallel to what we have already noted as the reordering of celestial power (the church) implied by this new matrix. In *Pepi, Luci, Bom*, for instance, the narrative is set in motion by the heroine's desire for elaborate revenge against the police detective who had raped her. In *Dark Habits*, Sor Estiércol (Sister Manure) declares, "the police are the natural enemies of nuns," suggesting that the progressive, liberating activities of the Humbled Redeemers are in direct opposition to the repressive tactics of the law.

The characterization of the police begins to undergo a transformation in *What Have I Done?*, where Polo, an impotent police detective who keeps crossing Gloria's path, turns out to be the onscreen witness and authenticator of the heroine's actions. Near the film's end, when Polo dismisses Gloria's confession of murder as merely an emotional outburst, the law seems to valorize her spiritual and social rebirth in the city, and to help reconstitute the family around a new matriarchy.

A somewhat similar dramatization of the valorizing glance of the law occurs at the end of *Matador*. After a prolonged car chase, the police finally arrive at María's country home and view the bodies of the two murderous lovers lying naked on the floor in rapturous embrace. Inspector del Valle speaks the last line of the film as if expressing the community's approval of sexual excess: "I've never seen anyone so happy!"

Law of Desire contains two distinct expressions of this valorizing process by representatives of the law. When Pablo arrives at the village where his lover, Juan, has been murdered, a young member of the Guardia Civil identifies himself as a childhood friend of Juan's. He tells Pablo he knows that Juan really loved him. This gentle characterization of what has been traditionally one of the most repressive and feared of Spanish institutions of authority suggests the changing spirit of the time. A more sustained narrative focus on the law as an agency of toleration comes toward the end of the film with the appearance of the father and son investigators who pester Pablo and Tina in an effort to solve Juan's murder. No longer menacing, they appear to be parodies of the hard-boiled urban detective of American genre films, particularly when the father advises his son: "In order to be successful in this profession, you need to be more than unscrupulous; you need to have a sense of humor." That "sense of humor" also prescribes a distance for the spectator, a way of seeing without the authoritarian impulse to judge and condemn that for so long ordered Francoist society.

That is the logic of the constant appearance of the guardians of social morality in Almodóvar's films. Like the detectives and police congregating on the street below Tina's apartment, where Pablo and Antonio experience their final hour of love, these officials become the audience that authorizes the new moral order of post-Francoist Spain. In positioning the law to witness and valorize murder, gay love, or any of the other countless acts that defy the "earthly" and "celestial" powers of the old

Spain, Almodóvar's cinema continues to engage its audience in the project of imaging Spain's present by rewriting the social and moral logic of its past.

NOTES

1. The American filmic influences on Almodóvar's development are abundant. The most often noted are Billy Wilder comedies and the films of Alfred Hitchcock. In terms of the depictions of the narratives of families in urban space, Almodóvar cites the examples of Francis Ford Coppola's *Cotton Club* and *Rumble Fish*. See Nuria Vidal, *El cine de Pedro Almodóvar* (Barcelona: Destinolibro, 1988), 225–226.

2. To one interviewer Almodóvar observed, "I think that since Franco died, new generations have come to the fore that are unrelated to the 'progressive' generations that appeared during the last years of the dictatorship. How do people twenty-one years old live in Madrid? It's quite complex." Peter Besas, *Behind the Spanish Lens* (Denver: Arden Press, 1985), 216.

3. For an insightful discussion of the political and sexual agendas in post–Civil War Madrid, see Carmen Martín Gaite, *Usos amorosos de la postguerra española* (Barcelona: Editorial Anagrama, 1987), 93–96.

4. John Hopewell sees in the insistent location shooting of recent Spanish films in and around Madrid—that is, in "the symbolic heartland of the Francoist state"—the stabilization of symbolic and allegorical readings of national culture. See John Hopewell, *Out of the Past: Spanish Cinema After Franco* (London: British Film Institute, 1986), 72.

5. Marsha Kinder, "Pleasure and the New Spanish Mentality: A Conversation with Pedro Almodóvar," *Film Quarterly* 41. 1 (Fall 1987): 40.

6. Michel Foucault, *Language, Counter-Memory, Practice*, trans. Donald F. Bouchard and Sherry Simon (Ithaca, N.Y.: Cornell University Press, 1977), 154.

7. Foucault, 155.

8. Linda Hutcheon, *A Poetics of Postmodernism: History, Theory, Fiction* (New York: Routledge, 1988), 35.

9. Hutcheon, 36.

10. Kinder, 37.

11. Vidal, 15, 41–42. See also Miguel Albaladejo, Mario Arias, and José A. Hergueta, "Conversación con Pedro Almodóvar," in their *Los fantasmas del deseo*, ed. Miguel Albaladejo et al. (Madrid: Aula 7, 1988), 46; and María Antonia García de León and Teresa Maldonado, *Pedro Almodóvar, la otra España cañi* (Ciudad Real: Biblioteca de Autores y Temas Manchegos, 1989), 55–56.

12. Vidal, 42.

13. Hutcheon, 61.

14. Besas, 216.

15. Vidal, 75.

16. Vidal, 72.

17. Vidal, 68–69.

18. Kinder, 38.

19. Albaladejo et al., 47.

20. Speaking of a similar film-within-the-film scene in *Matador*, Almodóvar says that when the ex-bullfighter and the lawyer go into a Madrid movie theater to see *Duel in the Sun*, "they look at the screen and they see their future. . . . When you go to the cinema, the cinema reflects not your life but your end." (Kinder, 41).

21. Hopewell, 240.

22. Vidal, 168.

23. Vidal, 168–169.

24. Vidal, 177.

25. In the press book for *Matador*, Almodóvar flippantly claimed that he made the film to show that you could dress as well in Spain as anywhere else. He would later say of the "thesis" of *Matador*: "I wanted everyone to be beautiful, tall and spectacular, as if, amidst those ruins [of the city], human beings had . . . acquired a kind of physical splendor" (Albaladejo et al., 46).

26. Teresa Maldonado has suggested that the union of the male and female *matadores* is an intentional mark of sexual ambiguity in the film, inspired by the type of weakening of traditional identities that was the centerpiece of *Some Like It Hot*, by one of Almodóvar's favorite directors, Billy Wilder. See García de León and Maldonado, 195.

27. From the press book for *Matador*.

28. Pedro Almodóvar, "Los directors cuentan su película: *Matador*," *Fotogramas*, March 1986, 7.

29. Vidal, 194.

30. Vidal, 205.

31. Kinder, 40.

32. Vidal, 209.

33. Vidal, 208.

34. Vidal, 308–309.

35. The image of the hens appears to be an homage to Buñuel's *Los olvidados*, which, like *Women*, plays with melodramatic tropes. Following the religious motif of Buñuel's film, Pepa later says to herself: "I'm tired of being good." Her line is a parody of the line in *Los olvidados* spoken by Pedro, the young hero of the film: "I want to be good but I don't know how." *Women*, in effect, will be a rewriting of the bourgeois and phallocentric system of morality that marginalized Buñuel's characters and comes increasingly to be seen as the snare for Almodóvar's heroines.

36. Albaladejo et al., 46.

From Matricide to Mother Love in Almodóvar's *High Heels*

Marsha Kinder

When I interviewed Almodóvar in 1987, I asked him why in Spanish oed-ipal narratives the erotic desire for the mother is frequently redirected toward the father and the patricidal impulse displaced onto the mother. After first claiming he didn't know, he then went on to describe a forth-coming film project called *Tacones lejanos* (*Distant Heels*). He said it was about two sisters from the south of Spain who run away from home because their Bernarda Alba-type mother frightens them by prophesying they will be guilty of destroying the world. Once they flee to Madrid, their parents perish in a fire. And once they become women, whenever they have sex, their mother's ghost appears, which drives the sisters crazy. Finally, they have a duel with their mother's ghost and, after killing her, discover that she was really alive and only pretending to be a ghost. So they inadvertently commit matricide. But, consistent with the surrealists' hatred of the patriarchal mother, Almodóvar claimed that "the mother's behavior is actually more murderous than that of the girls." He explained:

The idea of motherhood is very important in Spain. The father was frequently absent in Spain. It's as if the mother represents the law, the police. . . . When you kill the mother, you kill precisely everything you hate, all of those burdens that hang over you. In this film, I'm killing all of my education and all of the intol-erance that is sick in Spain. . . . It's like killing the power.[1]

When I finally saw *Tacones lejanos* four years later, at a screening at the Directors Guild in Los Angeles (with Almodóvar and two of his stars in attendance), I reminded him of our earlier conversation in Madrid and asked him how an outrageous story of matricide had been converted into an equally outrageous melodrama about mother love. He claimed that he had only "borrowed" the title from that other project, which remained undone.

Yet clearly there was more to it than that, for he had also turned that inverted oedipal narrative inside out. The subversive goal was no longer to destroy the maternal, but rather to marshal melodrama's full arsenal of emotional excess in order to eroticize and empower it for those traditionally marginalized under patriarchy—or, in other words, to liberate the maternal from the dreaded image of the repressive patriarchal mother, which frequently haunts Almodóvar movies.

Tacones lejanos (literally *Distant Heels*, but retitled *High Heels* in English) is still a story about a passionate daughter (now a TV news broadcaster named Rebecca, brilliantly played by Victoria Abril) who is haunted by a powerful mother (played equally brilliantly by Marisa Paredes) (Plate 22). The matriarch is no longer a repressive Bernarda Alba, but an aging, promiscuous pop singer named Becky Del Paramo (a name evoking the windy moors of *Wuthering Heights*), with whom the androgynous daughter is erotically obsessed and for whose love she jealously kills two patriarchs—her stepfather and her husband, Manuel (the owner of a TV network and her mother's former lover). As if working her way toward phallic empowerment, Rebecca uses sleeping pills in the first murder (a weapon frequently associated with women) and her husband's little snubbed-nose gun in the second. As in the original matricidal story of *High Heels*, the murderous daughter (a conflation of the two sisters) is sympathetic, but this time, so is the mother—despite her narcissicism and adultery. When Becky learns that her daughter has committed these two murders, she comically advises her in a warm, motherly tone, "You need to find another way of solving your problems with men," and then adds, as if to counter any lingering phallocentric assumption, "You need to choose your weapons more carefully." Finally, like Mildred Pierce, she's willing to take the rap. But neither of these crimes is punished or condemned.

The fact that Becky sleeps with her daughter's husband hardly raises an eyebrow, especially since the daughter has chosen to marry Manuel (Fedor Atkine) precisely because he had been her mother's lover. This marriage enables her finally to best her mother in the traditional female rivalry and also to replay the murderous oedipal drama that is represented in the film's prologue (where a freckled little Rebecca kills her stepfather after he tried to sell her into white slavery to swarthy natives in the islands).

Apparently, René Girard's thesis (which foregrounds the homoerotic backstory of the Oedipus myth) also applies to the oedipal heroine—namely, that it is the homoerotic desire to love/imitate/become the parent of the same sex (in this case, the mother) rather than the heterosexual desire for the other (in this case, the father) that really drives the oedipal narrative.[2] In *The Acoustic Mirror: The Female Voice in Psychoanalysis and Cinema*, Kaja Silverman argues that this "negative Oedipus complex" is essential to feminism because it "make[s] it possible to speak for the first time about a genuinely oppositional desire which challenges dominance from within representation and meaning, rather than from the place of a mutely resistant biology or sexual 'essence.' "[3] In other words, it allows the daughter to voice her love for the mother, as is clearly the case in powerful feminist oedipal narratives like Helma Sanders-Brahms's *Deutschland, bleiche Mutter* (*Germany, Pale Mother*; 1980) and Chantal Akerman's *Les rendezvous d'Anna* (*The Meetings of Anna*; 1979). In contrast to Almodóvar's previous homoerotic variations on the oedipal narrative (such as *La ley del deseo*), *High Heels* (like many subversive feminist texts) boldly proclaims that mother love lies at the heart of all melodrama and its erotic excesses, for it is a passion with primal appeal to all genders and sexual persuasions. As Almodóvar puts it in the press kit, "*High Heels* would be nothing without the powerful virtuosity of Marisa Paredes and Victoria Abril. For me, the greatest spectacle of the film . . . is watching these two animals confronting each other. The magnitude of their talent is contagious and impregnates every scene in which they appear." Therefore, the rebellious patricidal impulse must be redirected toward the father, who remains a mere pawn or minor obstacle in the women's game. As Almodóvar quipped in the 1987 interview: "Fathers are not very present in my films. I don't know why. . . . This is something I just feel. When I'm writing about relatives, I just put in mothers."[4]

As in other Almodóvar films, although the patriarchs are soon dispatched, the police endure to the bittersweet end. *High Heels* also adopts the mother/police dyad that Almodóvar mentioned in the 1987 interview. But, instead of making the police a patriarchal mother like Bernarda Alba, Almodóvar creates a maternal police detective frequently referred to as "the Judge" and who doubles as a female impersonator called Femme Letal (Plate 23). With this false persona, he specializes in impersonating Rebecca's mother on stage and also succeeds in impregnating Rebecca in his dressing room. As if that weren't sufficiently confusing, this protean figure masquerades as a drug dealer and other informants fabricated for his various police investigations. Given this endless chain of impersonations, even his role of detective becomes suspect—especially since he wears a false beard and appears to be a mild-mannered young bachelor named Eduardo Dominguez living with his bedridden mother who imagines she has AIDS (as if she believes it is the modern version of the Theban plague), and with no father in sight. His perpetual slippage of identity is heightened by the casting of Miguel Bosé, a well-known Spanish pop singer and sexual icon. Clearly, Bosé's symbolic function in the oedipal narrative is not to be a seductive or castrating patriarch like Laius or Creon but rather an androgynous hybrid like the mysterious Sphinx or the protean seer Tiresias who both poses and solves the narrative enigmas. Yet instead of being an obstacle to the oedipal hero or testifying to his guilt, this investigator falls in love with the oedipal heroine and insists on her innocence under patriarchy, even when he discovers that she deliberately murdered her husband and father.

After tracing Almodóvar's representations of policemen from the odious villain in his debut feature, *Pepi, Luci, Bom y otras chicas del montón* (*Pepi, Luci, Bom and Other Ordinary Girls*, 1980) to the sympathetic spectators in the closing scene of *La ley del deseo*, Marvin D'Lugo concludes that he positions the law "to witness and valorize murder, gay love," and other acts that defy the old Spain. He claims, "The characterization of the police begins to undergo a transformation in *What Have I Done?* where Polo, an impotent police detective who keeps crossing Gloria's path, turns out to be the on-screen witness and authenticator of the heroine's actions."[5] It obviously reaches a new stage of inversion in *High Heels*, where the glamorous androgynous hero is a cop and where virtually all policemen are tenderhearted souls who identify with those marginalized under patriarchy. In this way, Almodóvar subverts dominant ideology by realigning the center with the marginal.

Along with the title, the film version of *High Heels* retains the central importance of the audio fetish, which is grafted over the traditional visual fetish of the woman's shoe. Even though its reverberations are somewhat diminished in the translation from the Spanish title "Distant Heels" to the English "High Heels," the audio fetish dominates the primal scene. In 1987, Almodóvar said:

I remember when I was a child, it was a symbol of freedom for young girls to wear high heels, to smoke and to wear trousers. And these two girls are wearing heels all the time. After running away, the two sisters live together, and the older remembers that she couldn't sleep until the moment that she heard the sound of distant heels coming from the corridor.[6]

In the film, this memory is eroticized and attributed to Rebecca. It is also paired with a primal tale of poverty (evocative of vintage maternal melodramas like *Stella Dallas*) told by her mother, Becky, who replaces the missing sister. As an impoverished child of janitors, Becky watched the well-heeled feet of bourgeois passersby, which could be seen through the window of her humble basement flat, a space that she nostalgically reappropriates, redecorates, and reoccupies (just as her daughter compulsively replays the murderous oedipal narrative). In the passionate scene in the family basement where Rebecca describes her aural memory to her mother (like a lover confessing her love), we actually witness how the daughter's primal story appropriates the fetishized visual images from her mother's earlier memories, which are still visible through the basement window in the background but which now acquire new erotic associations with mother love.

The power of the audio fetish is also strengthened by giving both daughter and mother oracular professions that rely on their voice and by implying that their speech is connected with their status as sexual subjects pursuing their own desire. Both use the airwaves, ordinarily controlled by the patriarchy, to address their passion to a privileged female listener. In one hilarious scene, Rebecca nervously flubs the news, giggling at disasters, because she thinks her mother may be listening; clearly, it is her mother who is both Model and Other, the privileged spectator for whose loving gaze and sympathetic ear she always yearns. Yet the TV network and its hardware are owned by her husband, Manuel, who has hired both her and his current "bimbo," Isabel (Miriam Díaz Aroca), to do the evening news. Rebecca succeeds in dismantling his power over the airwaves by murdering him and by using his medium to broadcast her "live" confession nationwide. Conversely, her more conventional rival, Isabel, who had sex with Manuel shortly before he was murdered, is forced into silence: she stands by Rebecca, signing the news for deaf viewers, fearful that her impersonation of a deaf-mute will be misread as the real thing and that the murder confession will be taken as her own.

Almodóvar claims that Rebecca's TV confession was the germinal idea for (what he calls) this "tough melodrama," as well as its "emotional high-point":

Television is a medium I hate but what Rebecca does on the news program is something I've dreamed about a lot: after reading the news of a death, the presenter confesses that she is the culprit and gives all the details with complete naturalness. But the real key to the scene is what follows . . . she goes on to show the news audience an envelope of ordinary looking photos, explaining that after the murder she photographed all the objects she shared in common with the victim, punishing herself with the terrible awareness that, from now on, their only meaning would be as memories.[7]

She turns these frozen photographic images into fetishistic substitutes for her dead husband (a strategy of the masochistic aesthetic, at least, according to Gilles Deleuze), who proves to be merely a secondary fetish for mother love.

The voice of sexuality is strongest in Becky, whose masochistic torch songs (actually performed by Luz Casal) are primarily addressed to her tormented daughter. This is particularly true when she dedicates the heart-wrenching "Think of Me" to Rebecca, who is temporarily in prison for the murder of her husband. Rebecca is so disturbed by this song that she tries to buy the radio (the patriarchal apparatus on which it is being transmitted) so she can turn off its erotic force. Not only are these musical numbers particularly appropriate to the romantic excesses of melodrama (as Thomas Elsaesser and Geoffrey Nowell Smith have persuasively argued),[8] but they are also resonant in the context of the new feminist theorization of sound, particularly in the work of Silverman and Amy Lawrence, who have emphasized the importance of the maternal voice in subject formation.

The mother . . . is traditionally . . . the one who first organizes the world linguistically for the child, and first presents it to the Other. The maternal voice also plays a crucial part during the mirror stage, defining and interpreting the reflected image, and "fitting" it to the child. Finally it provides the acoustic mirror in which the child first hears "itself." The maternal voice is thus complexly bound up in that drama which "decisively projects the formation of the individual into history," and whose "internal thrust is precipitated from insufficiency to anticipation." Indeed, it would seem to be the maternal rather than the paternal voice that initially constitutes the auditory sphere for most children, although it is clearly the latter which comes to predominate within the superego.[9]

Thus, the women's subversion of the patriarchy (what Almodóvar calls in the press kit "act[ing] behind the back of the law of man and that of God") is achieved primarily by fetishizing the maternal voice, which is amplified through media transmission and hardware as well as through dubbing and impersonation. In this way, it succeeds in replacing the unspoken Name-of-the-Father and the hollow voice of God.

The subversive potential of the maternal voice under patriarchy becomes most compelling in two brilliant comic scenes where the gender of the maternal performer is most ironically compromised through a dazzling chain of masquerades. In one scene, sexy transsexual actress Bibi Andersen leads an extravagant musical dance number in the women's prison yard. This statuesque beauty plays an "idealized" maternal lesbian who has broken into prison (by nearly killing a cop with a brick) so that she can protect her daughter-like lover. Thus (like Bosé) Bibi performs a triple impersonation—of a woman, a mother, and a criminal. It is a performance that mocks the symbolic order of the patriarchy and dissolves the boundaries between allegedly incompatible genders and genres (the women's prison picture and the musical). It also implies that the opposition between outlaw/lawman is as arbitrarily constructed and gendered as that between female/male and that the boundaries between both sets need to be transgressed as thoroughly as those between genres.

Although the genres hybridized in *High Heels* are limited primarily to the maternal realm of melodrama, the film's intertextuality is pointedly international. There is an explicit reference to *Autumn Sonata* when Rebecca tells her mother how much they resemble (Ingmar/Ingrid) Bergman's talented mother artist and her mediocre daughter. There are also parallels to Hollywood's celebrity versions of that genre like *Mommie Dearest* and *Postcards from the Edge*, and many implicit allusions to classical mother/daughter weepies like *Mildred Pierce, Imitation of Life*, and *Stella Dallas*, and to Hitchcock's latent lesbian thrillers *Marnie* and *Rebecca* (particularly through the doubling of the name for mother and daughter). There are even a few allusions to Spanish classics, like Juan de Orduña's popular musical melodrama *El último cuplé* (*The Last Song*, 1957), where an aging popular singer makes a comeback and collapses on stage in midsong, and Edgar Neville's *El crimen de la calle de Bordadores* (*Crime on Bordadores Street*, 1946), where the mother similarly saves the daughter she once abandoned by falsely confessing to a murder on her deathbed. And, of course, there are echoes of earlier Almodóvar hits, like *Entre tinieblas* (*Dark Habits*, 1983), where extravagant Mexican boleros are similarly used to fetishize an erotic passion between two women—a torch singer doing Gilda and a smitten Mother Superior—or *¿Qué he hecho yo para merecer esto?* (*What Have I Done to Deserve This?*, 1984), where another woman who kills her husband is united in the end with an androgynous love (in this case, her homosexual son rather than the impotent cop whom she tries to fuck in the opening comic sex scene), or even *La ley del deseo* (*Law of Desire*, 1986), where Bibi Andersen plays not a model maternal lesbian (as in this musical interlude) but a bad mother lesbian model who (like Becky) runs off to a foreign country with a lover, leaving her daughter behind.

The other comic musical performance in *High Heels* is the most brilliant sequence in the film. It is the scene where Rebecca takes her mother and husband to the Club Villa Rosa to see Femme Letal do an impersonation of Becky. The chain of simulations is dazzling, for the impersonator is really a male pop star (Miguel Bosé) doing an impersonation of an ordinary man (Eduardo) doing an impersonation of a detective ("the Judge") doing an impersonation of a female impersonator (Letal) doing an impersonation of a female pop singer (Becky), who is there in the audience with her daughter, Rebecca, who has been impersonating her mother all her life. When the camera cuts to a reverse shot of the spectators, we see that Becky watches the performance with narcissistic fascination, Rebecca with erotic desire, and Manuel with hostility and contempt. Meanwhile, three anonymous "female" spectators sing along with Letal, imitating his every gesture and taking great pleasure in impersonating the impersonator.

Whenever we cut back to the transvestite, we notice that he is performing against a painted backdrop decorated with images of gypsies and matadors—the old *españolada* stereotype of Spain promoted for foreign consumption, which Almodóvar's postmodernist transsexuals have come to replace in the post-Franco era. This image takes on even greater irony when we recall that Bosé is the offspring of the famous union between Italian actress Lucia Bosé (the beautiful star of *Muerte de un ciclista* [*Death of a Cyclist*, 1955], which mocked that bullfighting stereotype) and Spanish matador Luis Miguel Dominguín (who embodied it), as well as the godson of Pablo Picasso (who helped popularize it worldwide). As in a palimpsest, one national stereotype (or generation or genre) is grafted over the other—just as the sound fetish is mapped over the visual fetish. This constant slippage of meaning evokes not only the endless chain of simulations that characterizes postmodernism but also the endless chain of substitutions and fetishization that characterizes primary process thinking.

After this dazzling performance, when Letal finally meets Becky, he proposes that they exchange mementos—her earrings (like the earrings made of horn that she had earlier given little Rebecca in the primal scene from the pretitles prologue) for one of his falsies. This exchange of fetishes reveals that their referents come from the mother's body, which is the point of origin for all fetishes—a revelation that contradicts the co-optive phallocentric theories of Freud and Lacan. Consistent with Georges Bataille's emphasis on exchange as fundamental to eroticism, this act empowers the extraordinary nonphallic sex scene between Femme Letal and Rebecca that immediately follows in his dressing room. It begins with a wild gymnastic form of cunnilingus (a sex act that could just as easily occur between two women) and ends with impregnation and a proper proposal of marriage (even though the petitioner is still partially in drag and the petitionee is already married). What is most remarkable about the encounter is that it is simultaneously very erotic and hysterically funny, a combination that is very difficult to achieve but that Almodóvar consistently masters.

It is this eroticized exchange, not only between two bodies but also between opposing genders and sexual orientations, conflicting tones and genres (screwball comedy, maternal melodrama, and softcore porn), that finally fulfills Rebecca's subversive dream of maternal plenitude, of becoming the powerful sexual mother she so ardently desires. By celebrating the love between mothers and daughters and giving new meaning to the epithet "Mommie Dearest," *High Heels* provides a new erotic fantasy for empowering a strategic alliance among straight women, lesbians, gay men, transvestites, transsexuals, and all other forms of nonpatriarchal androgynes. And it adds new maternal resonance to Almodóvar's ongoing project of making the "marginal" central to mainstream cinema, not only in Spain but worldwide.[10]

NOTES

1. Marsha Kinder, "Pleasure and the New Spanish Mentality: A Conversation with Pedro Almodóvar," *Film Quarterly* 41.1 (Fall 1987): 43.

2. René Girard, *Violence and the Sacred* (1972), trans. Patrick Gregory (Baltimore: Johns Hopkins University Press, 1977), see ch. 3.

3. Kaja Silverman, *The Acoustic Mirror: The Female Voice in Psychoanalysis and Cinema* (Bloomington: Indiana University Press, 1988), 124.

4. Kinder, 43.

5. Marvin D'Lugo, "Almodóvar's City of Desire," *Quarterly Review of Film and Video* 13.4 (1991): 63. This essay is also included in the present volume.

6. Kinder, 43.

7. Press kit for *High Heels*.

8. Thomas Elsaesser, "Tales of Sound and Fury: Observations on the Family Melodrama," and Geoffrey Nowell-Smith, "Minnelli and Melodrama," both in *Movies and Methods*, vol. 2, ed. Bill Nichols (Berkeley: University of California Press, 1985).

9. Silverman, 100. Also see Amy Lawrence, *Echo and Narcissus: Women's Voices in Classical Hollywood Cinema* (Berkeley: University of California Press, 1991).

10. See also my discussion of the film in *Blood Cinema: The Reconstruction of National Identity in Spain* (Berkeley: University of California Press, 1993), 250–262.

Almodóvar's Postmodern Cinema: A Work in Progress . . .

Víctor Fuentes

The tremendous success of Pedro Almodóvar in the eighties can be tied, in large part, to the emergence on the cultural and artistic scene of the postmodern generation. Born under the sign of heterotopia, into a world in which "everything has already been said," their lives and life-styles an endorsement of the attitude "anything goes," these young people opened the door to an unlimited pluralism regarding modes of life and creation.[1] Almodóvar's personal origins provide a paradigmatic example of one key phenomenon of these times, the displacement of the center by the margin or periphery. Leaving behind his birthplace in a small provincial town, and without benefit of professional training in film, he achieved a startling string of cinematic successes, both national and international, over the course of a decade: from *Pepi, Luci, Bom y otras chicas del montón* (*Pepi, Luci, Bom and Other Ordinary Girls*) in 1980 to *Mujeres al borde de un ataque de nervios* (*Women on the Verge of a Nervous Breakdown*) in 1988. Nevertheless, his most recent films appear to mark a halt in what had been the irresistible ascension of Pedro Almodóvar. After the virtually unanimous popular and critical acclaim that greeted *Women on the Verge*, the response to these latter films has seemed tepid in comparison.

Thus it would appear that the Almodóvar tide has reached its high-water mark. The apparently unlimited flood of his creative imagination has begun to ebb precisely at the moment when the doors of the world-wide film market have opened wide to welcome and distribute his films, a case without equal among Spanish directors, with the possible excep-

Translated by Kathleen M. Vernon and Barbara Morris.

tion of Luis Buñuel. How, then, to interpret the signs of this relative decline? Can it be attributed to a certain change of sensibility brought by the conflicts and crises of the nineties that has escaped Almodóvar? Has he surrendered to the temptation of fashion, to the logic of the market, and begun to repeat himself? Is it possible that the total artistic control he exercises as scriptwriter, director, and producer of his films, in the absence of outside critical mediation, has come to function not as a stimulus but as a restriction on his creative freedom?

These and similar questions indicate this as an appropriate point at which to evaluate Almodóvar's contribution, as a product and promoter of the postmodern condition, to Spanish as well as global cinema and culture. It is also the moment to consider the limitations inherent in the director's work, limitations that may also be those of some of the presuppositions most fundamental to the notion of postmodernity itself.

THE INFLUENCE OF THE LATIN AMERICAN "BOOM"

As virtually all the early interviews with the director note, in 1969 Almodóvar arrived in Madrid, where, as he tells us, he encountered "two big explosions in social and literary terms . . . on the one hand the hippie movement and on the other the boom in Latin American literature."[2] Indeed, much has been made about the extent to which the director's first forays into filmmaking—beginning in 1974 with a series of short films shot in Super-8 and culminating in 1982 with his second film, *Laberinto de pasiones (Labyrinth of Passions)*—represent a version of sixties American underground or counterculture as interpreted through Madrid's Rastro flea market. However, there has been no mention of another source, not as obvious but no less important: the writers of the "Boom" who gave back to Spanish-language narrative a love for telling stories, for the mixing of reality and fantasy, that originated with Cervantes. The young Manchegan director brings that same fascination with the power of the storyteller to the film screen. Scattered throughout his films are a series of homages to those writers whose works, Almodóvar tells us, dazzled him. Speaking of Jorge Luis Borges, he notes that the discovery of the writer "was sensational for me, although it probably doesn't show in my films."[3]

However, the lessons learned not only from Borges but also from Gabriel García Márquez, Julio Cortázar, Guillermo Cabrera Infante, Severo Sarduy, and Manuel Puig are in fact evident in his works. In Almodóvar's films, as in the writings of the "Boom" novelists, the opposition between fiction and reality, and high and low culture, is repeatedly violated. The Borgesian title "The Garden of Forking Paths" could serve as an emblem for the bifurcated structure of postmodern narrative, translated by Almodóvar to the film screen along with the specular refractions learned from the great Argentine writer.[4] From García Márquez, on the other hand, comes a source for his extravagant mastery of the storyteller's art, while the influence of Cabrera Infante and Puig is felt in the director's eclectic embrace of all manner of popular culture, most notably his love of boleros and classic Hollywood films. But perhaps the primary lesson in postmodern artistry that Almodóvar learned from the Latin Americans is the possibility of combining quality with popularity so as to appeal to the broadest audience of film viewers, from the most demanding critics to the general public.

THE CARNIVALESQUE: DIONYSIAN
STRATEGIES OF SUBVERSION

As regards the other, social, explosion, Almodóvar's cinema was to emerge as an expression of the hippie counterculture that, as it developed and expanded into its diverse Spanish permutations—*el underground, el rollo*—would eventually blossom into the postmodern *Movida* of the late seventies and early eighties. Indeed, *Pepi, Luci, Bom* and *Labyrinth* in many ways represent a cinematic chronicle of the imaginative life possibilities charted by the young Spanish postmodern generation.[5] Steeped in this generational imagery, those first two films possess a freshness and exuberantly subversive vitality never to be equaled in his subsequent pictures. His *Atame (Tie Me Up! Tie Me Down!)* in particular seems to cast a retrospective, critical glance at the orgiastic excesses of the *Movida*. With much of "what were they thinking" this film signals the disenchantment with the *Desencanto*.

At the time when Almodóvar was making his first films, the "end of history" proclaimed by postmodernism had a special meaning in Spain; it signified the end of Francoism as well as the fratricidal legacy of the two Spains. Thus Spanish postmodernism took on an air of carnival, a *fiesta popular*, lived out, like the *Movida*, in the streets and public spaces.

Almodóvar brings this festival to the film screen. Partially inspired by the American underground of Andy Warhol and John Waters, but anchored in the Spanish literary-artistic tradition, from the Arcipreste de Hita, Miguel de Cervantes, Francisco de Quevedo, and Francisco de Goya to Pablo Picasso, Ramón del Valle-Inclán, Ramón Gómez de la Serna, and Luis Buñuel, Almodóvar's films are the most recent Hispanic contribution to cinematic representations of the carnivalesque. Indeed, Almodóvar's explorations of the phenomenon are entirely consistent with Mikhail Bakhtin's analyses of the genre, and his films offer what might be considered a catalogue of carnivalesque elements: the joyful embrace of an unbridled disorder affecting all aspects of life, a liberating parodic and comic attitude regarding the most sacred and taboo topics, transvestism in all its forms, grotesque realism, and a view of the world turned upside down. In sum, there reigns in his cinematic universe a cult of profanation and ludic subversion, a countermodel of cultural and libidinal production. It is not for nothing that his production company bears the name El Deseo, although the harnessing of desire to the market carries the risk that desire will be reduced to a mere trademark, its liberating force contained under the cover of a commercial label.

Virtually all the elements of the carnivalesque are already present in his first film. In *Pepi, Luci, Bom* the scatological, with its Hispanic antecedents in Cervantes and Quevedo, is brought to present-day Madrid in an affirmation of the material and corporal foundations of life that Bakhtin traces in the traditions of an originary popular culture and its festivals.[6] *Tie Me Up*, in contrast, marks the ebbing of carnivalesque celebration. The two sisters in the film go to the toilet, but this is no longer the celebration of the *materia alegre* as indulged in by the piss-happy heroines of his first film, over whose bodies streams the verse from César Vallejo's *Trilce*: "divinamente meado y excrementido" (divinely pissed and excremented). Similarly, the mother and daughter of *Tacones lejanos* (*High Heels*) neither pee nor laugh; they dissolve in a flood of tears.

Almodóvar's willful, postmodern disavowal of the historical memory of the Civil War and Francoism is a trait he shares with other young Spanish *cinéastes* of the eighties, such as Fernando Trueba and Fernando Colomo.[7] In *Matador* he dismisses the theme of the "two Spains," the source of so much bloodshed over the years, with two lines of dialogue during the sequence devoted to the fashion show, "España Dividida" (Divided Spain). Almodóvar himself, playing the designer Montesinos, tells a young reporter that he gave the show that title because Spain is a nation divided into two groups, "the envious and the intolerant." When asked to which he belongs, the director replies, "I belong to both." That he had already arrived at such an ironic synthesis of the two Spains (revolutionary, heterodox Spain vs. orthodox, reactionary Spain) is evident in the imagery of *Dark Habits*; instead of burning virgins or adoring them piously, he dresses them in Montesino's postmodern fashions.

In *Tie Me Up*, however, there is an attempt to recover historical memory in the person of the orphaned protagonist, Ricky. Abandoned by his father and devoid of connections to previous generations, Ricky is portrayed as an amnesiac sunk in the ecological disaster of his hometown. His confrontation with the effects of this historical and ecological vacuum is expressed graphically in the scene in which he peers through the vacant window frame of his parents' former home, a ruined heap in the abandoned and destroyed village.

Almodóvar's late films find us far from the celebratory extremes of the earlier works, whose festive, active nihilism effected a revival of the dadaist and surrealist rebellions, their shock tactics designed to mobilize ecstatic, intoxicating life forces against the imperatives of usefulness and normality. There the slogan of the *Movida*, "Madrid me mata" (Madrid kills me), receives allegorical expression in the orgiastic excesses of his protagonists. The "kill me" with coke uttered by Tina, the transsexual heroine of *Law of Desire*, evokes Saint Teresa's "I die because I do not die," parodically reincarnate in the Mother Superior of *Dark Habits*, who achieves mystical-amorous ectasy with the help of heroin. The excesses of drugs, alcohol, and sex in Almodóvar's films prior to *Tie Me Up* have an emblematic meaning within the context of that Dionysian, carnivalesque exaltation with which the postmodern generation celebrates the death of modern Spanish history, embracing the present tense of desire and pleasure.

The "mátame" of *Atame*, on the other hand, while maintaining the drive of desire and amorous passion, has lost the collective-orgiastic dimension of the postmodern generational celebration. The same is true of the deaths in *High Heels*; although they continue to function within the dynamic Eros-Thanatos that presides over Almodóvar's cinema from *Dark Habits* on, such scenes no longer correspond to the vitalist ecstasy of that previous celebration. Instead, in his last three films, set in a Madrid shadowed by the worldwide economic crisis and its consequences, the celebration takes on a decadent connotation.

POSTMODERN PLURALITIES

The eclecticism or hybridism so characteristic of the poetics of postmodernism achieves its cinematic hour of glory in Almodóvar's films. Consistent with their reflexive character, the films flaunt this dimension. Yolanda, the nightclub singer-protagonist of *Dark Habits*, remarks that she specializes in cultivating hybrids, while the taxi driver husband and father of *¿Qué he hecho yo para merecer esto? (What Have I Done To Deserve This?)* brags of his skill as a forger, a talent inherited by his son.[8] With total lack of inhibition and a properly postmodern sense of the ludic, Almodóvar recycles styles and genres from different periods and directors. Parody, pastiche, *mise-en-abime*, and intertextuality characterize all his films. Together with the carnivalesque, the cannibalization of diverse subjects, styles, and modes of representation is a constant in his films.

In his earliest films Almodóvar appropriated elements of American underground cinema as well as other manifestation of popular counterculture—punk styles, pop art, rock music, commercial design, and television advertising—to subvert and fragment traditional film narrative. Yet, beginning with *Dark Habits* his films emerge from the underground to seek a wider audience, targeting the public's emotions and those of female spectators in particular. Additional Latin American influences show up increasingly in the form of sentimental music. As Yolanda notes, "I adore any music that talks about feelings—boleros, tangos, merengues, salsa, rancheras." Abandoning, for the most part, the off-putting extremes of the underground, the hybridism of this phase embraces (1) popular Hollywood cinema, especially the melodramas and comedies of the forties and fifties (William Wyler, Douglas Sirk); (2) sentimental Hispanic music from the same period; and (3) a particularly Spanish, corrosive *costumbrismo* that, combined with a postmodern visual sense, gives shape and color to an explicitly hybrid whole.

The richly creative, hybrid diversity common to all Almodóvar's films has its roots in classic Hollywood cinema. In *What Have I Done?*, for example, the sixties American melodrama *Splendor in the Grass* serves as a subtext to this melodrama of Madrid's working-class housing projects, which is then grafted onto the neorealist subtext of Spanish films like *Surcos (Furrows)* or *El pisito (The Little Apartment)*. But here the apartment, with the television set dominating the entire living space, corresponds to Jean Baudrillard's "hyperrealism of simulation." Almodóvar has stated that in this film he was able to change genres within a single sequence; indeed, one can find a kaleidoscopic fusion of genres: neorealism, hyperrealism, melodrama, *film noir*, the foreign intrigue thriller, and the horror film featuring a child with telekinetic powers, as in Brian de Palma's *Carrie*.

The artificiality of the studio sets, an inheritance of the Hollywood dream factory's dominion over time and space, is also appropriate to the postmodern exaltation of artifice that serves to create a space of heterotopia, an access zone where diverse worlds coexist without transition. In *What Have I Done?*, we move from Madrid's M-30 freeway to the Berlin superhighway and back to the working-class Concepción quarter, an exterior setting that could just as well be the desolate urban landscape of *Blade Runner*—as the director himself notes—and that will return in *Tie Me Up*.

Almodóvar's biggest international success, *Women on the Verge of a Nervous Breakdown*, is a palimpsest upon which is inscribed an outrageous comedy of manners of postmodern Madrid. The successive layers reveal the strata of previous film and theatrical works: Jean Cocteau's *La voix humaine*, Sirk's melodramas, Billy Wilder's comedies, and underneath them all, that black-and-white forties Hollywood melodrama, *Now, Voyager*, starring Bette Davis. Ever conscious, like all postmodern authors, that imitation is not replication, the director is happy to declare his sources and has often expressed his admiration for Bette Davis films. It was *Now, Voyager* that popularized the expression "woman on the verge of a nervous breakdown," referring to the Bette Davis character, a phrase that Almodóvar would appropriate as the title of his film, this time with greater popular resonance.

Women on the Verge is rife with references, though often by way of reversals, to the Davis film. The psychiatrist of *Voyager* returns, for example, in the role of Julieta Serrano—the former mental patient wife of protagonist Pepa's (Carmen Maura) lover; the affection felt by Pepa toward her lover's son recalls that of Bette Davis for her lover's daughter; the Brazilian taxi driver is a distant precursor of the mambo taxi driver of *Women on the Verge.* However, the most resonant intertextual borrowing can be located in the artificiality of the luxurious balcony in Rio that is the site of a single, memorable scene for the lovers in *Voyager.* Almodóvar transposes that tropical Hollywood balcony to postmodern Madrid, thus creating one of the most striking "zones-collages" found in postmodern cinema. In the leafy and luxuriant vegetation of Pepa's penthouse balcony, smack up against an impossible, idealized Madrid skyline, there meet several realms of incompatible "reality": Rio de Janeiro, as imagined by Hollywood; Hollywood of the fifties and sixties; and eighties postmodern Madrid.

The common denominator behind the eclecticism and artifice of Almodóvar's films may be that of a postmodern, quasi-mannerist style. Indeed, many critics have seen postmodernism as neobaroque or mannerist. As Umberto Eco observes, relating the baroque to mannerism, the latter is born out of the discovery that the world has no center, that we must find it by inventing our own points of reference.[9] The comments of novelist and essayist Severo Sarduy, whose sensibility anticipates and echoes Almodóvar's in so many ways, on neobaroque simulation are equally relevant for Almodóvar's films. For Sarduy, simulation acts as a drive or force that connects diverse phenomena of apparently disparate origins, thus suppressing the differences between copy and original, true and counterfeit, real and imaginary.[10]

Sarduy, a recent victim of AIDS, ends *La simulación* by pointing out that beyond pleasure, just as in so many Almodóvar films, simulation yields emptiness and death. Like the historical baroque, the Spanish director's postmodern/neobaroque extravagance hides a horror of the void, traceable in the series of high-angle shots that mark his films' camera work. The meaning behind this stylistic trait is brought home in *What Have I Done?* and *Women on the Verge,* in which the characters Gloria and Candela regard themselves in the bottomless mirror of a suicidal urge.

THE SUBVERSION AND/OR INVERSION OF HOLLYWOOD'S MASCULINE VISION

As already noted, Hollywood cinema of the forties and fifties offers Almodóvar a nearly unlimited source of creative plunder in his cannibalization of filmic styles and ideas. For instance, three representative examples of the genre known as "woman's pictures"—*Love Letters, A Letter to Three Wives*, and *Letter from an Unknown Woman*—films in which telephones and letters play a decisive role, provide an unlikely intertextual source for the interlocking homo/heterosexual love triangles of *Law of Desire*, where two men exchange love letters under the cover of a woman's signature, the unknown Laura P.

Now, Voyager, another paradigm of the woman's picture, represents a fundamental source not only for *Women on the Verge* but also for *High Heels* in its treatment of one of the principal themes of this woman-oriented genre: the mother-daughter relationship and its generally harmful effects on the latter. The originality of Almodóvar's appropriation lies in his parodic treatment of its foundations in Freudian theories of the terrible, phallic mother.[11] Through parody and humor the director reveals the ideological underpinnings of this type of melodrama as a support for the masculine discourse of power.

Almodóvar's films treat questions of sex and gender within the context of a postmodern decentering of traditional notions of social-sexual identity. Indeed, one of the constants of his cinema is the emphasis on sex and gender role reversals, whether masculine or feminine. Emblematic of this concern is the presence and sometimes proliferation of homosexual, transvestite, and/or transsexual characters. Through and with them, the films celebrate, in carnivalesque form, the polymorphous perversity of the human body, the declining power of masculine discourse and the Father's Law, and the almost infinitely plural "I" of the postmodern subject signified in the transsexual as signaled by Baudrillard.

In the central, protagonizing role accorded to his female characters, Almodóvar effects a further reversal of societal and cinematic hierarchies. Beginning with *Pepi, Luci, Bom*, his largely female company of postmodern movie stars brings heat and light to his films. From Pepi to Pepa, these women affirm their female identities, their right to control their own bodies and to attend to the law of their own sexualities and heterogeneous desires. Despite the director's satiric asides regarding militant feminists (recall the unsympathetic feminist lawyer of *Women on the Verge*), and more disturbing—although couched in comic terms—the recurring scenes of violence toward women, his films reveal a general feminization of culture. A number of Almodóvar's films resolve with scenes portraying friendship between women. Thus, the ending of his first film shows Pepi and Bom crossing an overpass that spans the M-30 highway, the shot a visual metaphor for the power of female friendship as a palliative to the urban hell of the technology-driven modern city. Similarly, the conclusion of *Women on the Verge* finds Pepa (once again, Carmen Maura, who also appeared as Pepi) finally free of the faithless Iván and at peace with herself, her impending maternity, and her women friends, secure in her penthouse terrace surrounded by rabbits and plants.

In a related vein, Almodóvar parodies the classic Spanish manifestation of masculine sexual potency, the macho Don Juan, in a number of his films: in *Women on the Verge* he satirizes the figure of the Don Juanesque Iván, while the Don Juan "matador" of the eponymous film meets his match in a female "Doña Juana," likewise a "matadora." Significantly, the figure of the "matadora" returns in *High Heels*, where Rebecca—first as a child and later as a grown woman—kills her stepfather and then her husband. Such crimes announce, allegorically, the triumph of matriarchy, thus delivering the final, subversive blow against the masculine ideology of power that prevailed in the Hollywood "woman's film," the ironic source of Almodóvar's inspiration.

THE SUBVERSION OF THE SIMULACRUM

Much of the emphasis on the cultivation of deceptive surfaces associated with the postmodern neobaroque derives from the fact that its historical referent lies in a world where reality and fiction are intermingled. The artifice and self-referentiality so characteristic of Almodóvar's cinematic universe continually point to that world of "simulacra and simulations," to use Baudrillard's title. Thus, it can be said that in Almodóvar's films we witness a celebration of the "ecstasy of the object" evoked in Baudrillard, as when the camera, on occasion, adopts the point of view of objects; the crystal of the camera lens (personified in the names of at least two of his characters, Cristal and Máximo Espejo [literally, Maximum Mirror]) looks at us.

The television set present in so many of the director's interiors, together with windows and mirrors, functions as a kind of frame for the image within the image or series of Chinese boxes nested one within the other that would enclose the postmodern but also baroque, and very Spanish, nothingness that threatens character and spectator alike. The empty insides of objects—washing machine, oven, and refrigerator—look at Gloria, the anguished heroine of *What Have I Done?*, raising echoes of Federico García Lorca's "Romance sonámbulo": "las cosas la están mirando y ella no puede mirarlas" (things are looking at her and she cannot look back at them). Lorca's Granadan plain is represented in the film in the form of the plastic, pastiched decor of a kitsch Alhambra that adorns the walls of a neighborhood bar by way of homage to the hyperrealism of a sort also found in the writings of Sarduy.

Also a constant in Almodóvar is the subversion and parodic recycling of the simulacra and simulations of mass media. The repeated appearance of various forms of the cinematic apparatus—film cameras, dubbing equipment, as well as television, video, typewriters, and telephone answering machines—points to his awareness of the power of these communication networks and the control exercised by such "telematics." In two of Almodóvar's films, the protagonists end up throwing the instruments of (their lack of) communication out the window: the typewriter in *Law of Desire* and the answering machine in *Women on the Verge*. It is as if they were trying to exit the information superhighway that—as Baudrillard writes about television—has turned our bodies and the surrounding universe into a control screen.[12] The openings of many of Almodóvar's films situate us within the circuit of Baudrillard's "pornography of information and communication," a network that threatens to envelop his characters completely until its tentacles are broken at the end of the film by life or death. Such is the case in *Law of Desire, Women on the Verge, Tie Me Up*, and *High Heels*. The theme reaches its culmination in this last film when Rebecca abandons her passive role as television anchorwoman in the middle of the evening news and declares herself responsible for her husband's death.

POSTMODERN REVISIONS OF ROMANTIC LOVE

Life and death, as linked by love, constitute the vital-mortal thematic center of Almodóvar's cinema, before which the simulacrum must ultimately give way. In the treatment of this theme his hybridism reaches its paroxysmal extreme. There the characteristic visual features of the comic strip and the soap opera meet the most exquisite aspects of mannerist-baroque iconography; the sentimentality of the bolero and melodrama fuses with the emotional depths of the baroque mystical experience, romantic passion, and surrealist "amour fou." The title of Lucho Gatica's bolero, "Historia de un amor" (History of a Love Affair), could well serve as the subtitle for almost all of the director's films.

Almodóvar's vision of eroticism recalls Buñuel's as well as the discussions of Bataille in *L'Erotisme*.[13] *Matador, Law of Desire*, and *Tie Me Up* evoke Bataille's formulations, to the effect that "eroticism is the affirmation of life, even in death," or "that which identifies passion is the halo of death."[14] The soap opera imagery of *Dark Habits* reveals the obvious similarities and even equivalencies between erotic and mystical passions and their expression analyzed by Bataille.[15] In her love for Yolanda, the Mother Superior offers an allusion to Bernini's sculpture *The Ecstasy of Saint Teresa*, reproduced on the cover of the paperback edition of Bataille's book. The dark blue tones that dominate the film's color scheme evoke the symbolism of night, sky, and tempestuous seas, an appropriate framework for that "dark night of the soul" and body lived out in the four above-mentioned films and expressed in the filmmaker's pop-baroque visual stylization. In a similar vein, the closing images of *Dark Habits* and *Law of Desire* allude to the iconography of the *Pietà*, although their deliberately kitsch stylings serve to represent the pain of an explicitly lesbian and gay passion (Plate 16). A variation on the same image appears in *Tie Me Up* as Marina embraces the wounded Ricky before their reflection in a mirror (Plate 20).

The heart—symbol of our innermost life feelings, according to Spanish philosopher María Zambrano—functions as the circulatory center of Almodóvar's cinema. Thus, *Tie Me Up*, interpreted through Zambrano's notion of the "metaphor of the heart," loses much of its offensive edge as opposed to when it is taken literally as a story of forced captivity. Pain and suffering, not violence, is what joins the couple in love. Thus, early in the narrative, Ricky, heart in hand (in the form of a box of candy), sets out in pursuit of Marina's heart, not Marina herself. The religious imagery of the Sacred Heart of Christ and the Sorrowful Virgin that presides over the bedroom where Marina is held captive underscores this sense of the film (Plate 21). Seen in the light of Zambrano's metaphor, Marina's abduction becomes withdrawal from the world into an inner abode; similarly, the characters' wounds, blood, and pain are revealed as attributes of the glowing ring around the heart that is offering and vessel as well as center through which the river of life passes.[16] Marina and Ricky let themselves go in this river, together with Marina's sister, as the three of them join in a unison rendition of the upbeat song that concludes the film, in a parody of the traditional "happy ending."

Almodóvar contrasts this life-affirming realm of romantic passion with the "other world" that is the setting for the main action: the film studio and the streets of present-day Madrid peopled by "replicants." Collapsing interior and exterior, the film refers us to the world of science fiction and terror, already frighteningly present in contemporary social reality. It is no coincidence that a poster for *The Invasion of the Body Snatchers* hangs prominently in the office of director Máximo Espejo and that Picassoesque Rossy de Palma from *Women on the Verge* here takes on a role that seems modeled on the replicants of *Invasion* or *Blade Runner*.

The ending of *High Heels* provides a similar demonstration of the powers of love and life over the world of the simulacrum that had threatened to envelop the characters. The final scenes reveal a series of significant plot reversals as Becky, the terrible phallic mother, lies prostrate in her daughter's arms, the two linked in love and womanly solidarity, while the judge-female impersonator sheds his mask, offering himself as lover to Rebecca. The mother's impending death and Rebecca's pregnancy (like Pepa's at the end of *Women on the Verge*) announce the continuity of the life-death-life cycle.

A POSTHUMANISM FOR OUR TIME OR THE COMMERCIALIZATION AND BANALIZATION OF THE POSTMODERN?

Almodóvar's last three films represent a coda to the successes generated by his postmodern cinema of the eighties. The success that carried him from the margins, the site of his original triumphs, to the hollow center (a vacuum around which he once knowingly spun his narrative webs) now finds him threatened by the conformity decreed by the logic of the marketplace, with its stress on quantity over quality.

Tie Me Up and *High Heels* present us with a more abstract, essentialized Almodóvar, whose vision of the world is now fixed. They also betray a certain loss of creative energy and imagination. As noted before, the shock value of these most recent films is much diminished compared with the earlier ones. More significantly, they no longer communicate humor and passion with the same force that was felt in *Women on the Verge* or *Law of Desire*, despite the excellent performances that the director still manages to coax from his actors. The cultivation of nostalgia and pastiche, once confined to his appropriations of Hollywood models, seems to have affected his attitude toward his own work, as the director and his characters circle endlessly in their own "labyrinth of passion." The simulacrum now threatens to envelop Almodóvar himself, like the closed spaces of the psychiatric hospital, the law court, and the prison that have replaced the open urban celebrations of the Madrid *Movida* as the primary setting of his most recent films.

Thus, themes and images repeat themselves without any net gain in creative or critical reverberations: love and passion against an artificial backdrop, women urinating, television commercials, leafy and luxurious balconies, bolero singers, cameo appearances by his brother Agustín. At times Almodóvar seems caught up in his own kitsch, in the eclectic buzz of a series of self-referential tics. The quotations from other films, the parody of famous directors—where do they lead? *High Heels*'s Máximo Espejo in his wheelchair evokes the journalist-voyeur of *Rear Window* played by Jimmy Stewart. But the most telling, though surely unintentional, allusion would seem to point to Almodóvar himself: immobilized by market forces, relying upon formulas of proven success, trapped in his own specular game.

Nevertheless, despite these harsh criticisms of his latest films, the legacy of Almodóvar's cinema is on balance an important one. His insistent questioning of the simulacra of patriarchal society, his joyous affirmation of the plural and even transsexual subject, and his celebration of freedom of expression and of passion and desire are contributions that gesture toward a posthumanism in keeping with the present *fin de siglo*: that is, a humanism unburdened by the dead weight of classical, and homocentric, humanism.

A POSTSCRIPT ON *KIKA*

It is impossible to watch Almodóvar's tenth film, *Kika*, which had its Madrid premiere in October 1993, without noting its retrospective quality, the sense of an ending or at least a pause in the career of one of the world's preeminent postmodern filmmakers. Indeed, the signs are clear that in *Kika*, despite the carnival atmosphere of the film's well-publicized opening night festivities, the party is definitively over.[17] Or rather, that the urban carnival of the earlier films has become a "Dance of Death," in an ironic convergence of Almodóvar's postmodern grotesques with the "Black Spain" of painter José Gutiérrez Solana. Thus the references to the religion and folklore of traditional, rural Spain, a subtext in previous films, come to the fore through the televised images of a procession of sadomasochistic penitents venerating the Virgin Mary—as if in a kind of a return of the repressed of the director's own small-town origins.

Nevertheless, the city, embodied here as the ultimate "society of the spectacle," of the simulacrum and simulation, continues to occupy center stage in *Kika*. The film-within-a-film parody of tabloid television "reality shows," *Lo peor del día* (*The Worst News of the Day*), hosted by Andrea Caracortada (Victoria Abril) functions not merely as a voyeuristic window on a world of crime, corruption, and human misery but also as a replacement for the "reality" it purports to report. Caracortada, her slashed face reminiscent of the bloody bride of *Matador*'s fashion show scene, is perhaps the film's most genuinely felt character. Pursuing the news in her cyborglike, Gaultier black leather biker outfit—the TV journalist as human Minicam—Andrea offers an image of the frustration and impotence of the dehumanized postmodern subject trapped in the telematic web and reduced to the role of voyeur.

The film itself has something of the collage effect of television news as it veers between upbeat human interest and the truly terrifying while many of the signature characters and characteristics of Almodóvar's cinematic successes of the eighties parade before the spectators' eyes in what may be their curtain call. From cast to mise-en-scène to musical sound track, the viewer finds himself or herself on familiar ground, a territory whose census include those longtime "chicas Almodóvar," Verónica Forqué as Kika and Rossy de Palma as her housekeeper; appearances by the director's brother and mother; the "matador" Don Juan or Iván personified here by a womanizing American (Peter Coyote); the phallic mother (Charo López, quickly dispatched) and voyeuristic oedipal son (Alex Casanovas); the postmodern design of the apartment shared by Kika and Ramón (Casanovas), the abundant references to cinema, video, and photographic apparatuses, the Madrid skyline where the moon dissolves into the image of a washing machine; and the bolero ("Luz de luna" by Chavela Vargas) performed here by transsexual Bibi Andersen in full frontal nudity.

What is new in *Kika*, even given the hybridism of Almodóvar's cinema, comes in the second half, the postmodern comedy of manners left behind, when the picture turns toward a parodic variation on the Hollywood "slasher film." Unlike his previous appropriation of the subgenre in *Matador*, where the horrorific did ironic service to the film's elegant choreography of erotic passion, in *Kika*, Almodóvar offers a glimpse of an authentic *cine negro* that evokes as an antecedent, despite obvious differences, Goya's "Black Paintings." It remains to be seen whether Almodóvar will muster the creative courage necessary to pursue this line of approach at the risk of alienating the mass commercial audience that his films have attracted since *Women on the Verge*. Nevertheless, it is evident that he is deeply troubled by the technological "sleep of reason" that, in the present *fin de siglo* perhaps even more than in Goya's day, begets monsters.

Kika's conclusion, like the other apparently happy endings of Almodóvar's previous films, raises more questions than it answers. On a country highway against a backdrop of yellow sunflowers in bloom, Kika, the indomitable survivor of the film's bloody climax in which Caracortada and serial killer Coyote battle to the death, gamely embarks on another amorous adventure with a winsome young man who invites her to his sister's wedding in the *pueblo*. Despite the willfully upbeat tone, the final scene strikes a false, unsatisfying note. A field of sunflowers and an irrepressible "chica" ready for fun in spite of the blood just shed don't offer much in the way of closure, let alone an opening or insight—contrary to what the director would have us believe—into the reality that awaits the spectator just beyond the door of the theater.

With *Kika*, as the director himself seems to recognize, Almodóvar's cinema has reached a crossroad. From the margins the director fashioned a unique product that reached out to a mainstream audience who then demanded more of the same. As the law of desire gave way to that of diminishing returns, the filmmaker found himself caught up in his own *laberinto almodovariano*, the balance between his effervescent imaginary and equally penetrating sense of the real tipped decisively in favor of the former. In my opinion, what is missing from Almodóvar's cinema of the nineties is the corrosive spark generated by the onscreen clash between imaginary and real, desire and history, precisely at the moment when our convulsive *fin de siglo* social reality demands the luxury of a dialogue with the world of film and culture.

NOTES

1. More than any internationally known director's of the eighties, Almodóvar's cinema has given visual form to the *realidad aligerada* (lightened reality) that, according to Gianni Vattimo, is characteristic of the postmodern era. Gianni Vattimo, *El fin de la modernidad. Nihilismo y hermeneútica en la cultura posmoderna* (Barcelona: Gedisa, 1986), 158.

2. Miguel Albaladejo et al., *Los fantasmas del deseo. A propósito de Pedro Almodóvar* (Madrid: Aula 7, 1988), 37.

3. Albaladejo et al., 37.

4. A number of the images/symbols of Borges's works show up in Almodóvar's films: the mirror, the tiger—although the latter, which figures in *Dark Habits*— as well as the rabbits in *Women on the Verge* and the lizard in *What Have I Done?*, owe more to Cortázar's *Bestiario* than to Borges.

5. As Francisco Umbral observed regarding Almodóvar: "He was, and is, the only coherent, plastic, lasting, ironic, and accurate summary of the 70's and 80's [in Spain]." Francisco Umbral, "Almodóvariana," *ABC*, 26 September 1993, 19.

6. In line with this interpretation, some of the film's most scandalous scenes embrace this scatological-carnivalesque dimension: Bom urinating on the ecstatic Luci, the farts and snot, the phony commercial for the all-absorbent women's panties "Ponte," the "Erecciones Generales" (General Erections) contest in which Almodóvar himself plays the master of ceremonies. Among its deliberately provocative points, the title of the latter scene, a parody of "General Elections," issues a clear, comic challenge to a number of the director's contemporaries, still engaged in creating a political cinema more in tune with the anti-Francoist concerns of previous decades than with the generally apolitical attitudes of the *Movida* generation.

7. Almodóvar has spoken of his intention to make films as if Franco had never existed, films designed to mirror the lives of young people in their twenties. Peter Besas, *Behind the Spanish Lens* (Denver: Arden Press, 1985), 216. The danger of this "youth cult"—Almodóvar himself was in his thirties when *Pepi, Luci, Bom* appeared—lies in remaining fixed on a particular moment in both one's personal history and that of the larger society. Such a fixation has marked the work and attitudes of much of the historical avant-garde.

8. In a plot element reminiscent of Borges's "Pierre Menard, Author of *Don Quijote*," the former emigrant and continuing Germanophile has forged an edition of Hitler's love letters.

9. Umberto Eco and Stefano Rosso, "A Correspondence on Postmodernism," in *Zeitgeist in Babel: The Postmodern Controversy*, ed. Ingeborg Hoesterey (Bloomington: Indiana University Press, 1991), 244.

10. Severo Sarduy, *La simulación* (Caracas: Monte Avila, 1982), 61.

11. The director fires his first satiric salvo at psychoanalysis in *Labyrinth*, via the character of Susana, the Lacanian psychoanalyst.

12. Jean Baudrillard, "The Ecstasy of Communication," in *The Anti-Aesthetic*, ed. Hal Foster (Port Townsend, Wash.: Bay Press, 1983), 128.

13. Of Buñuel one might recall *Abismos de pasión (Wuthering Heights)*, *La vida criminal de Archibaldo de la Cruz (The Criminal Life of Archibaldo de la Cruz)*, and *Ese oscuro objeto del deseo (That Obscure Object of Desire)*, whose titles echo throughout Almodóvar's films.

14. Georges Bataille, *El erotismo*, trans. Toni Vicens, 2nd ed. (Barcelona: Tusquets, 1982), 135.

15. Bataille, 372.

16. María Zambrano, "La metáfora del corazón," in her *Claros del bosque* (Barcelona: Seix Barral, 1977), 63–77.

17. While Spanish film critics (with some exceptions) have never been excessively kind to Almodóvar's films, the response to *Kika* has been stunningly negative. See, for example, the review by Angel Fernández-Santos, "La ley del

desastre," *El país*, 30 October 1993, 27. On the preceding page, in contrast, the full-page chronicle of the film's postpremiere extravaganza, as expertly choreographed and even rehearsed by Almodóvar at the cost of some $75,000, is celebratory in tone. Rocío García, "En bandeja española," *El país*, 30 October 1993, 26.

Afterword: From Rough Trade to Free Trade: Toward a Contextual Analysis of Audience Response to the Films of Pedro Almodóvar

Wendy Rolph

As 1993 drew to a close and around the world the media began the ritual dissemination of the results of their annual tallies of the year's triumphs and disasters, the snazzy new weekly entertainment supplement to *El país*, Spain's most prestigious daily newspaper, informed its readers that once again in 1993 Pedro Almodóvar had easily topped the lists of the country's most cinematically hot. Not only did Almodóvar outdistance by a considerable margin all competition for the title of best Spanish film director, but his recently released film *Kika* emerged as the best Spanish film of the year and two well-known members of its cast (Verónica Forqué, who plays the title role of Kika, and Victoria Abril) between them captured 47.7 percent of the votes for the year's best Spanish female actor.[1] Deprived of a context, such journalistic polls of public enthusiasms are, of course, almost totally meaningless. Even in context, it could be argued that their meaninglessness is their most appealing virtue. Yet despite their absence of scientific rigor either by intention or by implementation, as instruments of entertainment propaganda these surveys and opinion samplings are rarely as innocuous as they might seem. Even when not planted by canny publicists, the statistical summaries they inevitably contain invite their invocation as indisputable evidence of the claims of the lucky chart toppers to continued pride of place within the iconography of contemporary popular culture.

The extent to which cultural production in individual countries such as Spain needs such blatant publicity and marketing devices if it is to survive, let alone thrive, in the emerging global audiovisual economy is now well recognized in the film, video, and television industries. Whether audiences are fully aware of the extent to which what they view is controlled by multinational interests that are increasingly dominated by huge monopolies is unclear. Nor is there any effective way of determining whether, knowing, the average filmgoer or television spectator does or does not care. Spanish viewers, long accustomed to the ready availability for their enjoyment of Spanish-dubbed versions of popular Hollywood films, have in recent years welcomed with enthusiasm a virtual deluge of American material onto the national screens. Comparative attendance figures for the past decade also show that, as theater audiences get younger and viewers' appetites for a steady diet of Americanized forms of entertainment increase, these same viewers tend to find other forms of cultural nourishment less and less appealing. Questioned, they simply state the obvious: "What we like are American films" ("A nosotros, lo que nos gusta es el cine americano").[2]

Whether countries can use legislation to remodel the tastes of a public thoroughly conditioned by market saturation and state-of-the-art promotion to give first preference to blockbuster American films and international superproductions is dubious. Certainly the sharply escalating controversies provoked by a series of emergency measures first invoked in 1982 by Pilar Miró as Director General of Cinematography and subsequently by a succession of Ministers of Culture in the final two years of the eighties and again in December 1993 do not encourage the optimistic view.[3] But even though the government's packages of incentives, challenges, and ultimatums to Spanish filmmakers and producers, distributors, and exhibitors to date have failed to resuscitate an increasingly moribund industry, there have been exceptional cases of individual filmmakers who have succeeded brilliantly in creating highly enjoyable, profitable, and eminently exportable indigenous Spanish productions. None, it would seem, more spectacularly than Pedro Almodóvar.

The ten feature films that Almodóvar has directed from 1980 to the present anticipate, interrogate, and hyperbolically replicate many of the most significant changes wrought on contemporary urban Spaniards' lives and value systems during an intense period of sociocultural adaptation to the modalities and configurations of a totally liberalized postmodern capitalist state. *Pepi, Luci, Bom y otras chicas del montón* (*Pepi, Luci, Bom and Other Ordinary Girls*, 1980), Almodóvar's first film in a standard professional format, was like the amateur Super-8 endeavors that preceded it, made with, by, and for his friends and acquaintances living in the epicenter of the Madrid *Movida*. Sketchily conceived and roughly executed, it was completed on an extremely small budget and modestly promoted as an innovative example of a fresh new talent. Niche market audiences reacted positively to it, and Almodóvar's reputation soared among the artsy habitués of the bars and coffeehouses of Malasaña and Chueca.

Two years later, in 1982, his second feature, *Laberinto de pasiones*

(*Labyrinth of Passions*) opened commercially at the Alphaville Cinema in Madrid and subsequently enjoyed a truncated tour of the festival circuit. The Alphaville, a relatively small art cinema adjacent to the Plaza de España, was at the beginning of the eighties virtually unique in the range and seriousness of its commitment to innovative filmmaking and repertory programming. As well as screening original-language versions of important films by internationally significant filmmakers, the Alphaville produced and exhibited new and experimental works by young, local Spanish filmmakers. *Labyrinth* was an ideal film for the Alphaville to promote. Testing the limits of the permissible, flaunting convention, and mocking the pretensions and hypocrisies of "good taste," it brought the delight of recognition to art house audiences who saw themselves on the sociocultural cutting edge and who either were, or desperately wanted to be, identified as part of the still-swirling Madrid *Movida*. Although, predictably, the film was not chosen for screening at Cannes, it was presented out of competition at Venice, where it attracted some interest and its first international sales. Later that fall, at the annual film festival of San Sebastián, audience response to a screening of *Labyrinth* was enthusiastic but the established critics and reviewers were more subdued in their praise, limiting themselves to the standard phrases of acknowledgment of a fresh and original young talent—someone to watch, perhaps, but one whose promise one should be careful not to exaggerate.[4]

Such comments set a pattern for subtle detraction that was never completely broken, even in the heady days of 1988 and Almodóvar's seeming unassailability following the phenomenal national and international commercial success of *Mujeres al borde de un ataque de nervios* (*Women on the Verge of a Nervous Breakdown*). Evidence would seem to suggest that in the early years, the opinions of the critical cognoscenti on the relative paucity of cinematic merits of Almodóvar's films exerted an inverse pressure on audiences, for whom late-night screenings of *Labyrinth* and *Entre tinieblas* (*Dark Habits*) became Spanish cult equivalents of *Eraserhead* or the *Rocky Horror Picture Show*. Almodóvar's cachet was becoming such among the students and mimics of the *Movida* that even uniformly negative critical response would not have dampened their enthusiasm.

During the decade from *Labyrinth* to *Tacones lejanos* (*High Heels*, 1991), the productivity of many Spanish filmmakers decreased dramatically as the total output of an industry beset by deepening crisis fell sharply. From a high of 118 features made in Spain in 1982, only 38 features were completed in 1992. Not only were fewer and fewer Spanish films being made, but over the decade a discouraging 10 percent of those made never found a distributor. Furthermore, few of those that did achieve theatrical release attracted large audiences in the nation's rapidly shrinking inventory of cinemas. Audiences, too, were shrivelling, from

176 million in 1980 to 83 million in 1993, and their preferences were clearly and increasingly for American films. By the end of 1993, Spain's own films accounted for only 7 percent of the national box office, and the country shared with Germany and Holland the dubious distinction of being the most attractive European markets for American films.[5]

In such a context, the trajectory of Pedro Almodóvar is doubly anomalous, both in terms of his record of sustained production and in terms of audience engagement with his films. During the eighties, Almodóvar was one of the few Spanish filmmakers able to maintain a constant creative momentum, revising and professionalizing his production arrangements from project to project and managing to complete films at an average rate of one feature per year. And while public interest in Spanish film in general may have been decreasing alarmingly, the number of spectators of Almodóvar films (including television and video viewing) has increased with every film he has made since 1980. At first, those films played in small and specialized cinemas and their audiences, like the films themselves, were predominantly the self-styled avant-garde. Records of box office statistics show that *Labyrinth* attracted a respectable 234,263 paying spectators, a figure that for *¿Qué he hecho yo para merecer esto?* (*What Have I Done to Deserve This?*, 1984) increased to 391,513. (It should be kept in mind that the incidence in Spain of inaccurate and even fraudulent reporting of theater attendance and box office receipts is high, rendering any and all attendance figures somewhat unreliable.) With *Matador* (1986), Almodóvar's success with a broader public began to be assured. Under skilled promotion by the experienced production company Iberoamericana, *Matador* was guaranteed access to more central channels of distribution and exhibition, beginning with its simultaneous premiere in Madrid's Proyecciones, Rex, and La Vaguada movie houses.

Positive response to Almodóvar's films in Spain was beginning to be supported by critical enthusiasm abroad (for example in France, in Canada at international festivals in both Montreal and Toronto, in New York), and Almodóvar's appeal to a more demographically representative domestic audience was building as a result. In Spain the release of *La ley del deseo* (*Law of Desire*) in 1987 by his own production company capitalized brilliantly on a combination of Almodóvar's growing reputation, the provocative subject matter, and the stylish ensemble acting of its talented cast to attract the fourth largest number of spectators (638, 646) of any Spanish film exhibited in that year. Like *Matador*, *Law of Desire* was restricted to spectators eighteen years and older, a fact that should be borne in mind when its attendance figures are compared with those for Almodóvar's later films, which did not, in Spain, carry a similar restricted rating. *Women on the Verge*, the filmmaker's most commercially profitable film, became the country's top-grossing film of 1988, attracting more than a million spectators nationally while repeating its domestic successes internationally, particularly in the United States.[6]

In the early years, the shock value of Almodóvar's themes, the visual stylishness of the films, and the outrageous antics of the filmmaker himself had found a small but eager audience of nonconformists. By 1988 and afterward, it seemed that the vast majority of Spain's young and urban population, having successfully exorcised the ghosts of the previous generation's repressed and repressive past, were reveling in their own versions of the totally liberated life-style celebrated in Almodóvar's cinematic romps and rampages. It consequently becomes of some interest to examine public reaction within Spain in 1990 to reports that the American release of *Atame* (*Tie Me Up! Tie Me Down!*) had been threatened with the dreaded X rating, a threat Almodóvar chose to fight in the courts. His lawsuit and its eventual outcome were widely reported on both sides of the Atlantic, but in Spain the reporting reflected concerns and attitudes toward gendered behavior considerably different from those expressed elsewhere. From the Iberian perspective, the primary hardship imposed on Almodóvar by any kind of restrictive classification for *Tie Me Up* was not ideological but essentially economic. Economic not because certain kinds of ratings would deny the film access to advertising in prestigious New York newspapers, and so circumscribe attendance, but because, by limiting admission to those over the age of seventeen, the classifiers would be excluding large numbers of American teenagers from a film with "obvious juvenile audience appeal."[7] This was the same film that had excited hostile demonstrations during screenings in Berlin, where festival goers angrily declared themselves offended by its acquiescent portrayal of violence against women.[8]

Over a ten-year period, Almodóvar's films have undergone a metamorphosis from minor marginal diversions into mainstream mass entertainments, produced with an eye not only to theatrical exhibition but also, increasingly, to videotape and television rerelease in recognition of the massive assimilation of contemporary viewing habits into the small-screen mode. In the second half of the eighties, Spain's Ministry of Culture moved to embrace audiovisual policy changes that implicated television heavily in the financing and subsequent exhibition of film productions and convinced not only Almodóvar but other Spanish filmmakers as well of the prudence of designing their projects with a view to their future dissemination on the small screen. As one after another the large cinemas were transformed into minicinema complexes or simply closed; as video sales, rentals, and piracies skyrocketed; and as the privatization of television and the introduction of satellite capability and a free-trade mindset dramatically increased the number of choices available on the small screen within the comforts of home, viewers' tastes in films were being remolded along with their viewing habits. In response, Almodóvar the filmmaker, even while polishing his cinematic craft on increasingly expensive and glossy productions such as *Kika*, has kept open his options for a multiscreen exposure in which, paradoxically, his "difference" is becoming less indelibly "marked" and the large-screen format perhaps serves him less well. There is irony in the fact that *High Heels* finally cracked the monopoly of the multinationals on premium screen space with a premiere screening in one of the few remaining picture palaces of the Gran Vía of Madrid, but audience attendance at its large-screen run fell well short of matching earlier records set by *Women on the Verge*. Does this film, do Almodóvar's films, finally fit better on the small screen, or is it just that contemporary viewers have become more at ease with experiencing their cinema that way?

NOTES

1. *El país de la tentaciones* 10 (31 December 1993): 14–15.
2. *El país*, 27 December 1993. Statistics analyzed by Ramiro Gómez B. de Castro in *La producción cinematográfica española* (Bilbao: Mensajero, 1989) show the gap between the box office receipts of Spanish and U.S. films beginning to widen significantly in 1982, and continuing throughout the decade with only a brief, minor correction in 1987. *Estudio base sobre el comportamiento de los españoles ante el cine* (Madrid: Ministerio de Cultura, 1986), an influential and much-quoted government survey of the film viewing habits and attitudes of Spaniards, profiled the average filmgoer at middecade as young (under thirty), male, not unknowledgeable about Spanish cinema but predisposed (77.3 percent) toward American entertainment models. Since that time, the Americanization of daily life throughout Spain, particularly in its major cities, has escalated dramatically. This is reflected in the disproportionate attention devoted to U.S. productions and personalities in such widely circulated popular film magazines as the monthly *Fotogramas & Video* or *Dirigido por: Revista de cine*.
3. The Miró law of 1983, characterized by a generous state subsidy system designed to enhance "quality" filmmaking and encourage new talent, ultimately failed, for a variety of complicated reasons, in its ambitious attempt to energize the production and especially the reception of Spanish films. Policy changes proposed by Minister of Culture Jorge Semprún, intended to address issues of capitalization and market viability, were unpopular among many vocal sectors of the film community and failed to receive effective implementation. One positive result was the formation of lobbying groups such as the Fundación Procine, a consortium of film and television producers concerned with devising collaborative means of solving the cinema crisis and meeting the challenges of competing in international markets. In December 1993, Minister of Culture Carmen Alborch introduced, in the most recent legislative attempt to resuscitate the audiovisual industry, a series of emergency measures that produced a violent schism between the production sector and the distributors and exhibitors. The latter darkened all of the screens in the country for a day on 20 December, in protest against the legislation, and the issues surrounding the imposition of stricter import licensing

controls and a preferential quota system became the subject of vigorous debate throughout the Spanish media.

4. In fact, sharp disjunctures between viewer response and critical assessment have tended to repeat on the release of almost every Almodóvar film. The critical assessments of *Laberinto de pasiones*, written from San Sebastián by Diego Galán and Angel Fernández Santos for *El país* (25 September 1982) are typical early examples. Brief samplings of the opinions of reviewers, arranged chronologically by film, are included in María Antonia García de León and Teresa Maldonado, *Pedro Almodóvar, la otra España cañí* (Ciudad Real: Biblioteca de Autores y Temas Manchegos, 1989).

5. These data are available annually from such English-language sources as *Variety* and *Screen International*. For a useful summary of industry issues from 1977 to 1990, see John Hopewell, " 'Art and a Lack of Money': The Crises of the Spanish Film Industry, 1977–1990," *Quarterly Review of Film & Video* 13.4: 113–122.

6. *Women on the Verge of a Nervous Breakdown* continues to attract large numbers of viewers in video release. In an informal survey conducted at four video outlets in Toronto, Canada, over a four-month period in 1993, it remained in the top spot among Spanish-language films at three of the outlets, and in the second spot at the fourth.

7. *El país*, 16 April 1990.

8. It is encouraging to see the extent to which recent analyses of *Atame* by feminist scholars have recontextualized spectatorial responses to the film in constructive ways. See, in particular, the extended study of the film in terms of sadism and masochism by Martha J. Nandorfy, *"Tie Me Up! Tie Me Down!* Subverting the Glazed Gaze of American Melodrama and Film Theory," *Cineaction* 31 (1993): 50–61.

Filmography

SHORT AND FEATURE-LENGTH FILMS NOT RELEASED COMMERCIALLY

Film político (*Political Film*) 1974 (Super-8, 4 mins.)
Dos putas o historia de amor que termina en boda (*Two Whores or Love Story Ending in a Wedding*) 1974 (Super-8, 10 mins.)
El sueño or *La estrella* (*The Dream* or *The Star*) 1975 (Super-8, 12 mins.)
La caída de Sodoma (*The Fall of Sodom*) 1975 (Super-8, 10 mins.)
Homenaje (*Homage*) 1975 (Super-8, n.a.)
Blancor (*Whiteness*) 1975 (Super-8, 5 mins.)
Trailer de "Who's Afraid of Virginia Woolf?" (*Trailer of "Who's Afraid of Virginia Woolf?"*) 1976 (Super-8, 5 mins.)
Las tres ventajas de Ponte (*The Three Advantages of Ponte*) 1977 (Super-8, 5 mins.)
Sexo va, sexo viene (*Sex Comes, Sex Goes*) 1977 (Super-8, 17 mins.)
Folle . . . Folle . . . Fólleme, Tim (*Fuck Me, Tim*; the title in Spanish is also a play on the word *folletín* or feuilleton) 1978 (Super-8, 90 mins.)
Salomé (16mm., 11 mins.)

FEATURE-LENGTH FILMS RELEASED COMMERCIALLY

Pepi, Luci, Bom y otras chicas del montón (*Pepi, Luci, Bom and Other Ordinary Girls*) 1980 (16mm. blown up to 35mm.)
Laberinto de pasiones (*Labyrinth of Passions*) 1982
Entre tinieblas (*Dark Habits*) 1983
¿Qué he hecho yo para merecer esto? (*What Have I Done to Deserve This?*) 1984
Trailer para amantes de lo prohibido (*Trailer for Lovers of the Prohibited*) 1985 (medium-length for TVE)

Matador 1986
La ley del deseo (*Law of Desire*) 1987
Mujeres al borde de un ataque de nervios (*Women on the Verge of a Nervous Breakdown*) 1988
¡Atame! (*Tie Me Up! Tie Me Down!*) 1989
Tacones lejanos (*High Heels*) 1991
Kika 1993

Selected Bibliography: "Almodóvar in America"

In compiling this selected bibliography, we have sought to provide a research guide for the English-language reader. Nevertheless, given the dearth of serious critical material on Almodóvar in English, we have included a list of books in Spanish devoted to the director and his films. Those by García de León and Vidal are particularly useful for their bibliographies on Almodóvar in the Spanish press, which also include extensive quotations from representative sources. The material included in the criticism section is drawn from a range of American publications on film as well as weekly and monthly magazines directed at a general audience. Because our concern is to give an account of the American reception of Almodóvar and his films, we have not included Canadian or British sources. Recognizing a practical need to observe certain limits on length, we have omitted reviews from daily newspapers such as the *New York Times* and *Los Angeles Times*. Although the importance of the former in the dissemination of "foreign film" culture (especially European) in the United States should not be underestimated, reviews are readily available in the *New York Times Film Reviews* volumes, found in most university and even local public libraries.

BOOKS IN ENGLISH ON SPANISH CINEMA

Besas, Peter. *Behind the Spanish Lens: Spanish Cinema Under Fascism and Democracy*. Denver: Arden Press, 1985.

Cabello Castellet, George, Jaume Martí-Olivella, and Guy H. Wood, eds. *Cine-Lit: Essays on Peninsular Film and Fiction*. Portland: Portland State University: 1992.

Caparrós-Lera, J. M., and Rafael de España. *The Spanish Cinema: An Historical Approach*. Translated by Carl J. Mora. Barcelona: Centre for Cinematic Research "Film-Historia," 1987.

D'Lugo, Marvin. *The Films of Carlos Saura: The Practice of Seeing*. Princeton: Princeton University Press, 1991.

Fiddian, Robin W., and Peter Evans. *Challenges to Authority: Fiction and Film in Contemporary Spain*. London: Tamesis Books, 1988.

Higginbotham, Virginia. *Spanish Film Under Franco*. Austin: University of Texas Press, 1988.

Hopewell, John. *Out of the Past: Spanish Cinema After Franco*. London: British Film Institute, 1986.

Kinder, Marsha. *Blood Cinema: The Reconstruction of National Identity in Spain*. Berkeley: University of California Press, 1993.

Molina Foix, Vicente. *New Cinema in Spain*. London: British Film Institute, 1977.

Smith, Paul Julian. *Desire Unlimited: The Cinema of Pedro Almodóvar*. London: Verso, 1994.

BOOKS IN SPANISH ON ALMODÓVAR

Albaladejo, Miguel et al. *Los fantasmas del deseo: A propósito de Pedro Almodóvar*. Madrid: Aula 7, 1988.

Blanco, Francisco [Boquerini, pseud.]. *Pedro Almodóvar*. Madrid: Ediciones JC, 1989.

García de León, María Antonia, and Teresa Maldonado. *Pedro Almodóvar, la otra España cañí*. Ciudad Real: Biblioteca de Autores y Temas Manchegos, 1989.

Vidal, Nuria. *El cine de Pedro Almodóvar*. 2nd ed. Barcelona: Destino, 1989.

CRITICISM ON ALMODÓVAR IN U.S. PUBLICATIONS

Interviews

Appell, David. "Why I Wear What I Wear: Man of La Mania." *GQ: Gentleman's Quarterly* 59.11 (November 1989): 104–108.

Bronski, Michael. "Almodóvar: Post-Franco American?" *Zeta Magazine* 2.4 (April 1989): 64–67.

Fernández, Enrique. "Off-screen: The Lawyer of Desire." *Village Voice*, 7 April 1987, 54 (2pp.).

Kinder, Marsha. "Pleasure and the New Spanish Mentality: A Conversation with Pedro Almodóvar." *Film Quarterly* 41.1 (Fall 1987): 33–44.

Lida, D. "Pedro Almodóvar." *Interview* 18 (July 1988): 27.

Schnabel, Julian. "Pedro Almodóvar." *Interview* 22 (January 1992): 78.

General Essays and Reviews

Allen, G. L. "*Tie Me Up, Tie Me Down*." *Premiere* 3 (July 1990): 107.

Allen, M. "*Law of Desire*." *Film Journal* 90 (May 1987): 19.

"Almodóvar Brothers Riding High." *Variety*, 23 September 1991, 48.

Ansen, David. "Consider the Alternatives." *Newsweek*, 6 January 1992, 52. [Review of *High Heels*].

————. "Let Us Loose." *Newsweek*, 7 May 1990, 65. [Review of *Tie Me Up*].

————. "The Man of La Mancha." *Newsweek*, 5 December 1988, 88.

————. "Outrageous *Matador*." *Newsweek*, 18 July 1988, 57.

Arroyo, J. "Pedro Almodóvar: Law and Desire." *Descant* 20.64–65 (1989): 52–70.

Ayscough, S. "*Pepi, Luci, Bom y otras chicas del montón (Pepi, Luci, Bom and Other Girls)*." *Variety*, 3 December 1990, 81.

Barasch, Amy. "Preview: All Tied Up." *Interview* 20 (January 1990): 26. [On *Tie Me Up*].

Bartholomew, D. "*High Heels*." *Film Journal* 95 (January 1992): 40–41.

Berman. M. "Miramax to Reopen *Tie Me Up* with NC-17." *Variety*, 15 October 1990, 40.

Besas, Peter. "*Atame (Tie Me Up, Tie Me Down)*." *Variety*, 31 January 1990, 31.

————. "*Entre tinieblas (Dark Hideout)*." *Variety*, 23 May 1984, 23.

————. "*La ley del deseo (Law of Desire)*." *Variety*, 18 February 1987, 20 (2 pp.).

————. "*Matador*." *Variety*, 9 April 1986, 13.

————. "*Mujeres al borde de un ataque de nervios (Women on the Verge of a Nervous Breakdown)*." *Variety*, 6 April 1988, 12.

————. "*Tacones lejanos (High Heels)*." *Variety*, 21 October 1991, 72.

Blake, Richard. "Franco Is Dead." *America* 160.2 (21 January 1989): 41. [Review of *Women on the Verge*].

Brantley, Ben. "Spain's Bad Boy Grows Up." *Vanity Fair* 53 (April 1990): 182–187+.

Buck, Joan Juliet. "*High Heels*." *Vogue*, January 1992: 61 (2 pp.).

Cadalso, I. "Pedro Almodóvar: A Spanish Perspective." *Cineaste* 18.1 (1990): 36–37.

Cardullo, B. "Lovers and Other Strangers." *Hudson Review* 43.4 (1991): 645–653. [On *Tie Me Up! Tie Me Down!*].

Corliss, Richard. "*High Heels*." *Time*, 10 February 1992, 76.

Corliss, Richard, and M. Hornblower. "Pedro on the Verge of a Nervy Breakthrough." *Time*, 30 January 1989, 68.

Denby, David. "No Exit." *New York*, 14 May 1990, 103 (3 pp.). [Review of *Tie Me Up*].

————. "Success de Scandale." *New York*, 29 April 1985, 76 (2 pp.). [Review of *What Have I Done?*].

————. "There's a Girl in My Gazpacho." *New York*, 21 November 1988, 115 (3 pp.). [Review of *Women on the Verge*].

Dieckmann, Katherine. "Obscure Objects of Desire: The Films of Pedro Almodóvar." *Aperture* 121 (Fall 1990): 74–76.

Edelstein, D. "Junk Bonds." *Village Voice*, 10 May 1988, 62. [Review of *Dark Habits*].

————. "Wooly Bully." *Village Voice*, 7 April 1987, 54 (2 pp.). [Review of *Law of Desire*].

Fernández, Enrique. "Miami Film Festival: Desire Under the Palms." *Village Voice*, 17 March 1987, 62 (2 pp.). [Review of *Law of Desire*].

Frascella, Lawrence. "*Kika*." *The Advocate*, 3 May 1994, 75–76.

Geist, K. L. "Pedro Almodóvar." *Films in Review* 40 (January 1989): 12–13.

Giddins, Gary. "Corpus Interruptus." *Village Voice*, 8 May 1990, 72. [Review of *Tie Me Up*].

————. "The Reine in Spain." *Village Voice*, 23 January 1990, 78. [Review of *Labyrinth of Passions*].

Giobbe, Dorothy. "*New York Times* Rejects Movie Ad, Says It Would Have Offended Readers." *Editor and Publisher*, 30 April 1994, 29. [On advertising for *Kika*].

Gold, R. "Mainstream Style Release for *Women on the Verge*." *Variety*, 14/20 December 1988, 10.

————. "*Matador*." *Variety*, 26 November 1986, 16.

Gooch, Brad. "The King of Kink." *Out* (May 1994): 53–57, 114.

Hart, Patricia. "*Patty Diphusa y otros textos* by Pedro Almodóvar." *World Literature Today* 66.3 (Summer 1992): 485.

Haskell, Molly. "*Tie Me Up! Tie Me Down!*" *Video Review* 11 (January 1991): 60.

Hivnor, M. "The Baroque Equation in Spanish Films." *Partisan Review* 57.4 (1990): 616–620.

Hoberman, J. "Mamas and Papas." *Village Voice*, 24 December 1991, 67 (2 pp.). [Review of *High Heels*].

————. "Mambo Dearest." *Village Voice*, 22 November 1988, 59 (2 pp.). [Review of *Women on the Verge*].

————. "True Glitz." *Village Voice*, 10 May 1994, 54. [Review of *Kika*].

Kael, Pauline. "The Current Cinema." *New Yorker*, 3 June 1985, 116–120. [Review of *What Have I Done?*].

————. "Manypeeplia upsidownia." *New Yorker*, 20 April 1987, 80–83. [Review of *Law of Desire*].

————. "Red on Red." *New Yorker*, 16 May 1988, 96–97. [Review of *Matador*].

————. "Unreal." *New Yorker*, 14 November 1988, 124 (4 pp.). [Review of *Women on the Verge*].

Kauffman, Stanley. "Anarchies and Devotions." *New Republic*, 20 May 1985, 24–25. [Review of *What Have I Done?*].

————. "Bound for Love." *New Republic*, 14 May 1990, 30–31. [Review of *Tie Me Up*].

————. "*High Heels*." *New Republic*, 3 February 1992, 28 (2 pp.).

————. "Jokers Wild." *New Republic*, 6 June 1994, 26–27. [Review of *Kika*].

————. "*Pepi, Luci, Bom*." *New Republic*, 29 June 1992, 28 (2 pp.).

————. "Strong Reactions." *New Republic*, 6 June 1988, 28–29. [Review of *Dark Habits*].

————. "Talents in Transit." *New Republic*, 12 December 1988, 24–26. [Review of *Women on the Verge*].

Kissen, E. "*Women on the Verge of a Nervous Breakdown*." *Films in Review* 40 (February 1989): 108–109.

Kissinger, D. "*Tie Me Up* Distributor Could Have Its Hands Tied by Tough New York Rule." *Variety*, 4 July 1990, 7 (2 pp.).

Klawans, S. "*Tie Me Up, Tie Me Down*." *Nation*, 28 May 1990, 75 (4 pp.).

————. "*Women on the Verge of a Nervous Breakdown*." *Nation*, 5 December 1988, 626–628.

Lane, Anthony. "Shock Treatment." *New Yorker*, 16 May 1994, 106–108. [Review of *Kika*].

Leavitt, David. "Almodóvar on the Verge." *New York Times Magazine*, 22 April 1990, 36 (5 pp.).

Levy, Shawn. "Almodóvar's *Kika*. You Can't Keep a Good Woman Down." *Film Comment* 30.3 (May–June 1994): 59–62.

———. "King of Spain." *American Film* 17 (January–February 1992): 38–43.

Lida, David. "Fast Track: The Spain Event." *New York*, 26 September 1988, 32. [On *Women on the Verge*].

MacPherson, M. "Director on the Verge." *Premiere* 3 (June 1990): 130–134.

Minx, Paul. "Breaking the Law." *Village Voice*, 4 December 1990, 19. [Review of *Law of Desire*].

Mitchell, E. "Foreign Films with a View." *Rolling Stone*, 8 May 1986, 31–32. [Review of *What Have I Done?*].

Murphy, Ryan. "A Spanish Fly in the Hollywood Ointment." *The Advocate*, 19 June 1990, 37–40.

Pally, Marcia. "Camp Pedro: Picador, Any Door." *Film Comment* 24.6 (November 1988): 18–19. [On the making of *Women on the Verge*].

———. "The Politics of Passion: Pedro Almodóvar and the Camp Esthetic." *Cineaste* 18.1 (1990): 32–35+.

Puffer, Christian. "*Patty Diphusa and Other Writings*." *Variety*, 24 August 1992, 79.

Rafferty, Terrence. "Conspicuous Consumer." *New Yorker*, 17 May 1990, 88–91. [Review of *Tie Me Up*].

———. "Unnatural Acts." *New Yorker*, 10 February 1992, 81–84. [Review of *High Heels*].

Reynaud, Berenice. "Close-Up: Pedro Almodóvar." *American Film* 13.5 (March 1988): 72.

Russo, Vito. "Man of La Mania: Pedro Almodóvar on the Verge. . . ." *Film Comment* 24.6 (November 1988): 13–17.

Sante, Luc. "Over the Verge." *Interview* 18 (November 1988): 142. [Review of *Women on the Verge*].

Sarris, Andrew. "*Women on the Verge of a Nervous Breakdown*." *Video Review* 10 (January 1990): 55.

Schaeffer, Stephen. "Spanish Gadfly: Hilarious Hedonist." *Harper's Bazaar*, December 1988, 82.

Schwarzbaun, Lisa. "Kika." *Entertainment Weekly*, 27 May 1994, 66.

Silverthorne, J. "Onwards and Sideways." *Artforum* 28 (March 1990): 146–150.

Simon, John. "Willing Victims." *National Review* 42, 9 (July 1990): 55 (3 pp.). [Review of *Tie Me Up*].

"Spain's Pedro Almodóvar on the Verge of Global Fame." *Variety*, 24 August 1988, 42 (2 pp.).

Stratton, D. "*¿Qué he hecho yo para merecer esto?* (*What Have I Done to Deserve This*)." *Variety*, 29 August 1984, 23.

"The Talk of the Town: Cocoon." *New Yorker*, 5 October 1992, 59–60. [On *Patty Diphusa*].

Taubin, Amy. "The Red and the Black." *Village Voice*, 20 September 1988, 65. [Review of *Matador*].

Toumarkine, D. "*Women on the Verge of a Nervous Breakdown*." *Film Journal* 91 (December 1988): 15–16.

Travers, Peter. "*High Heels*." *Rolling Stone*, 9 January 1992, 56.

———. "*Matador*." *People*, 1 August 1988, 23.

————. "*Tie Me Up, Tie Me Down.*" *Rolling Stone*, 17 May 1990, 28.

————. "*Women on the Verge of a Nervous Breakdown.*" *People*, 14 November 1988, 24.

Tusher, W. "*Up* Loses Fight, Judge Comes Down on MPAA." *Variety*, 25 July 1990, 5 (2 pp.).

Villarubia, José. "Review of *Patty Disphusa and Other Writings.*" *Lambda Book Report* 3.8 (January 1993): 49.

White, Armond. "The 16th New Directors." *Film Comment* 23.3 (May 1987): 64, 69+. [Review of *Law of Desire*].

Williamson, Bruce. "Kika." *Playboy* (June 1994): 21.

————. "*Tie Me Up! Tie Me Down!*" *New Woman* 20.6 (June 1990): 36.

————. "*Women on the Verge of a Nervous Breakdown.*" *Playboy*, January 1989, 28.

Young, Deborah, and Moore, Linda. "Brothers' Keepers." *Variety*, 8 March 1993, 33–34. [On Almodóvar's brother and producer, Agustín].

Young, Tracy. "¡¡Almodóvar!! Who Inspires Spain's X-rated Director? Doris Day, for One." *Vogue*, June 1990, 124–125. [On *Tie Me Up*].

Index

About the Contributors

MARVIN D'LUGO is professor of Spanish and director of the screen studies program at Clark University. His essays on Spanish and Latin American cinema have appeared in *Quarterly Review of Film and Video, Film Quarterly*, and the collection *Mediating Two Worlds* (BFI). He is also the author of *The Films of Carlos Saura: The Practice of Seeing* (1991) and coauthor of *Theories of National Cinema* (forthcoming).

BRAD S. EPPS is currently assistant professor in Romance languages and literatures at Harvard University. He has published numerous articles on contemporary Spanish literature and film, focusing on questions of gender, sexuality, and politics. His book *Significant Violence: Oppression and Resistance in the Narrative of Juan Goytisolo* is forthcoming.

VÍCTOR FUENTES is professor of Spanish at the University of California, Santa Barbara. He has written extensively on nineteenth- and twentieth-century Spanish and Latin American literature and film. His publications include *El canto material y espiritual de César Vallejo* (1981), *La marcha al pueblo en las letras españolas 1917–1936* (1986), *Benjamín Jarnes: Bio-grafía y metaficción* (1988) and *Buñuel en México* (1993).

MARSHA KINDER is professor of film and critical studies at the University of Southern California. A member of the editorial board of *Film Quarterly*, she has written extensively on Spanish and world cinema. In 1991 she edited a special issue of *Quarterly Review of Film and Video* devoted to Spanish cinema of the last decade. Her most recent books include *Playing with Power in Movies, Television and Video* (1991) and *Blood Cinema: The Reconstruction of National Identity in Spain* (1993).

LEORA LEV is currently assistant professor of Spanish at Northern Arizona University, and has published on fetishism in Ramón del Valle-Inclán. Her work in progress includes a book on the representations of cruelty in early-twentieth-century Spanish and French vanguard cultures.

JAMES MANDRELL teaches Spanish and comparative literature at Brandeis University. His recent publications include *Don Juan and the Point of Honor: Seduction, Patriarchal Society and Literary Tradition* (1992) and essays in *Comparative Literature, Novel, Hispanic Review, Bulletin of Hispanic Studies*, and *MLN*.

BARBARA MORRIS is an independent scholar working in contemporary Spanish film. She has taught at UCLA, Rutgers University, and Fordham University. Her articles, reviews, and translations have appeared in *Revista de estudios hispánicos, Critical Inquiry, Letras peninsulares, España contemporánea*, and *Anales de la literatura española contemporánea*. She is currently writing a book titled *Configurations of Gender in Post-Franco Spanish Cinema*.

WENDY ROLPH is chair of the Department of Spanish and Portuguese at the University of Toronto. Her writing and research have focused on the interactions between Spanish literature and cinema. Her publications have appeared in *Anales de la Literatura Española Contemporánea, Hispanic Review, Words and Moving Images, The Canadian Modern Language Review*, and *Scripta Mediterranea*.

PAUL JULIAN SMITH is professor of Spanish at Cambridge University. He is the author, most recently, of *Representing the Other. "Race," Text and Gender in Spanish and Spanish American Narrative* (1991) and *Laws of Desire: Questions of Homosexuality in Spanish Writing and Film* (1992). His book on Almodóvar, *Desire Unlimited: The Cinema of Pedro Almodóvar* was published in 1994.

KATHLEEN M. VERNON teaches Hispanic literature and film at the State University of New York at Stony Brook. Her publications on Spanish cinema include *The Spanish Civil War and the Visual Arts* (1990) and essays in *Film Quarterly, Film and History, Quarterly Review of Film and Video, Hispania*, and *Rewriting the Good Fight: Critical Essays on the Literature of the Spanish Civil War* (1989). She is currently completing a book on the representation of history and memory in post–Civil War Spanish narrative, novel, and film.

Recent Titles in
Contributions to the Study of Popular Culture